Kathryn Bigelow: Interviews

Conversations with Filmmakers Series
Gerald Peary, General Editor

Kathryn Bigelow
INTERVIEWS

Edited by Peter Keough

University Press of Mississippi / Jackson

www.upress.state.ms.us

The University Press of Mississippi is a member of the Association of American University Presses.

Copyright © 2013 by University Press of Mississippi
All rights reserved
Manufactured in the United States of America

First printing 2013

∞

Library of Congress Cataloging-in-Publication Data

Bigelow, Kathryn.
  Kathryn Bigelow: interviews / edited by Peter Keough.
    pages cm. — (Conversations with filmmakers series)
  Includes bibliographical references, filmography and index.
  ISBN 978-1-61703-774-0 (cloth: alk. paper) — ISBN 978-1-61703-775-7 (ebook) 1.
Bigelow, Kathryn—Interviews. 2. Women motion picture producers and directors—
United States—Interviews. I. Keough, Peter, 1952– editor of compilation. II. Title.
  PN1998.3.B565A5 2013
  791.4302'33092—dc23   2013009244

British Library Cataloging-in-Publication Data available

Contents

Introduction

Despite the millions of viewers and all the hoopla, the Academy Awards rarely amount to much of cultural significance. Not so the 82nd annual Oscar ceremony, which took place on March 7, 2010.

Though there were ten nominees for Best Picture, the first time more than five had competed since 1944, the contests had come down to only two films and two directors, who, adding to the drama, were also formerly husband and wife. They were James Cameron with his sci-fi epic *Avatar*, and his ex-spouse Kathryn Bigelow with her tale of bomb disposal crews in Iraq, *The Hurt Locker*.

The films had much in common. Both drew on anxieties about the ongoing wars in Iraq and Afghanistan—though, as Bigelow would insist to Scott Tobias on the *A. V. Club* website in 2009, her film was "nonpartisan." Both explored the nature of heroism and the attraction of danger and violence while attempting to re-create the subjective experience of the protagonist. And both sought to elevate popular entertainment into art.

Then there were the differences.

Cameron's *Avatar* cost $200 million to make, consisted almost entirely of special effects, and employed state-of-the-art 3-D. Bigelow's budget for *The Hurt Locker*, on the other hand, was minuscule and she achieved her effects the old-fashioned way, employing hand-held cameras, long takes, and meticulous sound design. "I wanted to give the audience a real, boots-on-the-ground, you-are-there look at what it would be like to have the world's most dangerous job," she told Ryan Stewart on the *Slant* website in 2009. "So, that necessitated a kind of presentational, reportorial, immediate, raw, visceral approach." So where Cameron exalted fantasy, Bigelow aspired to reality.

The contest could be seen, then, as a battle between two philosophies of filmmaking. But the main reason people were excited about this Oscar race was that if Bigelow won, she'd be the first woman to receive an Academy Award for Best Director.

In true Hollywood fashion, Bigelow triumphed. She won the Oscar for Best Director and *The Hurt Locker* won for Best Picture and in four other categories. But if Bigelow felt her victory marked a turning point for women filmmakers in Hollywood, she didn't mention it in her acceptance speech. She refused to identify herself as a woman filmmaker. For her, the Oscar was not a landmark for women, but "the moment of a lifetime."

You can hardly blame her. For twenty-five years she had been patiently fending off questions about being a beautiful woman who makes bloody films. Interviewing her in 1987 for the *Chicago Tribune* about her second feature, the vampire thriller *Near Dark*, Marcia Froelke Coburn asked, "What's a nice woman like Bigelow doing making erotic, violent vampire movies?"

Four years later, Mark Salisbury wrote in the *Guardian*: "Why does she make the kind of movie she makes? . . . 'I don't think of filmmaking as a gender-related occupation or skill,' Bigelow recites in response. It's an answer she must have given many times before."

And over two decades later this writer tried to obliquely broach the subject in the *Boston Phoenix* by writing, "Everyone makes a point of Bigelow's gender and height and good looks, [but] what's germane is that even if she was short and had bushy eyebrows like Martin Scorsese, she still would be directing action pictures like no one since Sam Peckinpah and Sergio Leone."

So by the time she received her Oscar, Bigelow probably thought it was time for people to get over her gender and appearance. Instead, a more fruitful discussion might focus on how an academically trained artist ended up making genre films for a mass audience. Her being a woman who makes violent movies makes for a less engaging story than how she evolved from the avant garde to the mainstream.

Born in San Carlos, California, on November 27, 1951, Bigelow's first vocation was to be a painter. "When I first started painting, I loved the Old Masters," she told Gavin Smith in a 1995 *Film Comment* interview. "When I was thirteen or fourteen, I was . . . blowing up a corner of a Raphael. I loved doing that, taking a detail and turning it into twelve by twelve feet."

This love of painting took her to the San Francisco Art Institute in 1971. While there the Whitney Museum Program in New York offered her a fellowship. "I was nineteen years old," she told Kenneth Turan in an October 1989 *GQ* interview, "and Susan Sontag, Richard Serra, and Robert Rauschenberg were commenting on my work."

The prototypical starving artist in Manhattan, she scrambled to make ends meet, in the process rubbing elbows with the great and soon to be great. As she recalled for Carrie Rickey in the *Philadelphia Inquirer* in 2009, she, along with painter Julian Schnabel, crashed in the loft of performance artist Vito Acconci. Doing odd jobs, she rehabbed an apartment with one of America's up-and-coming composers. "I did the drywall," she remembered. "Philip Glass did the plumbing."

The possibilities of art expanded for her after she discovered the power of film. "Acconci hired me to film some material to be projected behind his performance piece," she told Gerald Peary in a March 30, 1990, interview in the *Toronto Globe and Mail*. "For me it was a revelation. I said, 'Ah hah! Movies!'" As she explained to Smith, "I just opened up Pandora's box. I'd see everything, from going to 42nd Street to see a Bruce Lee movie to *The Magnificent Ambersons* in Andrew Sarris's class to Fassbinder at Lincoln Center. That would be a day. *Year of 13 Moons*—I thought I'd died and gone to heaven when I saw that film."

Who could settle for "Ad Reinhardt's black-on-black paintings" (as she mentioned to Gavin Smith) after an afternoon with Bruce Lee and Rainer Werner Fassbinder? Not Bigelow; she had a new calling. "I became dissatisfied with the art world," she told Andrew Hultkrans in a 1995 interview with *Artforum*. "The fact that it requires a certain amount of knowledge to appreciate abstract material . . . I felt that film was more politically correct."

She'd get a chance to put that theory into practice when she entered the Columbia Graduate Film School in 1978, where her teachers included Milos Forman, Andrew Sarris, and Peter Wollen, and where she made her first student short, *Set-Up* (1978). It consisted of two actors beating each other up for twenty minutes while Marshall Blonsky and Sylvère Lotringer, two semiotics professors, deconstruct the action in voiceover.

"I began with *Set-Up* to provide a physiological and psychological connection between the audience and the screen," she later recalled for Paul Hond in the *Columbia Magazine* in 2009. "While you're watching it, you're deconstructing the connection. In a perfect world, theoretically, you're *experiencing* that connection."

At the time, however, she was still finding her way from the conceptual to the concrete, from abstraction to narration. She was also discovering her affinity for classic Hollywood directors. "I just love to see action films by George Miller, Sam Peckinpah, Martin Scorsese, [James] Cameron, Walter Hill," she told Ana Maria Bahiana in *Cinema Papers* in 1992. "These are great filmmakers. It's high impact with emotional involvement." Her love for such movies only grew stronger over the years. In 2009 she told Richard Natale in the *Los Angeles Times Calendar*, "I love B-movies. They are pure expression like the works of Jackson Pollock or Willem de Kooning. There is a wildly chaotic rawness to them. And they're not self-important."

Her first feature, however, still had roots in academia. Co-directed with Monty Montgomery, *The Loveless* (1982) starred Willem Dafoe in his big screen debut as a mopey biker passing through a hick town in the fifties. It's a kind of lethargic *The Wild One* with fetishized Harleys. "What I was interested in was a Kenneth Anger *Scorpio Rising* kind of thing," she told Gavin Smith. "Images of power and a skewed perspective of it."

As a first film *The Loveless* might not have had the impact of, say *Citizen Kane*, but some important people saw it and were impressed. Like Bigelow's maverick director idol, Walter Hill. After a series of frustrations ("It's a long story," Bigelow tells Victoria Hamburg in 1989 in *Interview*), the influence of Hill and later Oliver Stone helped make her third feature *Blue Steel* (1989) possible. But by that time she had already experienced similar difficulties while making her breakthrough second movie, *Near Dark* (1987).

"The company that made it lost its distribution [deal] while we were cutting the movie," Bigelow recalled for Bahiana. "They sold it to Dino de Laurentiis, but DEG went bankrupt while it was releasing the picture. So it happened twice on the one film! That's terrifying for a filmmaker."

A hybrid of the vampire movie and the Western, *Near Dark* grew into a cult and cinephile favorite. In it, Bigelow (and co-director Eric Red) developed her fascination with genre and in manipulating conventions and expectations into a subversive entertainment.

"What interests me is treading on familiar territory," she explained to Hamburg. "I try to turn the genre on its head or make an about-face, and just when I make the audience a bit uncomfortable, I go back and reaffirm [the genre conventions]."

With its sly intelligence and visceral energy, *Near Dark* grabbed the attention of another Hollywood player, producer Ed Pressman. He joined Oliver Stone in backing *Blue Steel*, the story of a female rookie NYPD cop who is stalked by a serial killer. The clout of Pressman and Stone guaranteed a big budget and drew an A-list cast that included Jamie Lee Curtis and Ron Silver.

Was Bigelow selling out her independence for Hollywood opportunities? Clarke Taylor brought up the question in 1988 in the *Los Angeles Times Calendar*. "I want more access," she told him. "I can't just ask for money to fulfill my own creative desires. And yet I want to be able to continue to make films I can live with."

Nick James, writing in the *City Limits* in 1990, also wondered if Bigelow had lost her edge. But he noted that she still indulged in the lurid fetishization of *Loveless*, particularly in *Blue Steel*'s opening shot in which the camera caresses a .44 Magnum in extreme close-up. More unconventionally, she featured a woman in the traditionally macho role of a gun-slinging vigilante, which might have inspired later heroines such as those in Ridley Scott's *Thelma and Louise* (1991) and James Cameron's *Terminator 2* (1991).

Blue Steel's premise of a heroine gunning for a villain may have epitomized patriarchal power, but Bigelow downplayed the picture's sexual politics. As she told Peary in the *Globe and Mail*, "I subscribe to feminism emotionally. And I sympathize with the struggles for equity. But I think there's a point where the ideology is dogmatic. So I'm not saying that *Blue Steel* is a feminist tract, per se. But there's a political conscience behind it."

In 1989 Bigelow married another one of her filmmaking idols, James Cameron. Though they divorced in 1991, their professional alliance continued for some time, starting with *Point Break* (1991), which Cameron produced. Like *Blue Steel*, this film featured a tough female character (played by Lori Petty), though she offers scant competition to the male bonding between FBI undercover agent Johnny Utah (Keanu Reaves) and Bodhi (Patrick Swayze), the guru-like leader of the outlaw surfer gang Utah has infiltrated. Utah's straitlaced ethics fray as Bodhi tempts him with the pleasures of surfing, sky-diving, and robbing banks.

"It's not about good guys and bad guys," she explained to Mark Salisbury in the *Guardian*. "It's a little more complicated when your good guy—your hero—is seduced by the darkness inside him and your villain is no villain whatsoever, he's more of an anti-hero."

Bigelow's most commercially successful film, *Point Break* also expresses a theme that transcends both genre and gender and goes to the heart of cinema itself. As she told Gavin Smith: "It's . . . transgression; the desire to escape through watching, to cross over, can be insidious, and comes with its own price—just like the price that's paid in *Point Break*, or the price [Megan—Jamie Lee Curtis] pays in *Blue Steel*, or the price you pay for immortality in *Near Dark*."

After her biggest hit came her biggest bomb, the unfairly maligned *Strange Days* (1995). Ironically, though it fared badly at the box office and at the hands of many reviewers, it inspired more in-depth interviews than any of her films except for *The Hurt Locker*. As she explained to Smith, it was her most personal film:

"It's a synthesis of all the different tracks I've been exploring, either deliberately or unconsciously, ever since I started making art. Of reflexive ideology, something that comments on itself; a kind of political framework; a narrative that uses classical forms. At the heart of it, it's a love story. And then you have the architecture of a thriller or noir. . . . And there's something very beautiful or serene at the heart of the film that's antithetical to the environment, which is grim, brutal, disturbing, [with] the hideous creativity of the killer."

Hugely ambitious with its themes of Apocalypse (remember Y2K?) and racial strife (remember the Rodney King riots?), *Strange Days* taps into a murderous narcissism, a lethal voyeurism. "Like the brilliant *Peeping Tom*," she told Roald Rynning in 1996 in *Film Review*, referring to the 1960 Michael Powell film, "*Strange Days* utilizes the medium to comment on the medium."

As it turned out, *Strange Days* would come close to derailing her career, just as *Peeping Tom* did Powell's. Five years would pass before she made her next film, *The Weight of Water* (2000), an adaptation of the novel by Anita Shreve. In it, a modern-day journalist researches a nineteenth-century murder mystery involving a Norwegian immigrant family, finding in the case parallels with her own unhappy marriage to an alcoholic poet.

Talky and set mostly on a yacht (could Roman Polanski's *Knife in the Water* have been an inspiration?), the film did not seem an obvious choice for Bigelow. She told Peter Howell of the *Toronto Star* that she initially became interested in the story because of its similarities to her own mother's background.

"Her side of the family was all Norwegian, so I grew up with these incredible stories of coming to America and trying to make a life here, what they were leaving behind and how difficult that was for them. Their hunger for a new reality kind of overrode everything."

The studio shelved *The Weight of Water* until 2002 when it was given a perfunctory, limited release. By that time Bigelow's *K-19: The Widow-maker* (2002) had surfaced, with its $90–$100 million budget, its big stars Harrison Ford and Liam Neeson, and a PR campaign that involved a junket and numerous interviews.

Based on a 1961 Cold War incident in which the captain and crew of a Soviet nuclear sub heroically stopped a reactor meltdown and possibly prevented World War III, the film took seven troubled years to reach the screen. But Bigelow persevered and ultimately completed the film on time and under budget. The studio, Paramount, released it in the summer, putting it up against blockbusters like *Spider-Man* and *Men in Black II*. Bigelow was dismayed. "I think it's not necessarily well-suited for a summer release," she told Stuart Jeffries in the *Guardian* interview. "It's the kind of film that's going to have a long life. I see it as more of a *Schindler's List* than a *Spider-Man*. Call me crazy."

They didn't call her crazy, but after the film flopped, grossing $30 million, for a long time they didn't call her at all. Seven more years would pass before she would return to the big screen triumphantly with *The Hurt Locker*. Though *K-19* did not endear Bigelow with the studios, it did seem to focus her areas of interest: military men in life-or-death situations depicted in a gripping, detailed, cinema verité style with journalistic verisimilitude. And, as she reported to Scott Tobias on the *A.V. Club* website in 2009, she did not spend those fallow years idly.

"I became familiar with [screenwriter Mark Boal's] journalism and turned one of his articles into a television series [Fox's *The Inside*]," she said. "That took a fair amount of time. And then it was a short-lived series, so it's not one to dwell on. But then at that time—it was 2004, so two years after *K-19*—I realized he was going off to do an embed in Baghdad with a bomb squad. I think it's a war that has been underreported in many respects, so I was extremely curious, and I kind of suspected that, providing he survived, he might come back with some really rich material that would be worthy of a cinematic translation, and that's what happened. So then he came back and we started working on the script in 2005, raised the money in 2006, shot in 2007, cut it, and here we are."

Tobias's interview with Bigelow about *The Hurt Locker* was one of hundreds; after years of zero coverage, everyone wanted to talk to her, from *Salon* to *60 Minutes*. I've tried to include in the book those interviews that bring up topics not covered in other articles. For example, Kyle Buchanan in *Movieline* asking her about rumors that she was going to direct the third *Twilight* episode, *Eclipse* ("I've done my vampire film") and about attending *Point Break Live!*, a dinner theater parody of her film ("very surreal . . . having someone play you jumping onto that set with a megaphone going, 'Cut! Cut! Cut!'").

These interviews took place prior to Bigelow's Oscar win, so she does not comment on that award's significance or its impact on the future of women in Hollywood, and gave no interviews prior to the release of her next film, *Zero Dark Thirty*. She made a rare public appearance at her career retrospective at New York's Museum of Modern Art in June 2010. As recorded by Brett Michel, during the Q&A she was asked about how winning Oscars changed her life. "If there are differences," she said. "I'd have to ask my friends. It was such a surreal moment."

Her next film, which opened in New York and Los Angeles on December 14, 2012, took on an even more ambitious subject, the ten-year CIA mission to find Osama bin Laden, ending with the Navy SEAL raid that killed the Al Qaeda leader on May 1, 2011. More than any of her other films, this one has encountered difficulties. During its production Republican Representative Peter T. King of New York conducted a Congressional investigation into her alleged access to secret CIA materials on the operation. And since its release, though numerous critics groups have named it best picture, some have accused Bigelow of condoning torture because of the brutally objective depiction of such scenes in the film. Consequently, though the film received five Oscar nominations, including one for Best Picture, Bigelow herself was not nominated for Best Director, and the film ended up with only one award, tying *Skyfall* for Best Sound Editing.

Despite the hostile reaction, Bigelow stands by the truth of the film, and in the press conference promoting it she described her process as a "reported film" in which "the story and the film are sort of contemporaneous."

As such, it represents a step further into the meticulous realism begun with *K-19*. It's a progression that began with the formal experiments of her art school days and the genre metamorphoses of her earlier career. "Having gone through different permutations," she said during the *Zero Dark Thirty* press conference, "I've been fascinated by different schools of filmmaking. . . . There's something very freeing about constantly, well, moving forward? But at the same time, I'm very excited by this kind of reportorial filmmaking. I think it sort of fills a space . . . a kind of imagistic living history."

As her experience following the film's release suggests, however, reporting the truth has its cost. Years earlier, in 1995, a similar backlash occurred with the release of *Strange Days*. What Bigelow said then is equally true today. "They're [politicians] using the movie industry in a political game," she told Sheila Johnston in *Index on Censorship*. "Rather than turning their attention to the cause of the . . . ills that are being represented in a film they fault the errand-boy."

The interviews in this collection have been lightly edited to avoid repetitions. Also, Bigelow can be cagy in her answers. I have therefore chosen whenever possible those interviews in which she opens up and ventures into new areas of discussion. Perhaps her guardedness comes in part from her own experience in interviewing filmmakers. In 1979 she interviewed Nicholas Ray for *Cinematographe*, and in 1982 she interviewed Douglas Sirk for *Interview*. I have included those articles here; sometimes Bigelow's questions for other filmmakers are as revealing as the answers she gives when she is interviewed herself.

Many thanks for their help and support to Ava Aguado, Gary Arnold, Rebecca Arzoian, Ana Maria Bahiana, Jay Carr, Ed Gonzalez, Brittany Gravely, Trevor Hogg, Ole Pijnacker Hordijk, Robert Horton, Sarah Jarvis, Zak Jason, Brian Kolb, Sylvère Lotringer, Kingsley Marshall, Tom Meek, Carrie Rickey, Scott Sugarman, Michael Sragow, David Sterritt, and Kenneth Turan.

Also thanks to Leila Salisbury and Gerald Peary of the University Press of Mississippi. And in memory of Peter Brunette.

Finally, thank you Alicia, my best editor and true love. She's funny, too.

PK

Chronology

1951   Born in San Carlos, California, on November 27, daughter of a
        paint factory manager and a librarian.

1970   Enrolls in the San Francisco Art Institute. Graduates in 1972.

1972   Accepted into the Independent Study Program at the Whitney
        Museum of American Art. Among her advisers are Susan Son-
        tag, Richard Serra, and Robert Rauschenberg. Joins the concep-
        tual art collective Art & Language. Presents a show of her art
        work at the Whitney Museum. Completes the Whitney pro-
        gram and remains in New York. Begins to work with concep-
        tual artist Lawrence Weiner and the British collaborative Art &
        Language. Serves as an assistant to video artist Vito Acconci.

1974–79 Collaborates on Lawrence Weiner videos, including *Done To,
        Green as Well as Blue as Well as Red*, and *Psychological Operations
        in Support of Unconventional Warfare*. Appears briefly in a Rich-
        ard Serra video.

1976   Participates in "Art & Language" exhibit at the Venice Bien-
        nale. Applies for and receives an NEA grant to complete her
        short film, *Set-Up*, in which two men fight while two academ-
        ics, Sylvère Lotringer and Marshall Blonsky, deconstruct the
        action.

1978   Submits the unfinished *Set-Up* to Milos Forman, head of the
        film department at Columbia. Bigelow is accepted and given
        a scholarship for an MFA in film criticism. Her professors in-
        clude Edward Said, semiologist Sylvère Lotringer, Peter Wol-
        len, and Andrew Sarris.

1979   Works with other students on an issue of Lotringer's *Semiotext(e)*
        called "Polysexuality."

1981   Receives master's degree from Columbia University School
        of the Arts' Film Program. Her first feature, *The Loveless*, co-
        directed and co-written by Monty Montgomery, debuts in

	August at the Locarno Film Festival. There Bigelow meets and interviews Douglas Sirk for *Interview* magazine.
1982	*The Loveless* debuts at the Filmex Festival in Los Angeles in March. Bigelow and Eric Red start collaborating on *Near Dark* which survives the bankruptcy of two production companies. The De Laurentiis studio eventually releases it in 1987, and then also goes bankrupt.
1983	Teaches a six-month class on B-movie makers of the thirties, forties, and fifties at CalArts at the invitation of John Baldessari. Walter Hill sees *The Loveless*, helps Bigelow as she attempts to produce a Latino-gang version of *Romeo and Juliet* she wrote called *Spanish Harlem*. It ends up in turnaround. Acted in Lizzie Borden's *Born in Flames*. Oliver Stone offers to produce her project about gangs in South Los Angeles. This also ends up in turnaround. Bigelow starts writing and developing *Blue Steel* with Eric Red.
1987	*Near Dark*, co-written by Eric Red, debuts at the Toronto Film Festival on September 12. It is released in U.S. on October 2.
1988	Appears in music video for the band Martini Ranch's song "Reach," directed by James Cameron. After the property had passed through the ownership of three studios, Bigelow shoots *Blue Steel* for Vestron in the fall. Oliver Stone and Ed Pressman produce.
1989	Plans to make *New Rose Hotel*, an adaptation of a William Gibson short story, produced by Ed Pressman. The film is eventually directed by Abel Ferrara in 1998. Directs segment of music video compilation *New Order: Substance*. Marries James Cameron, August 17.
1990	Jury member, Sundance Film Festival in January. *Blue Steel*, co-written by Eric Red; produced by Edward R. Pressman and Oliver Stone, released in U.S., March 16.
1991	*Point Break* released, July 12. Bigelow and Jay Cocks collaborate on script for a Joan of Arc project. The *Strange Days* project is offered to Bigelow by James Cameron. Divorced from James Cameron.
1992	On April 29 a jury acquits four Los Angeles police officers accused of beating Rodney King, an assault caught on videotape. Six days of rioting follow, resulting in fifty-three deaths, thousands of injuries, and over a $1 billion in damages. Kathryn Bigelow, living in L.A. at the time, witnesses some of the violence

	and destruction, attributes part of the inspiration for *Strange Days* to this experience.
1993	Directs episode #4 from the *Wild Palms* TV series.
1994	Bigelow obtains the rights for Anita Shreve's novel *The Weight of Water*. Begins production of *Strange Days* in June.
1995	*Strange Days* premieres in U.S. at the New York Film Festival, October 7.
1996	Bigelow withdraws from a project to produce a film about Joan of Arc entitled *Company of Angels* when partner Luc Besson insists on casting his wife Milla Jovovich in the lead. The film would ultimately be released by Besson in 1999 as *The Messenger: The Story of Joan of Arc*.
1998–99	Directs three episodes of the NBC TV series *Homicide: Life on the Street*.
1998	Jury member, Venice Film Festival, in September.
1999	The production company Working Title puts Bigelow's project *K-19: The Widowmaker* into turnaround. It is ultimately picked up by Intermedia, with Paramount distributing. Bigelow shoots *The Weight of Water*.
2000	Universal Pictures releases a rival submarine drama, *U-571*, in April, stalling production of *K-19: The Widowmaker*. The Soviet nuclear submarine K-141, the *Kursk*, sinks in the Barents Sea on August 12. All 118 crew members perish.
2001	Bigelow shoots *K-19: the Widowmaker*.
2002	*K-19: The Widowmaker* released, July 19. *The Weight of Water* receives limited U.S. release on November 1.
2003	Jury member, Berlin Film Festival, in February. Develops adaptation of Erik Larson's bestseller *The Devil in the White City*, but the project is taken over by Leonardo DiCaprio in 2010.
2004	Bigelow develops *The Inside* with Mark Boal for Fox TV; the project is taken over by Tim Minear and is made into a 2005 series canceled after seven episodes. Bigelow directs "She Was a Friend of Mine," an episode for the ABC TV series *Karen Sisco*. Mark Boal is embedded with an EOD unit in Iraq.
2005	Bigelow and Boal begin preproduction for *The Hurt Locker*.
2007	*The Hurt Locker* is shot in Jordan in July.
2008	*The Hurt Locker* debuts at the Venice Film Festival, September 4. Bigelow and Mark Boal begin plans to produce a film about the hunt for Osama bin Laden.
2009	*The Hurt Locker* is released in the U.S., June 26. Bigelow wins

numerous critics' groups awards for Best Picture and Best Director and in other categories for *The Hurt Locker*. Bigelow and Boal start preparations for *Triple Frontier*, a big-budget action picture about the war against drug traffickers in South America, for Paramount. The potential cast includes Tom Hanks and Johnny Depp.

2010   Bigelow becomes the first woman to receive the Directors Guild of America's "Outstanding Achievement in Motion Pictures" award for *The Hurt Locker*, January 31. Bigelow becomes the first woman to win the Academy Award for Best Director, March 7. The film also wins for Best Picture and in three other categories. Directs the TV pilot *The Miraculous Year* for HBO, but the series is cancelled before the program can be broadcast. In December Bigelow and Boal announce that they are putting off production of *Triple Frontier* until they finish a low-budget thriller about anti-terrorist special operations. That film is eventually titled *Zero Dark Thirty* and is about the actual mission to kill Osama bin Laden.

2011   Osama bin Laden is killed by U.S. commandos in Abbottabad, Pakistan, on May 2. Brazilian director José Padilha begins developing *Tri-Border*, a film similar to Bigelow's *Triple Frontier*, complicating and perhaps killing Bigelow's project. Sony Pictures picks up distribution rights for Boal and Bigelow's bin Laden project, *Zero Dark Thirty*. The U.S. release is planned for December 19, 2012, with a cast including Jason Clarke, Joel Edgerton, and Jessica Chastain. In August U.S. Rep. Peter King, R-NY, calls for Department of Defense and CIA investigations into possible collusion between the Obama administration and the makers of *Zero Dark Thirty* in which classified information may have been leaked.

2012   Bigelow begins shooting *Zero Dark Thirty* in northern India in February; radical Hindu groups protest the production. *Zero Dark Thirty* is released December 19 in New York and Los Angeles. On December 19 Sen. John McCain (R; AZ), Sen. Carl Levin (D; MI), and Sen. Barbara Feinstein (D; CA) of the Senate Intelligence Committee, in a letter to Sony Pictures, denounce *Zero Dark Thirty* for "grossly inaccurate and misleading information suggesting that torture resulted in information that led to the location of Osama bin Laden."

2013   The Senate Intelligence Committee opens an investigation into *Zero Dark Thirty* on January 2. The film is released wide January 11. The Director's Guild nominates Kathryn Bigelow as Best Director for *Zero Dark Thirty*, January 8. The Motion Picture Academy nominates *Zero Dark Thirty* for Best Picture and four other awards January 10. Kathryn Bigelow is not nominated for Best Director. *Zero Dark Thirty* receives one Academy Award, tying *Skyfall* for Best Sound Editing, February 24. On February 25 the Senate Intelligence Committee reports that the investigation into *Zero Dark Thirty* is closed.

Filmography

PSYCHOLOGICAL OPERATIONS IN SUPPORT OF UNCONVENTIONAL
WARFARE (1975)
Director: **Kathryn Bigelow**
Screenplay: **Kathryn Bigelow**

SET-UP (1978)
Director: **Kathryn Bigelow**
Screenplay: **Kathryn Bigelow**
Cast: Marshall Blonsky, Sylvère Lotringer
15 minutes

THE LOVELESS (1982)
Atlantic Releasing Corporation
Directors: **Kathryn Bigelow** and Monty Montgomery
Screenplay: **Kathryn Bigelow** and Monty Montgomery
Cinematography: Doyle Smith
Editing: Nancy Kanter
Producers: A. Kitman Ho, Grafton Nunes
Cast: Willem Dafoe, J. Don Ferguson, Robert Gordon
82 minutes

BORN IN FLAMES (1983)
First Run Features
Director: Lizzie Borden
Screenplay: Lizzie Borden and Ed Bowes
Cast: Honey, Adele Bertei, Jean Satterfield, **Kathryn Bigelow**
90 minutes

THE EQUALIZER, season one, episode five: "Lady Cop" (1985)
CBS
Director: Russ Mayberry

Screenplay: Michael Sloan, Richard Lindheim, **Kathryn Bigelow**,
Maurice Hurley, Joel Surnow
Cast: Edward Woodward, Steven Williams, Karen Young
60 minutes

NEAR DARK (1987)
De Laurentiis Entertainment Group
Director: **Kathryn Bigelow**
Screenplay: **Kathryn Bigelow** and Eric Red
Cinematography: Adam Greenberg
Editing: Howard E. Smith
Producers: Mark Allan, Edward S. Feldman, Diane Nabatoff, Eric Red
Cast: Adrian Pasdar, Jenny Wright, Lance Henriksen, Bill Paxton
94 minutes

REACH (1988)
Warner Brothers Records
Director: James Cameron
Cast: **Kathryn Bigelow**, Bud Cort, Lance Henriksen, Adrian Pasdar,
Bill Paxton
Cinematography: John R. Leonetti
Editing: Howard E. Smith
8 minutes

NEW ORDER: SUBSTANCE (1989)
Warner Reprise Video
Directors: **Kathryn Bigelow**, Robert Breer, Philipe DeCloufé, Jona-
than Demme, Rick Elgood, Robert Longo, Charles Sturridge, William
Egman
Cast: Gillian Gilbert, Peter Hook, Stephen Morris, Bernard Sumner
37 minutes

BLUE STEEL (1989)
MGM
Director: **Kathryn Bigelow**
Screenplay: **Kathryn Bigelow**, Eric Red
Cinematography: Amir Mokri
Editing: Lee Percy
Producers: Michael Flynn, Lawrence Kasanoff, Edward R. Pressman,
Michael Rauch, Diane Schneier, Oliver Stone

Cast: Jamie Lee Curtis, Ron Silver, Clancy Brown
102 minutes

POINT BREAK (1991)
20th Century Fox
Director: **Kathryn Bigelow**
Screenplay: Rick King, W. Peter Iliff
Cinematography: Donald Peterman
Editing: Howard E. Smith
Producers: Peter Abrams, James Cameron, Rick King, Robert L. Levy,
Michael Rauch
Cast: Keanu Reeves, Patrick Swayze, Lori Petty, Gary Busey
120 minutes

WILD PALMS, episode 3: "Rising Sons" (1993)
ABC TV Miniseries
Director: **Kathryn Bigelow**
Screenplay: Bruce Wagner
Cinematography: Phedon Papamichael
Cast: John Belushi, Dana Delany, Robert Loggia
45 minutes

STRANGE DAYS (1995)
20th Century Fox
Director: **Kathryn Bigelow**
Screenplay: James Cameron, Jay Cocks
Cinematography: Matthew F. Leonetti
Editing: Howard E. Smith, James Cameron (uncredited)
Producers: James Cameron, Steven-Charles Jaffe, Lawrence Kasanoff,
Rae Sanchini, Ira Shuman
Cast: Ralph Fiennes, Angela Bassett, Juliette Lewis, Tom Sizemore
120 minutes

UNDERTOW (1996)
Showtime Networks
Director: Eric Red
Screenplay: **Kathryn Bigelow**, Eric Red
Cinematography: Geza Sinkovics
Cast: Lou Diamond Phillips, Mia Sara, Charles Dance
93 minutes

HOMICIDE: LIFE ON THE STREET, season 6, episodes 22 and 23: "Fallen Heroes: Part 1" and "Part 2" (1998)
NBC
Director: **Kathryn Bigelow**
Screenplay: Paul Attanasio, Lois Johnson, Eric Overmyer, David Simon (novel), Darryl Wharton, Sean Whitesell
Cinematography: Alex Zakrzewski
Executive Producer: Barry Levinson
Cast: Richard Belzer, Andre Braugher, Clark Johnson
60 minutes each

HOMICIDE: LIFE ON THE STREET, season 7, episode 20: "Lines of Fire" (1999)
NBC
Director: **Kathryn Bigelow**
Screenplay: Paul Attanasio, Tom Fontana, David Simon (novel), James Yoshimura
Cinematography: Alex Zakrzewski
Executive Producer: Barry Levinson
Cast: Richard Belzer, Giancarlo Esposito, Peter Gerety
60 minutes

THE WEIGHT OF WATER (2000)
Lionsgate Films
Director: **Kathryn Bigelow**
Screenplay: Anita Shreve (novel), Alice Arlen, Christopher Kyle
Cinematography: Adrian Biddle
Editing: Howard E. Smith
Producers: Lisa Henson, A. Kitman Ho, Steven-Charles Jaffe
Cast: Sean Penn, Elizabeth Hurley, Catherine McCormack, Sarah Polley
113 minutes

K-19: THE WIDOWMAKER (2002)
Paramount Pictures
Director: **Kathryn Bigelow**
Screenplay: Louis Nowra, Christopher Kyle
Cinematography: Jeff Cronenweth
Editing: Walter Murch

Producers: **Kathryn Bigelow**, Harrison Ford, Steve Danton, Steven-Charles Jaffe, et al.
Cast: Harrison Ford, Liam Neeson, Peter Sarsgaard
138 minutes

KAREN SISCO, season 1, episode 10: "She Was a Friend of Mine" (2004)
ABC
Director: **Kathryn Bigelow**
Screenplay: Scott Frank, Peter Lefcourt, Elmore Leonard, Jason Smilovic
Cast: Carla Gugino, Bill Duke, Robert Forster
60 minutes

MISSION ZERO (2007)
Pirelli Film
Director: **Kathryn Bigelow**
Screenplay: Sofia Ambrosini, Sergio Rodriguez, Stefano Volpi
Cinematography: Janusz Kaminski
Cast: Uma Thurman, Jason Maltas, Mathew Vigil
8 minutes

THE HURT LOCKER (2008)
Summit Entertainment
Director: **Kathryn Bigelow**
Screenplay: Mark Boal
Cinematography: Barry Ackroyd
Editing: Chris Innis, Bob Murawski
Original Music: Marco Beltrami, Buck Sanders
Sound Design: Paul Ottosson
Producers: **Kathryn Bigelow**, Mark Boal, Nicholas Chartier
Cast: Jeremy Renner, Anthony Mackie, Brian Geraghty
131 minutes

THE MIRACULOUS YEAR (2011)
HBO
Director: **Kathryn Bigelow**
Screenplay: John Logan
Cinematography: Barry Ackroyd
Producers: John Logan, **Kathryn Bigelow**, Lydia Pilcher

Cast: Eddie Redmayne, Eric West, Susan Sarandon
60 minutes

ZERO DARK THIRTY (2012)
Columbia Pictures
Director: **Kathryn Bigelow**
Screenplay: Mark Boal
Cinematography: Greig Fraser
Editing: Dylan Tichenor, William Goldenberg
Producers: Kathryn Bigelow, Mark Boal, Megan Ellison
Cast: Chris Pratt, Jessica Chastain, Joel Edgerton
157 minutes

Kathryn Bigelow: Interviews

Nicholas Ray: The Last Interview

Kathryn Bigelow and Sarah Fatima Parsons / 1979

From *Cinematographe* magazine, May 1979. Reprinted by permission of the authors.

Nicholas Ray: You know, I hate watching *Johnny Guitar* on television. But I really appreciate what Andrew Sarris wrote in the *Village Voice*: "With *Johnny Guitar* Nick Ray reaches the absolute criteria of the auteur theory."

Question: What did you think when you went to Europe and noticed how filmmakers, especially, the French ones, were influenced by your work? Truffaut, for example?
NR: And also Godard, Rohmer. Yes, I did have a strong influence on their work. I'm not sure if it was always for the best. I remember one evening I was driving home during the filming of *Rebel Without a Cause*. We shot a scene between Jim and Plato. I was whistling. I was really thrilled thinking, "My God, the French will adore that scene."

Q: Your films have also influenced the new German and American cinema.
NR: I hear that Wim Wenders is going to start a new film soon, *Hammett*. He's a great guy. I think he's had a hard time with the screenplay.

Q: He originally wanted to write it with the author of the book, Joe Gores.
NR: He tried but it didn't work out. It seldom does with the author of a book. A lot of filmmakers have failed. I myself thought I could do it, but it was a failure. Authors fall in love with their own words, and you have to be pitiless as a director or screenwriter.

Q: So that it won't become literature?

NR: Yes, that's right. I mean it's another kind of literature. They tend to get excited about one sentence, visualize it, and then it becomes really monotonous. You should never talk about something you can show, and never show something you can talk about.

Q: Doesn't it have something to do with what actors bring to a film?

NR: Absolutely. An actor can be as talented as another, but if he doesn't stick to what the director's intentions are, it all falls down. I adore working with actors.

Q: You come from the theater. I would imagine you have a particular method of work.

NR: Yes, I do have my method, as other directors do.

Q: What do you think of all the different interpretations?

NR: It's one of the beauties of cinema, or of any kind of art for that matter. Sort of a contradiction. I don't try to manipulate people. You're on. Do what you want. Some interpretations are shocking to me because they are ridiculous, but then again, why not? I have entered the kingdom of contradiction, but it's just as well. It adds to the reflection, even if sometimes it drives me crazy.

Q: Are you painting these days?

NR: No, I haven't in a long time.

Q: What kind of painting are you interested in?

NR: I was always a fan of German and Swedish expressionism. Edvard Munch, and medieval art too. I think my films express this tendency.

Q: Yes, like the colors and set design of the saloon in *Johnny Guitar*.

NR: I had it built on the side of a mountain, in the desert, because I loved the shape and color of the rocks there. It's a kind of medieval Frank Lloyd Wright.

Q: For how long did you work with Frank Lloyd Wright?

NR: One year. I was studying theater in New York, but since I come from Wisconsin I would stop at his place once in a while. He came for a conference at Columbia University. I went to listen to him, and then congratulated him at the end. We took a walk together, and he asked me if I would become one of his first students, and I went over there to get a master's in theater.

Q: When you designed the sets for *Johnny Guitar*, did you harmonize the colors specifically after any painters?
NR: I wasn't inspired by other painters, but of course I followed a principle of pictures. I kept the posse in black and white during the whole film. Herb Yates, the studio owner who was in Europe during the shooting of the film, looked at the dailies when he came back. And he said, "Nick, I love what I'm seeing, but it's a Technicolor film and everything's in black and white."

Q: You have used stereotypes, black for evil, white for good, and with a lot of humor.
NR: But the black and white are combined within the posse. They are penguins.

Q: The same combination when Joan Crawford wears a white dress with a black shotgun.
NR: That's baroque.

Q: James Dean, who was an archetypal figure of the 1950s, has become trendy again in the seventies. What do you think of this cult of youth? Of the frustrated aspirations of teenagers?
NR: This is all due to the negligence of an opulent society, the non-involvement, the lack of progress.

Q: All those also characterized the fifties?
NR: Of course. It was a time of opulence. It's easy to put labels on things, but it shouldn't be that simple. I don't know all the different forces in the present. This period of searching that we are living now is quite positive, but at the same time there's a big waste of time, a great irresponsibility. All the rich kids (talking about film students) spending five thousand or six thousand dollars a year to make their films.

Q: Do you think someone who's rich or supported by their parents doesn't have the necessary energy to fight for work, or that urgency in the effort?

NR: It's not a question of being able to fight for work. They are given all possibilities. They can talk about any subject matter they want to. But that's the point. Those subjects are so trivial.

Q: Which projects would you like to achieve now?
NR: I try to imagine something new. It's very disappointing not to be totally excited of something. I need that.

Q: In your film *In a Lonely Place* Humphrey Bogart for the first time in his career played a fragile character.
NR: Yes, I thought Bogie was fantastic, and in both films I did with him I took the gun out of his hands. The gun was a constant prop for him. For him as well as for me. *In a Lonely Place* was a very personal film.

Q: Do you mean in terms of your marriage to Gloria Grahame? Didn't she leave you to marry your son?
NR: Oh, yes, it's good for the tabloids, but not very interesting. It happened years ago.

Q: Oedipus?
NR: No, there's nothing Oedipal about it. That is always what people believe, but it's not that terrible really. Oedipus's fate is to kill his father. But, shit, it's never been a bloody relationship. They are divorced today. Only two or three close friends have looked at the situation quietly. Everybody thought it was gloomy, and it made me feel like locking my door. And I don't think it was very healthy for my son.

Q: While shooting *In a Lonely Place* were you aware of Hollywood's cynicism as strongly as the Humphrey Bogart character is?
NR: No, I don't think it appears in the film. I tried to treat Hollywood the way I would a Pennsylvania cattle town. In Beaver, Pennsylvania, same things happen as in Hollywood. It's just not as much in the lights as it is in Hollywood.

Q: The real intensity of *In a Lonely Place* lies in the fact that there's no way for that man and that woman to get a fresh start. Suspicion triumphs.
NR: Yes, we don't really know anything about them. In the first draft of the screenplay that I had written with Bundy Solt the end was more clearly stated. He killed her and Frank Lovejoy arrested him. But I didn't

like that ending. So I kicked everyone off the set, except for the actors, and we improvised the ending. We don't know exactly what it means. It's the end of their love of course. . . . But he could also drive off in his car and fall off a cliff, stop over in a bar to get drunk, or else go home or to his old mother. Anything is possible. It's up to the imagination of the audience.

Q: Wim Wenders in *The American Friend* seems to use the narration as an excuse to displace highly complex characters in beautiful and elaborate backgrounds. The story becomes almost superfluous.
NR: And obscure.

Q: Is it important to break the narrative linear structure?
NR: It's the way I've chosen for my autobiographical project. It's not chronological but based on spontaneity. Because things that are of any interest to you, that you write about in the present form, you might as well have heard them half an hour ago on radio, or else when you were nine.

Q: Did you enjoy working on *The American Friend*?
NR: I loved it. I enjoy playing once in a while. It allows me to sum things up, to tell myself that my way of working is still the right one. On the first day I found myself doing what I always scream at my actors not to do. We broke it down and began writing my part while shooting. Wim is very patient, and I felt very good, which is not always the best thing for an actor, feeling at ease. Sometimes it's good to scare them to death.

Q: While shooting *Johnny Guitar* I read that you would bring flowers to Mercedes McCambridge but not to Joan Crawford, or vice versa, just to create a tension between them. Is that true?
NR: One night Joan Crawford got drunk and threw Mercedes McCambridge's clothes on the highway. She was absolutely great at work, but sometimes anger won over her temperament. They were very different and Crawford hated McCambridge.

Q: Your films come from a very precise cultural period, and yet they do have a profound influence on our times.
NR: Do you think so? You think my films influence the culture of our time?

Q: Yes.
NR: How is that?

Q: The media project a certain image.
NR: They are reflecting it.

Q: Both.
NR: That isn't influence.

Q: Doesn't it work both ways?
NR: The important thing is people.

Q: Aren't you talking about conformity?
NR: How far does conformity go? Only a small number of women have gone through the *Annie Hall* syndrome. You see very few of them in cities of fifty-thousand people or less.

Q: But *Rebel Without a Cause* has influenced the youth culture we were talking about.
NR: It got a lot of people excited over someone they rediscovered. After this resurrection we will need another twenty years to rediscover it in a cave.

Q: Nevertheless, does James Dean symbolize something out of the social order, a sort of rupture that we're still fascinated by? The film shows the symbols that society has attached to itself.
NR: The real interesting character of the film is Plato played by Sal Mineo. People wanted to believe in a story. There's no story. I just wanted to influence parents.

Q: To make them understand what they were doing to their kids?
NR: No, what they were doing to themselves. All the parents of that time had become a lost generation, and I always hear the same things about it, the same words. It's all so dated.

Q: In *Rebel Without a Cause* parents represent law and order.
NR: Yes, I characterized them very deliberately. I'm very prejudiced for young people. But it was hard to reach adults.

Q: Is it a political film?
NR: Yes, Abbie Hoffman said it. Fuck politics. Politics is living.

Q: But in *Rebel* Jim and Judy seem to rebel against law and order, only to return to that law and order at the end. . . . The film works within the space of that ellipse.
NR: That's when earthquakes happen.

Q: What did James Dean bring to the film?
NR: He didn't write the dialogue. Stewart Stern and myself did a lot of improvisations. Jimmy was immensely talented due to his open imagination.

Q: Did he imitate you?
NR: Oh, he would copy my mannerisms, but I don't think he ever imitated me because that's an aspect of directing I hate. I never try to show an actor what to do or what to say. He has to find out for himself. The role of the director is to guide him to that state, and then to implement it. Otherwise, everyone is going to imitate the director, and no director however talented can play all the roles.

Q: While directing are you often confronted by actors' weaknesses?
NR: Oh, yes, it's a great cathartic experience for them, and they tend to be stronger, becoming aware of their own limitations.

Q: Werner Herzog in *Heart of Glass* hypnotized his actors, which tends to increase the hierarchy.
NR: To hypnotize an actor is to tell him when to wake up, to walk left, and go down the stairs. An actor must somehow contribute to the direction. One must be able to trust in his spontaneity, to set it in motion. We must help him get there.

Q: The character played by James Dean is sort of a synthesis of his own catharsis, and your concept of what a character should be.
NR: Yes, of my own will to accept or dismiss the character.

A Visit with the Master of Melodrama: Douglas Sirk

Kathryn Bigelow, Matthias Brunner, and Monty Montgomery / 1982

Originally published in *Interview*, July 1982, 50–52. Reprinted by permission of Interview Inc.

On the terrace of the Sirk home overlooking Lake Lugano, situated against the base of the Alps in Lugano, Switzerland, Hilde Sirk (beautiful and gracious former stage actress in Germany), Mathias Brunner (Swiss film exhibitor and friend of the Sirks), Kathryn Bigelow (American film director), and Monty Montgomery (American film director) meet with the eighty-two-year-old film director Douglas Sirk. Born Hans Detlef Sierck in 1900, in Hamburg, Douglas Sirk entered a prewar America—1938—to become one of the great directors of Hollywood's last decade of studio grandeur. Sirk began his career with a classical education and maintained a conscious involvement with major theoretical developments of the twentieth century from Eisenstein (whose lectures he attended in 1921) through Levi-Strauss and the New Left. He worked for fifteen years as a theatre director in the turbulent atmosphere of Weimar Germany. He switched from theatre to film over a confrontation with the Nazis in a 1933 stage production of *The Silver Lake* by Georg Kaiser and Kurt Weill. Sirk turned to the UFA studios and achieved tremendous success as a film director until the German film industry became Nazified. In 1937, obtaining a passport under the pretext of looking for location abroad, Sirk left Germany and, after an interlude in France and Holland, wound up in Hollywood. There, in an Eisenhower America, Douglas Sirk, the European intellect, directed some of the decade's most beautiful melodramas such as *Magnificent Obsession, All That Heaven Allows, Written on the Wind, The Tarnished Angel,* and *A Time to Love and a Time to Die,* climaxing his career in 1959 with *Imitation of Life*, Universal's largest-grossing picture of the time. He then retired from Hollywood, ultimately to Switzerland, coming out of retirement to stage a few plays at the Residenz Theater, Munich, and in Hamburg, the last in 1969. More recently he has taught at the film school in Munich. There he made three short films, one of them with Hanna Schygulla and Rainer Werner Fassbinder.

In nature there is no defect but the mind. None can be called deformed but the unkind.
—*Shakespeare, Richard III*

Kathryn Bigelow: You've been quoted as saying that you learned to trust your eyes more than words. That the angles are the director's thoughts, the lighting is his philosophy.

Douglas Sirk: The director has to control everything. The movement of the camera is important because this is his style. Otherwise he just becomes a director of the people. With film, a director should be *in* on everything. Never give up and don't let them tell you *they* are the specialist. You don't want any special kind of work, you want *your* kind of work. You see, a film is a visual thing. It's not being told by words alone. Words are important, but almost to a minor degree. It's the lighting, the angling, and it's the cutting, too. I've always been from the first to the last minute, in the cutting room telling the cutter I want it this way and that way, because once in a while you take a whole sequence out of here and put it there and that makes a lot of difference. Believe me, maybe it will make the film.

Monty Montgomery: The mechanical aspects are just as critical as the conception.

DS: Yes, the mechanical things are very important. For instance, if I could, I would have the same cameraman because then you don't need explanations any more. Most of the time it was Russell Metty. I would arrange the set-ups, mostly moving shots. I always moved the camera with the people. The camera is a woman, so you have to be nice to your camera. I always embraced my camera after a shot and I would say, "Did you like it?" and if she liked it I'd say, "Okay, let's print it," I would arrange the set-ups and then ask Metty if he could do it. He would grumble a little, but then he would do it. Only with a cooperation between director and cameraman do you get a good result. The language of color, the language of movement is very important to me, also the lights and the mirrors.

There are so darned many mirrors in my films, perhaps because when a man looks into a mirror he gets frightened; he discovers who he is.

KB: Death, despair, and failure wind up at the center of most of your plots. This dark, seamy side is given the spotlight and everything "sweet" or "good" looks simplistic or banal in comparison.
DS: You see, psychoanalysis, all the time, was beginning to be *the* thing in America. For instance, those extreme characters in *Written on the Wind* are all psychoanalytical studies, and everything is based on a sexual drive.

KB: A frustrated drive—
DS: Very true, but motivated by a certain melancholic quality. You especially feel it when they talk about their childhood, about playing at the pond. It's that lost childhood, lost innocence, really. And Robert Stack was great for the film with his sad, crazy eyes.

KB: You opened the picture on his feet, moved with him as he staggers toward the doorway—then pulled back and his face tells you everything . . .
DS: My technique always has been not to wait for the bang of the finish. So I put the finish at the beginning of the film. And you know, that when he came out of the door, and the shot had been fired, he was finished. It was a tragic ending. Most scriptwriters insisted on letting the ending come as a surprise. I think it's wrong.

Hilde Sirk: Did you hear, the Parisians called and said that they are opening a new cinema in Paris with *Written on the Wind*?
Mathias Brunner: They are opening the cinema with a new print of *Written on the Wind*. I think it is Frederique Mitterrand, the nephew of the President of France, who requested it.

KB: Did Malone have to be taught how to dance for *Written on the Wind*?
DS: No. At first she didn't like the idea.

MB: Was it because it was too nude for her? She was wearing only a negligee.
DS: You never know with women, forgive me. You never get a glance into their dark interior, though she had been wax in my hands so far. I

talked to Zug [Albert Zugsmith], the producer, and he wanted to get it on film and then, if I didn't like it, it could be thrown out. She ultimately gave in and did it, as I wanted her to do it, beautifully, holding a large photo of Rock Hudson to her breast. I printed the first take because I had the feeling I wouldn't get her to do it a second time as well as she had done it the first. What really plagued her was that she was no dancer. But I thought it should not be a dance—this woman is not a dancer in the film—she is just crazy about Rock.

KB: Did you storyboard every shot?
DS: Yes.

KB: The shots are so perfectly constructed.
DS: That's because I often shot it with two cameras. And since I always did my own cutting, I could pick the best of every shot. It was a complicated thing.

KB: Didn't it restrict you?
DS: No, not really.

KB: Did you physically do a lot of your own cutting?
DS: Yes. I had learned cutting so I could supervise it.

KB: Douglas, what are your thoughts on the future of film, what do you anticipate?
DS: Very interesting and very difficult to answer. I have been talking to Susan Sontag about it. The way I feel is the following: Film needs, among other developments, a new era of technical progress. They tried the 3-D glasses and it never worked out. At any rate, film has always been searching for some new elements—be it technical or philosophical in nature. You see, right now film is going back to what has been done before; trying to digest it, to better it or to worsen it, but trying to play with it. Still, there is the overwhelming power of so much film having been done in the past. Of course, a director has to know about the past too, certainly, but film needs a *new* epoch. And so far, I could be wrong because I am not living in America, films are still being made like films were being made. New films, of course, are slightly different. One would tell *Taxi Driver* apart from films of the fifties, but still the elements of the fifties are in it—it is aesthetically the same.

KB: Structurally too—

DS: Yes. You see, so far my creed, and I think the creed of every artist, is that form, shape, is more important than content. The form shapes the content. But of course, content reflects on form, too. Take *Written on the Wind*, the form I have given this basically trite story is a personal style and this mark of handwriting has always been to me the most important thing about any work of art. But it's not form alone, certainly not anymore, because maybe it's time for content to come to the fore a little more than it has been so far.

KB: A psychoanalytic content?

DS: Maybe. You see, during my time at Universal I had to do things that I was not used to doing. Universal was the oldest of companies in America, the first to go to Hollywood and shoot films there, but also it was the most conservative and the most timid one, always insisting on the old values.

KB: Morality.

DS: Yes, of moralities, of happy endings. The father has to be good and the mother has to be even better. The stories that I got, without exception, were very trite, without any element of life to them. But still the content of a trite novel could be vivified—you could wake it up—you could put something into it. Take a story like *All That Heaven Allows,* for instance. It's a very trite story basically, it's a nothing story, but I got some fundamental American philosophy into it, and turned it into a meaningful film. Maybe there will be a new era . . . a previous era started when political films were being made. Take *Battleship Potemkin*, there the content is tremendously important. Happily enough, the form is just as good in that old film. Maybe to our modern eyes the film has aged, but still, for its time, it was a great picture. It had form. Now if you have that combination of both of them it's marvelous. But you rarely can have it. I do feel that now there is again a wish for content . . .

KB: Media has changed films, has created a new market for films. The media shapes our perception of reality and the film product is finding it harder and harder to compete. The news is very exciting.

DS: The media is danger. Formerly, the critics used to go more for content than for form. This is because they were literary critics and in a book the content is important. Proust wouldn't be Proust if his language wasn't the language of Proust. Certainly, what he is writing about,

French family affairs, society, would bore me to death if it wasn't for his marvelous language. I think form is, and remains, *the* thing . . . but I'm an old formalist. What I wanted to say is not that a new era of content *has* to come in, or must come in. Quite to the contrary, I do feel that a new era *wants* to come in. When you go back to the silent films, there was hardly any criticism at all. I remember when I was a little boy going to the cinema with my grandmother, thinking it was great, the guy hammering on the piano, etc. It was *beneath* criticism. This was a happy era for films. This is how film was born. Now things are different. Look, I think the world today is full of angst. Angst is a German word, as you know, and has entered the American language very quickly which proves it to be wanted. People accept it as a new word which expresses something which fear doesn't contain. Fear has to do with running away from something. But angst is something to be caught by, to be captivated by; you can't get out of it, you know. I think that's a great theme for new films: angst. The trap of humankind—the trap you put up for yourself. If you succeed in catching that, I think you can make great film. It's a new content, but it will breed a new form. At any rate, this is very important, and I do think it's *the* theme and attitude of our time. We are flying to the stars, we are flying into an eternity, and coming back we are just shaken with angst. I can't turn on the radio without hearing about that darned atomic bomb which is filling mankind with angst. This strange twist in the human mind never existed in America before. When I came to America the most frequent term was "keep smiling." No one dares to keep smiling today.

KB: That's the gap comedies try to fill—

DS: Right. But you see, it's no era for making the old kind of comedies. Today, you have to make gruesome comedies. . . . Comedies where between the laughter, angst stands up, takes off its mask and shows its haunting face.

(We break for lunch at the Grand Hotel Willa Castagnola Au Lac in Lugano.)

KB: A director has to be sort of set psychoanalyst; you have to play father, mother, daughter—

DS: And brother. Above all you have to encourage your actors. You have to love your actors. This is the most magnificent material you have; human beings. That's more than life, that's more than anything else; you have to be careful with them. Actors are overly sensitive people and the better they are the more critical they are of their own work. You must make even very experienced actors believe in themselves. They are always coming to you for advice and that's wonderful—never discourage an actor.

KB: There seems to be a trend right now toward films that are inspirational—a reaction to the glut of horror films and probably an attempt to salvage meaning. There are a lot more independents today, too.

DS: Yes, conditions are completely different from the time when I was working in the studios. In America as well as in Europe. Then it helped being with a studio. Today an independent director has a much tougher time to make a film. On the other hand, of course, he is much freer—nobody interferes with him and his work. But independent filmmaking is something like a Broadway producer's search for an "angel" who gives the money . . . and I understand, "angels" even in heaven have become a rarity.

Revamping Vampires

Marcia Froelke Coburn / 1987

From the *Chicago Tribune*, October 11, 1987. Reprinted by permission of the Chicago Tribune Company.

It's not that Kathryn Bigelow believes in vampires. Not exactly. And even though she has just directed an erotic vampire thriller, Bigelow says that's not really the reason she's wearing a gold cross around her neck now.

"Well," the thirty-five-year-old director of *Near Dark* admits, "I did think, 'I'm making this picture which is sort of blasphemous, so maybe I should cover my bets.'"

Still, Bigelow is quick to point out, that's her only concession to the idea of dark, supernatural powers. "I'm not carrying garlic or mirrors or stakes of wood."

None of which, by the way, would help if you ran into any of the bloodthirsty creatures from Bigelow's movie. In *Near Dark*, all of the gothic vampire mythology has been stripped away, leaving an intense, haunting story of sensual compulsion and anarchy. The outlaws live forever, by night and on blood, but the word "vampire" is never once mentioned.

"It was a deliberate choice," says Bigelow, who also co-wrote the script with Eric Red, author of the chilling nightmare movie *The Hitcher*. "We thought since we were reinventing vampires in a way, it would be a disservice to categorize them. And what are they, really? Modern-day pirates or cowboys. Nocturnal creatures. They're people you pass on the street when you walk through dark alleys."

The genesis for *Near Dark* came out of conversations the two writing partners kept having about vampires. "There's something so seductive about them, that we wanted to rework the image," says Bigelow. "It was an idea that just kept eating away at us." So to speak.

They started by getting rid of all the gothic underpinnings surrounding vampires—teeth, holy water, garlic, bats—and then merging that stripped-down essence of vampire with the classic elements of a western.

"The showdown, the shootout, the Midwest setting. We turned them into modern gunslingers traveling these deserted highways."

The concept of a vampire western, Bigelow admits, is an unusual one. "It sounds like a clash, or even a joke, but certain qualities make it work. The starkness of both their lives and the landscape, the wide open spaces, the pioneering aspect. If we'd kept all the mythic vampire details, then it would have felt like a transplant stuck on top of this landscape. You know, black capes and fangs in Oklahoma. It wouldn't have integrated. But since we reinvented them, are they still vampires? I don't know. They're more like pioneers, because anything is available to them, as long as it's not daylight."

Bigelow says she didn't approach this project by steeping herself in vampire lore. "I only read Bram Stoker's *Dracula* and Anne Rice's *Interview with a Vampire*. Stoker gave me the idea of reclaiming victims by draining them completely, almost to the point of death, and then infusing them with 'healthy' blood. What was appealing was the notion of redeemable vampires who give up the ability to live forever for mortality. Yet they're tainted by that knowledge. I wanted to explore that idea while putting an erotic charge into the material, sexualizing the violence."

And what's a nice woman like Bigelow doing making erotic, violent vampire movies?

"I think women are very interested in violence. They're certainly the victims of it a lot, so they're focused on it. Admittedly, movie-making is a male-dominated industry. And within the codes of who does what material, women are more associated with emotional material and men with the apparatus, the technology, the hardware. But I don't think of *Near Dark* as a violent movie, but, rather, an emotional, moral one."

Bigelow came to filmmaking through an indirect route. Growing up in northern California, her primary interest was in art. She attended the San Francisco Art Institute, where she concentrated on painting, specifically abstract expressionism. "Even then my work was large, dark, intense," she says.

A scholarship to an independent study program, connected with the Whitney Museum, brought Bigelow to New York. "They give you a studio and contemporary artists look at your work and talk to you," she says. "It was supposed to last for twelve months; I stayed about twelve years."

During that time, Bigelow began experimenting with various materials and methods. She got involved with a group called "Art and Language," conceptual artists who incorporated film into their works. "Their focus was language and the selling of culture. It was a bit lofty, but nonetheless, fascinating to me. So I began backing away from painting and into film."

Her first films, Bigelow says, were not the kind you'd see at your neighborhood theater. "They were completely analytical, totally within an art concept. One film, which played at the Whitney, analyzed violence within a cinematic context. Before this point, I was not a big movie fan. But I immersed myself into a sort of tunnel vision, watching everything."

Her favorite period, she decided, were the "noir" films of the forties— the "black" movies, a designation that describes their philosophical point of view. "I think I'll probably always be making movies with dark underpinnings and a main character who's trapped in a situation from which he can't extract himself . . . a fatalism combined with an adrenaline aspect. I'm interested in high-impact, high-velocity movie-making."

Certainly, that's what Bigelow presents in *Near Dark*, where a young man, Caleb, is seduced into a killing lifestyle by a sensual, other-worldly girl.

"The look of the film, where the night appears very seductive, was intentional. I wanted the lifestyle of these people to seem attractive. But I don't think this is a straight violence movie, nor is it a straight romance. There's a bittersweet quality here, because Caleb and his girlfriend have been tainted by their experience. And they have to decide whether to give up immortality for a 'normal' life.

"At the very least, we could say, they have a lot to talk about."

Black-Leather Director in a Business World

Clarke Taylor / 1988

From the Los Angeles Times Calendar, October 9, 1988, 28. Reprinted by permission of the Los Angeles Times Syndicate.

Bang! Bang! Bang!

Shots rang out along the dim paths into Central Park, reminding intrepid strollers and joggers of the danger that lay deep within the huge, cavernous park.

And then, a reassuring shout from within the park: "Cut! Print!"

Kathryn Bigelow, sinewy and dark-haired, stood in long shadows that streaked the floodlighted clearing, directing her third film. It's *Blue Steel*, an action thriller about a rookie police detective who becomes embroiled in the hunt for a serial killer. Jamie Lee Curtis is the detective in pursuit of psychotic murderer Ron Silver.

The camera operators, grips, and other technical personnel were easily identified as the crew. The bookish producer Ed Pressman—whose quirky range includes *Badlands*, *Plenty*, *True Stories*, *Conan the Barbarian*, and *Wall Street*—appeared strong and authoritative. The executives sent in from Los Angeles by Vestron Pictures, the film's distributor, looked and sounded like the Hollywood executive types they were (they wouldn't breathe a digit of the film's budget).

But Bigelow, in black pants and sweater and a black leather jacket, seemed more like one of the rockers or punkers who nest in downtown Manhattan and rarely venture into the park.

Then again, Bigelow, thirty-five, is not in the mold of many other working directors.

• • •

Bigelow appeared on the independent film scene several years ago with *The Loveless*, a biker movie set in the fifties and starring Willem Dafoe, which she co-directed with Monty Montgomery.

Talk of Bigelow and her highly stylized approach began to circulate within the independent film community, but not much beyond, until last year's release of *Near Dark*. A vampire Western about handsome, homoerotic, blood-drinking villains that seemed to blend the fated romanticism of Nicholas Ray, the poetic violence of Sam Peckinpah and the explosiveness of contemporary filmmaker James Cameron, *Near Dark* vanished quickly into videocassette stores.

However, the film, which she co-wrote with her *Blue Steel* co-writer, Eric Red (*The Hitcher*), also caught the attention of younger film buffs, *cineastes*—and producer Pressman.

"I thought her style was cinematically dynamic and her sensibility original," said Pressman, who compared his discovery of Bigelow to that of the young Brian De Palma (*Sisters*) and Terrence Malick (*Badlands*), whose early films Pressman produced. "Like them, I felt that she was trying to push the (film) form as far as she could. And my confidence in her has been reinforced on this location. She's bright, with a strong visual sense; she's totally in command; and the picture looks wonderful."

Pressman said he is committed to producing the next film slated for Bigelow. A futuristic film set in Japan, *New Rose Hotel* is based on a story by author William Gibson (*Necromancer*), who, as the "cyber-punk" king of science fiction, flourishes in the cult circle of fans who already surround Bigelow.

Bigelow was quick to acknowledge her influences and "the input" into her work from within this circle, as well as those who have gone on to commercial success such as Walter Hill and her friend Oliver Stone (who is co-producing *Blue Steel* with Pressman).

"There may be a certain relationship to other filmmakers, but she also paints a very different landscape, with color, light and dark, all to establish an atmosphere that deals with the darker side of America," said Larry Kardish, a film department curator at the Museum of Modern Art, where Bigelow's work, including her first twenty-minute short, *Set-Up*, is being added to the collection. "We think she's a significant talent."

Bigelow started out in the art world, first as a painting student at the San Francisco Art Institute and then, from 1972 to 1983, in New York, where she eventually showed her work at the Whitney Museum of American Art and edited a magazine devoted to art criticism. During this period she shot film backgrounds for a performance art piece, "fell in love" with the filmmaking process and enrolled in Columbia's graduate film school, headed by director Milos Forman.

A woman of few words who immediately comes across as bright and artistically motivated with an academic bent, Bigelow resisted analysis of her work, especially its categorization in the action/violence genre.

Acknowledging her fascination with "the impact" of violence on audiences (even her short-subject film consisted mainly of "two guys beating each other up," according to Kardish), Bigelow said: "It's not the violence, per se, it's the drama, with good, fleshed-out characters and a good story, that interests me. I'm interested in the art form. If I'm part of the action genre, then, well, I'm proud of that, and I love good action films. But I don't focus on my work in this way."

Bigelow also bristled at the suggestion that it is unusual for women directors to make their mark with action-packed or violent films. "There's nothing, culturally or socially, that would limit women to the more ephemeral, sensitive subjects—or men to hardware films," she said.

No one interviewed on location saw anything different about a woman's direction of what all referred to as a "graphically violent" action film. "When people bleed in this film, they really bleed," said Jamie Lee Curtis. "But this clearly isn't just a shoot-em-up, action film. It's not exactly an intimate, family drama either."

Both Curtis and Silver—who said he alone gets shot "about twelve times" during the course of the film—credited Bigelow for knowing "exactly what she wants and how to get it." And both actors said they never have worked with such a stylish director as Bigelow.

"She paints with light, rather than just lighting a set," observed Curtis.

Nobody on location was trying to distance the picture from Bigelow's last title. But everyone seemed to stress that the film was placed more in "the here and now" than her previous work and was cast with more familiar actors, including Oscar winner Louise Fletcher.

Was Bigelow attempting to move into the mainstream?

"What appeals to me in science fiction is the limitless possibilities," said Bigelow. "But the possibilities of exploring the human psyche are limitless too. This is a very psychological portrait of a very tragic mind— the killer's—and of our heroine, who, through adversity, comes to know a strength she never knew she had."

Bigelow said she was trying to "push the limits" of her subject, whether vampires or a police case. But she also acknowledged that she would like to reach beyond a "rarefied" audience toward a wider one.

"I've been very fortunate, getting producers, and it helps to write your own material—you've invented it. But I've had very limited access, in terms of audience, finances, options, and in film making, you have to justify the expenditures with wider audiences in order to continue. So I want more access.

"I can't just ask for money to fulfill my own creative desires. And yet I want to be able to continue to make films I can live with."

Happiness Is a Warm Gun

Phoebe Hoban / 1988–1990

From *Premiere*, April 1990, 45–46, 52. Reprinted by permission of Phoebe Hoban.

In a narrow cul-de-sac near Wall Street, a woman cop is fighting for her life. Jamie Lee Curtis, arm and hand bloodied, collapses against a car. Ron Silver's gun is aimed at her. It's the final showdown of a long, gory battle. Curtis, bleeding profusely from her ear and arm, gun clenched tight in her bloody hand, is struggling slowly to her feet.

"I'm in the wrong place," Curtis says, standing up suddenly. Her matter-of-fact voice is more jolting than gunfire. Silver, totally covered with blood, relaxes for a second. The makeup woman takes the opportunity to smear some blood on Curtis's wounded ear.

On the set of *Blue Steel*, there's more red than blue: Vials of blood. Gallons of it. Blood that's dribbled on with turkey basters and dabbed on with cotton balls. Stalking the actors with her camera is a tall, dark woman with the deadly concentration of a killer. Director Kathryn Bigelow is determined to nail this scene. "Action, three, two, one, FIRE!" Gunshots perforate the air. Bigelow gives a thumbs-up.

Blue Steel was shot on location in New York City over a period of nine weeks in the fall of 1988. It's a high-concept action-thriller about a rookie cop named Megan Turner and her nemesis, Eugene Hunt, a commodities trader turned serial killer who signs his crimes with bullet casings engraved with her name. Beside Curtis and Silver, the cast of *Blue Steel* includes Clancy Brown, Louise Fletcher, and Philip Bosco.

"When you are shooting in New York, you are shooting in spite of New York," says Bigelow, who already has a cult following for her trademark blend of violence and visuals. "It's like guerilla filmmaking. Sometimes we actually had to shoot between traffic lights." But, Bigelow insists, "this film couldn't have been done anywhere else. You need that sort of seething, boiling metropolis. This kind of psychosis, this ticking bomb–like character, is best suited to a schizophrenic environment like New York." The Wall Street area posed its own problems. "We probably had to deal with two million people over a three-hour period. But I was looking for canyons. . . . You can't get this kind of proportions anywhere else in the city. These narrow streets and that kind of height."

"Nice architecture," says Curtis, strolling over and twirling her blue-steel .38 Smith & Wesson. She delicately sprinkles bits of glass on herself in preparation for the next scene, in which she tries to ram Silver with a car. "I wouldn't want to come up against her in an alley with a gun," observes Edith Quiles, the real-life cop who taught Curtis to shoot.

It's after lunch, and Ron Silver is rehearsing. He's a bloody mess. The actor, who went from playing the hyperverbal movie producer in *Speed-the-Plow* on Broadway to playing this ultra-violent psycho killer (his recent *Enemies, A Love Story* was shot after *Blue Steel*), is kneeling in the middle of William Street, his gun pointed straight ahead. "Action!" Silver tries to fire the gun; he's out of bullets. He falls backward, and blood drips realistically from his prosthetic chest. "Cut!"

"I wasted the fucker," says Curtis, who's been schmoozing. Then she starts to sing. "I see a bad day coming / I see some trouble on the way / I see a Magnum in my future / I should have gone and done a play! / I see my body getting holey / I see me splattered somewhere soon / I see the gunfight needing Foley. I see me on the floor of the cutting room!"

It's one of several songs she and a few crew members have written as a part of a musical parody of *Blue Steel*. The song accompanies a scene from a bogus script: "INT. HERO'S BEDROOM—NIGHT. Megan (naked, bloodied, bruised, bullet-ridden, greasy, swollen, hungry, happy, sad, confused, sullen) (Ask K.B. to explain)."

"You know you're involved when you push it to the point of parody," says Curtis. She's been on the set for nearly forty-five days (many of them nights). Maybe she needs a break.

Blue Steel was finally scheduled for release by MGM/UA in March. The picture has been through the machinations of three studios. "It started out as a thriller and ended as an epic," says Bigelow with a laugh. Vestron Pictures originally bought the script (written by Bigelow and former partner Eric Red) for producers Edward R. Pressman and Oliver Stone from Paramount Pictures, where it was in turnaround with Bigelow attached as director. At about $10 million, *Blue Steel* was Vestron's most expensive property. It was scheduled for release last September, with much attendant hype; when the studio suddenly went under during the summer,

Blue Steel briefly fell into movie limbo before MGM/UA picked it up. Says Bigelow, "In a way we ended up having the best of both worlds. We made *Blue Steel* under the aegis of an independent, so we didn't have to compromise. Yet now we have the muscle of a major behind us." Meanwhile, Bigelow is working on her next two projects, *New Rose Hotel*, another Pressman production, based on a story by cyber-punk author William Gibson, and a Columbia script, *Johnny Utah*, which she is rewriting with her husband, James Cameron. (The two were married in August 1989.)

The word most often used in connection with Bigelow is "vision," and it's not just because of the way she looks. "Being near Kathryn, I feel like a fat dwarf," says Curtis, who obviously has nothing to worry about. "You don't like to be on a fucking set with her and be on the other side of the camera." A striking five foot eleven, Bigelow is long and lean and usually dressed in black leather and jeans. But that's not the reason she had become the darling of a coven of critics who went nuts for her previous movie, an arty vampire picture called *Near Dark*. It was because she has vision.

"One out of ten directors has vision," says Curtis. "Kathryn has it."

"I had lots of confidence in her vision," says Silver. "I was aware that we were pieces in a jigsaw puzzle. She knows frame by frame what she wants. She cares about the image a great deal, and I think she'd sacrifice aspects of her continuity and even perhaps character motivation if the image was cinematic and intriguing and exciting and striking enough. She has a vision."

Says co-producer Michael Rauch, "To me the most amazing thing about Kathryn is that she has a vision. That vision is exactly what you see onscreen."

You get the picture.

The thirty-eight-year-old Bigelow came by her vision via another medium: painting. From 1972 to 1983, she was part of the New York art scene, and her work was once included in an exhibition at the Whitney Museum of American Art. Her first brush with film came when she worked on a performance-art piece. She liked the experience enough to switch from canvas to celluloid and studied film at Columbia University's graduate film school.

Her first effort was a twenty-minute short called *Set-Up*, in which two men in an alley beat each other up to the drone of her professor's lecture. "I was trying to examine the nature of violence and why it can be seductive in a cinematic context," she says.

In 1981, Bigelow co-directed *The Loveless* a nihilistic reverie in a fifties biker gang, staring Willem Dafoe. A self-conscious exercise in retro iconography and attitude, the film started the word of mouth on Bigelow's bankability. In 1983, producer-director Walter Hill saw *The Loveless* and gave her her first development deal. It was four years before her next feature film, *Near Dark,* was released.

Near Dark became a cult classic when it hit video stores in 1988.

The film also caught the eye of Pressman and Stone, who had once worked on a script with Bigelow about south Los Angeles gangs. They decided to produce whatever project Bigelow wanted to do next. Says Pressman, "I think a director's main job is to inspire by the power of personality, often incarnated physically. Like John Huston, Otto Preminger. Kathryn has that in spades. Her being a woman and so, uh, forceful gives her a certain command."

Sheets of rain obliterate the breathtaking nighttime view from the City Midday Drug and Chemical Club on the fiftieth floor of 140 Broadway. Curtis and Silver are dining under the chandeliers, and a scrim and a smoke machine soften the light. "Perfect, we're ready. Picture," says Bigelow.

"I feel like I'm on top of the world," says Curtis.

"You want to get higher?" Silver asks seductively.

Curtis glows, then laughs hysterically. "I'm sorry Kathryn. I may have lost it. I'm sincerely fucked." Bigelow silently waits her out. A crew member mutters that Bigelow (all in black) looks like a vampire.

Silver takes a break while they do close-ups of Curtis. "When Rembrandt died, he gathered everyone around him and said, '*Mehr licht, mehr licht*'—'More light, more light.' When Kathryn dies, she'll be saying '*Mehr blut, mehr blut*'—' More blood, more blood,'" says Silver, smiling, one expensive shoe up on a table. "What's kind of nice about this is that when I was a kid, I used to play action scenes in bed with pillows. I'd pretend I was in war, and I'd die a million times. Then I went to acting school. Now my career consists of talking. So this is fun for me, because I get shot, I jump over cars. It really intrigued me that such a hard-ass script with really explicit, gory action scenes was written and directed by a woman. It was also one of the few scripts I've read where I could see the movie."

Curtis has retreated to the makeup room. "The camera definitely plays a big part in this film," she says. "This movie is shot so much in here"—she frames her face with her hands. "It's hard to act in this space, because you lose three quarters of your body. It takes away all the crutches and leaves you very exposed. But the challenge is to touch people in the midst of pretty pictures and beautiful light and action and adventure. This film is so spare, uncluttered, minimal, cool, stylized. It's about a woman warrior. Kathryn talked about [Sigourney] Weaver's role in *Aliens* and how a woman in a man's world almost doesn't look like a woman on the surface." Suddenly, a voice calls: "You don't have any blood in here, do you?"

In a quick scene that's quintessential Bigelow, the club's kitchen doubles as a morgue. On the counter, between steaming vegetables and soggy French fries covered with ketchup, are several plastic jugs of "blood." A big-bulbed baster is stuck in the red glop. The camera is shooting straight down an aisle of stainless steel. Clancy Brown, who plays detective Nick Mann, sticks a pencil into a plastic bag and extracts something tiny, which he holds up to the light: a bullet casing with Megan Turner's name carved on it.

It's the last day of shooting. A warm fall night with a nearly full moon. An ambulance is parked in front of a brownstone on East 82nd Street, its flashing red light streaks on the house. "These crime scenes are great," says Bigelow. "I love the way the red light looks on film. It's instant drama."

Curtis, dressed in spandex pedal pushers, staggers from the house, supported by Brown. He puts her in the back of an ambulance. "I gotta get you to the hospital," he says.

She clenches her teeth. "We're gonna get him. Now!"

By 2 a.m., the scene's been shot dozens of times. Co-producer Rauch tells Bigelow to wrap. "I just did the worst scene of my life!" says Curtis. Whoever's still left on the set straggles to the wrap party.

"I don't think a work of art is ever finished," says Bigelow. "It's only abandoned. You always try to negotiate for more—I'll be negotiating until it's been out in video for ten years. When Mike said 'Wrap,' I immediately recut the scene in my head. It's okay, I can live with it. I hope."

One afternoon last April. Bigelow's long legs are stretched out behind a desk in a New York editing room. Where she's been working on *Blue Steel* all winter. "It's very limiting just to work with a genre," she says. "I think it's important to work within an element that is familiar and comfortable and then take a left turn. And just when you take it a little too far, recoil a little. It's fun to kind of play with the genre, mutate it, refract it, challenge it. At the same time, it should be experienced on a very visceral level too. You should be able to chew popcorn and have a good time.

"I was really interested in making a movie with a woman at the center," Bigelow continues, "someone very strong but very vulnerable. You really ride her ride. And then there's this man who's like a ticking bomb. He has power, he has money, he has everything. But he has this psychosis. He's like a mental minefield that gets triggered by a traumatic event. Overall, what I'm most pleased with is the performances. I think that's where *Blue Steel* transcends its genre and becomes a character piece."

It's early June, and Bigelow is back in Los Angeles where she is screening a rough cut *Blue Steel*. From its emblematic opening scene in the police academy to the bloody climax in the financial district, the movie is a relentlessly stylized thriller. And if ever a writer exploited Chekhov's maxim—if you introduce a gun in the first scene, it should fire in the last—it's Bigelow.

"My interest was to sexualize the gun," says Bigelow, who films it like a gorgeous piece of sculpture. She even sticks a fiber-optic lens into the bullet chamber to show it from the inside out. Bigelow does beautiful things with light and shoots objects as if they've never been seen before. The movie is sleek and scary. It's how it looks that lingers in the mind's eye (even the blood seems decorative). While the premise lurches over the top, Curtis's lucid performance does not. And ultimately Good triumphs over Evil. But it's considerably less certain whether content wins out over form.

"The movie is a lean machine," says Bigelow. "If you want a ride, you get that. But I think if you are looking at it through other eyes, you'll also be satisfied."

Curtis says she's happy with the finished product too. "I was afraid that it was going to be like *Blade Runner*, with all these shafts of light, and ultimately it wouldn't be engaging." (Curtis needn't worry—the inimitable *Blade Runner* it's not.) "But I am pleased that it's more than that. It shows police officers in a really positive, heroic light. I'm really proud of that portrait. I told Kathryn, 'You really did this. You made your movie. Congratulations.' And she said, 'No, I didn't, you did.'"

Phoebe Hoban is a New York–based journalist who has covered art and culture for a variety of major publications, including the New York Times, New York Magazine, New York Observer, Vogue, GQ, *and* Vanity Fair. *She is the author of* Basquiat: A Quick Killing in Art *(Viking/Penguin, 1998) and* Alice Neel: The Art of Not Sitting Pretty *(St. Martin's Press, 2010).*

Dark by Design

Victoria Hamburg / 1989

Originally published in *Interview*, August 1989, 84, 85, 168. Reprinted by permission of Interview Inc. and Victoria Hamburg Cummings.

Writer-director Kathryn Bigelow makes tough, violent movies. Her first feature, *The Loveless* (1983), in which a motorcycle gang faces off against small-town rednecks, starred Willem Dafoe and rockabilly star Robert Gordon. Four years later she gained a small cult following with her second feature film, *Near Dark*, a mixed-genre tale about a young man who falls in love with a beautiful teenage vampire and joins her blood-sucking family on a gory rampage through the wild West. Bigelow's new picture, *Blue Steel*, co-produced by Oliver Stone, is an action thriller about a rookie cop, played by Jamie Lee Curtis, and a psychotic killer (Ron Silver), who become obsessed with each other.

The child of a paint factory manager and his wife, a librarian, Bigelow grew up in northern California and studied painting at the San Francisco Art Institute. She entered the Whitney Museum Independent Study program in 1972 and began experimenting with film while working as an assistant to Vito Acconci. Her first short, *Set-Up*, made at Columbia's graduate film school, is now part of the Museum of Modern Art's film collection.

Tall, willowy, and in her mid-thirties, Bigelow speaks in a surprisingly soft, girlish voice. We met in an empty production office in Manhattan while she was completing the final cut of *Blue Steel*. She was eager to return home to Los Angeles and be reunited with her fiancé, James Cameron, the director of *Aliens* and *The Abyss*.

Victoria Hamburg: It seems to me that you're exploring genre films in an interesting way. I'm wondering, are you defining ultimate archetypes?

Kathryn Bigelow: What interests me is treading on familiar territory. With the motorcycles and vampires, it makes the audience comfortable to know that there's something familiar; i.e., there's the genre thread through it. Then I try to turn the genre on its head or make an about-face, and just when I make the audience a bit uncomfortable, I go back and reaffirm—"Yes, it's all right." But it isn't necessarily conscious. I am keeping within the sense of something familiar, then trying to expand it, push its limitations. Maybe in the case of *Near Dark*, which is more like a vampire Western, there's a bit of hybridization of genre. I also think in *Blue Steel* there is a mutation that maybe implies a different genre.

VH: But instead of avoiding the issue, you embrace clichés. I think there is always some truth in clichés.

KB: Oh, absolutely. But again, the use of cliché is not a conscious approach. It's just a matter of working within a construct that is familiar and then subverting it in order to reexamine it.

VH: Do you think that by doing so you create a climate of safety that allows you to take the audience somewhere they might not ordinarily go?

KB: Possibly. Otherwise, I don't know if they'll take the ride with you. They want to; they're not going to balk at something new if you approach it in a certain way. Just when they think they know exactly what's going on in a story, something happens, and they say, "Wait a minute. I thought this was a horror movie." Suddenly, they're seeing a showdown, and it should be high noon, but it's midnight.

VH: I also think there's an amazing sense of space, a painter's composition, in your films—long horizontal lines. When I read the script for *Blue Steel*, I wondered how you would approach shooting in Manhattan.

KB: It's not a spacious landscape. In a way, the film's landscape is internal and psychological. It's a film of people—faces and eyes and behavior. *Near Dark* was a film about light and the absence of light—which implies great space and atmosphere. *Blue Steel* is really within the context of the mind, so it's telescoped, which doesn't immediately imply as visual a canvas. But it looks exquisite. It's clutter, an extraordinary sort of tribute to capitalism.

VH: It's also schizophrenic and psychotic—which is what New York is partially about.

KB: Yeah, it's an urban nightmare. There's this compression and a clutter of people and buildings. Whereas *Near Dark* takes place in the West, and there's an incredible expanse.

VH: Just from a nuts-and-bolts production standpoint, was *Blue Steel* harder for you?

KB: It was definitely physically and logistically tougher. So many productions take place in New York. New Yorkers know there is nothing novel about a film shoot—there's nothing educational or fun. They don't want their routine interrupted, because it's happened so many times. Whereas you go to a place like where we shot *Near Dark*—a town called Coolidge, Arizona, near Phoenix—and the entire town will bring box lunches and picnic trays and come watch the shoot for fun. There's a sense of camaraderie. Here, you work in spite of the city, but on the other hand, you have a sense of authenticity. This entire picture was shot on location—no studio sets at all, which can be very difficult.

The city is an incredible pool of talent, and as a city it tries to make things work for you. For example, we had a couple of shots down on Wall Street at rush hour. There were probably two million people walking within a single shot. There are logistic problems you would never face in any other situation.

VH: I wondered about that. There's this whole shoot-out scene right down on Wall Street.

KB: We made a lot of people very unhappy.

VH: How long did it take you to do that?

KB: About a week. We really did disrupt their world. Also, we actually shot in the commodities exchange during business hours, in the gold pit. The character Ron Silver plays is a trader. There we were—gold was being traded, we had an actor in the pit while people were trading, and I was thinking to myself, Am I affecting world commerce? Regardless of whether I am or not, I've got to get this shot.

VH: So when the gold market crashes, they're going to blame you.

KB: A couple of hundred people didn't realize Ron was an actor at all, because he was so effective. He'd done his homework. They would start trading with him, and then I'd say "Cut." One of the guys who actually tried to buy from him said, "Cut? What do you mean 'cut'?"

VH: What did you do?

KB: We . . . sorted it out. The president of the exchange was also in the shot. He was very helpful and explained everything to the trader—this guy had come in late, after everyone else had been alerted.

VH: Do you think the audience has reached a point where they're jaded by violence? It seems there's got to be a certain amount of violence in a cop movie or a psychological thriller before the audience will take it seriously. Otherwise, they'll say it's too arty.

KB: Yeah, I think you always tread that line. You also have to be careful not to make an exploitation film. You want to try to give it an edge, a kind of adrenaline, without compromising. You try to do it within a context that has integrity. So it's a fine line. You don't want to pander. On the other hand, if the audience is expecting something consistent with the genre that is defined, their expectations are going to be in contradiction to what you're delivering. I think if you can do it intelligently or give them the framework in which their expectations are being met, the violence might not be as gratuitous as it could be. Then I think that you are doing something.

VH: When you're doing scenes like the shootout on Wall Street, do you rehearse the actors a lot beforehand? Do you have much time on the set to work with them when there's so much going on logistically?

KB: It's difficult to rehearse something like that. In a way, that kind of thing is pure cinema. It's all constructed in the editing room. It's a series of shots. You're not actually letting the actors work to the best of their ability, the way you can in a dramatic scene, when they work with nuance. Character can evolve within the context of a scene with dialogue, but when you're in a situation where a person is simply surviving, it's very cinematic. I like to rehearse ahead of schedule—just go through the script and read it through. Not necessarily for performance, but for clarity and understanding, character, background. My fear—it's interesting, because this is a real departure from theater—is all of it might become mechanical. It's always a fine line.

VH: I wonder if you have any mentors, people who have protected you.

KB: Protected . . . I don't know.

VH: Or encouraged you.

KB: Yes. I mean, there are people whose work I truly admire and learn from. And, for instance, Oliver Stone helped *Blue Steel* get made. Without his involvement it would never have been made.

VH: How did that happen?
KB: It's a long story. In 1983, Walter Hill had seen *The Loveless* and cast Willem Dafoe in *Streets of Fire*. He was also setting up a producing deal at Universal and asked me what I was interested in doing. I pitched him a story about gangs in East Harlem, Spanish Harlem. I was interested in writing and directing, and he was to be the producer. Universal developed it, but various studio-head changes followed, and the project ended up gathering dust somewhere, I think at Columbia. Oliver Stone read the script, and he was interested in doing a project on South Los Angeles gangs. He asked me if I wanted to write it with him. We did research down in South Los Angeles, where there are like three hundred homicides a year. Extraordinary. Twenty minutes from downtown Los Angeles, you have this place where you think the National Guard should be brought in.

Anyway, just as we were about to begin that project, *Salvador* got underway, and then Oliver did *Platoon*. He saw it and called me up and said, "I'm interested in whatever you want to do next. If it helps, I'll produce you're next picture." I sent him *Blue Steel*, and he loved it. He shepherded it to Ed Pressman, who was able to get it financed. I guess having someone like Oliver behind it gives it a kind of credibility. To be out there solo can be difficult. It's a very tough piece, with a woman at the center of it who goes through hell. It's not a comedy. This is a tough sell.

VH: How do you feel about these projects that got shelved? It must be hard to be out there pushing one and the suddenly find it's on hold.
KB: The first few times it happens, you are emotionally devastated. Then you realize it's all a big waiting game. It's an inevitable process, and you just try to stay alive and not let it beat you. You have to triumph over it. It's simply the law of averages. You keep writing. It's a crapshoot and one script will ultimately make it.

VH: I always wondered how aggressive you have to be out there.
KB: It's like a feedback loop. There's a certain kind of aggression that's necessary. You're out there making a picture and trying to follow your schedule; you've got X number of shots to do. There's a certain kind of mind-set that you have to get into or you're not going to make it. You

see this kind of transformation, a metamorphosis, happening, but it's a necessary evil.

VH: Do you come from a big family?
KB: I'm the only child. What's interesting is that your parents become your peers, as opposed to sort of the "other." I'm obviously talking from only one perspective.

VH: When did you decide to become a filmmaker?
KB: Not until the mid-seventies. Up until then I was painting and thought I would make art of some kind. My understanding of film was cursory. I went to films as anybody does, purely for entertainment. After I moved to New York and started to make art seriously, I began focusing on European films rather than American cinema. With art everything had a big historical context, and I looked at film in the context of art. My knowledge of film was so limited that everything was exciting. I was just out there with a small crew. I didn't even know that what I was doing was called directing. I had the equipment, I had the camera, I had the lights. I kind of knew what I wanted to do, and was making these small films.

VH: Were you taking film courses?
KB: No, I did that after I started shooting. I really came into film as a naïf. And in a way I want to preserve that, because I was making art.

I came to New York when I was nineteen and somebody told me that the Whitney Museum had a great independent-study program. My teachers were Susan Sontag, Richard Serra, Robert Rauschenberg. Fantastic people would come down and give lectures. I took it so seriously, it was almost paralyzing. Then I got involved in conceptual art, so the hand, the colors, and all of that were dissipated. I had a series of odd jobs. One was working with Vito Acconci, putting together films that would run as loops for one of his shows at Sonnabend. He used to have these sayings on the walls. As I was filming them for him a light bulb came on.

Somehow I commandeered a camera, got a crew of friends together, and shot something. I was very interested in the idea of violence being seductive. Again, it was all from an analytical standpoint. I ran out of money and got a scholarship for graduate school at Columbia. Milos Forman was the co-chairman of the film division, and we had a lot of access. Peter Wollen was one of the teachers. He was great. He's illuminating.

Until I met him I was just looking at light reflected on a screen. After that it was more like a window. I graduated and wrote *The Loveless*.

VH: In *The Loveless*, after the young girl shoots her father, she comes out of the cocktail lounge and into his car. Then she puts the gun in her mouth and shoots herself. Willem Dafoe's character just stands there and does nothing. He's just been to bed with her, but he does nothing while she kills herself. What was that supposed to mean?
KB: Probably, only in retrospect, when you're asked questions like that, do you try to put references together. When you're writing, things are very abstract. There isn't the sense of a message, per se.

That character's story has more to do with the fact that she had triumphed over her father; suicide was for her a form of triumph. She did not want to be saved. Willem Dafoe's character respected her decision., even though it could be argued that she was too young to make a decision like that and desperately needed help.

VH: But how could another human watch and let her do that?
KB: It's very nihilistic—a certain kind of anger. But I really argued that her suicide was an act of triumph, even though in retrospect it seems very shocking. At the same time, given the future that she would probably face, maybe it was the strongest choice she could make. On the other hand, given that it was the 1950s, the nightmare she was in probably couldn't have been resolved any other way. It's just one of those things where you're writing and it's very intuitive, sort of abstract.

VH: When I read *Blue Steel* it also struck me that you're really hard on men. There's a sense of anger in both of these films. In *Blue Steel*, the cop's relationship with her father is bad—her father's very violent and beats her mother. She finally falls in love with a man who is a psychotic, who kills her best friend?
KB: *[laughs]* You think there's something the matter with that?

VH: It does seem a little angry.
KB: There's anger there, but I don't think of it that way. It's not like I'm channeling anger that should otherwise be focused on an individual. Not at all. It seems to be what is necessary for the character in *Blue Steel*, for the evolution of that story. In other words, her back story had to be very difficult. Becoming a cop probably gave her the strength, for the first time in her life, to stand up to somebody that she had wanted for

twenty-five years to stand up to. But now something has changed internally. The character in *Blue Steel* is interesting to me because she's very human. She's flawed; she makes mistakes . . . I think that's universal.

VH: Also when she makes mistakes, it's treated very harshly. She doesn't get away with it.
KB: No. *[laughs]*

VH: She gets suspended. Her best friend gets killed. Life goes really bad when she makes a mistake.
KB: *[laughs]* It's not a good day. Dark, dangerous situations. I try to ask myself why I'm drawn to that kind of material. It has an energy; it's very provocative. I think it's important to challenge.

VH: Her suicide made me wonder what kind of world you think we live in. It seemed hopeless.
KB: Ultimately, her decision over her life is her own responsibility. In other words, relinquishing that to somebody else would have weakened her.

VH: Would you make it differently if you were making it today?
KB: I don't know if I would. You know, with the flashback of her laughing, one can be left with an image of what is, in the context of the film, her happiest moment. I've never tried to argue the notion of triumph.
   In a way, *Blue Steel* has a little in common with *The Loveless*. It's about someone finally coming to terms with something that she has found impossible to come to terms with before. The circumstances she falls prey to give her a chance to act.

VH: Filmmakers who aren't just hired guns, who are doing movies that somehow relate to a personal view of the world, may, in a sense, find themselves making the same movie over and over again.
KB: I think even if you are a hired gun there's an obligation to personalize. On the other hand, it's the old paradox. If you're making art, you are truly investing your time and energy in a very personal creative desire. You can be very pure. On the other hand, there's art coupled with commerce. There's a point where your personal desires have got to work with respect to the economics.

VH: With *Blue Steel*, the stakes are higher than with your other films. The

people involved with it are on a much higher level. Did you have a sense of interference or strong guidance?
KB: Guidance, yes.

VH: So you didn't feel you had to compromise?
KB: No. I feel like when you get to the point you feel you are compromising, then you risk losing the thread of integrity that was the reason you wanted to make the film in the first place. If you're trying to satisfy too many different people's expectations, that poses a real risk to the material.

VH: Is there great pressure in Hollywood to compromise?
KB: Well, pictures ultimately have the tendency to be made by committee. You're trying to satisfy an audience that is perhaps a kind of animal that nobody can predict. It's really a judgment call. All you can do is hope and rely on the support of the people who hire you. If you've created the project and then taken it through to its realization, that gives you an important kind of leverage. Someone like Ed Pressman has a history of making films with people who have carried the project from inception to realization. He's been very outspoken about trying to protect that concept. But it's always tenuous, because you are at the service of an audience, which is fickle, and you're also in an industry that's very competitive.

VH: What are you doing next?
KB: *New Rose Hotel*, I hope, by William Gibson.

VH: What attracted you to that story?
KB: Probably its *noir* aspects. All of Gibson's material has incredible landscapes. To be honest, it was very hard to choose which story to do. He was particularly fond of this piece, so that also affected my judgment. It's about a character who is on a downward spiral from which he can't retrieve himself, no matter what he does. The more he tries to relieve himself, the more stuck he is. It's a wonderful ride.

VH: There's also an interesting relationship between a man and woman in that story.
KB: Wonderful. In the short story, she's a classic femme fatale, but as she is now in the script, she has incredible strength. And he benefits from that. So even though ultimately it's not a wise move when he throws

in with her for emotional reasons, it's completely understandable. You don't lose patience with the character, as you sometimes can with a femme fatale—you know, when you see it coming three miles away. It's also a character piece; it looks inside of a character who is without a country, without a home. The whole story takes place in Tokyo.

VH: It's difficult and expensive to shoot in Tokyo.
KB: I've heard stories. But I'm optimistic. Shooting is never easy.

VH: Will this be the first time that you will work with a script you didn't write?
KB: Yes. I'm thrilled. I really love Bill Gibson's world, and I love to be simply the translator and not necessarily put my stamp on it, whatever that stamp might be. I like to be just a conduit. That would be the ultimate objective on my part.

VH: I can't wait to see it.
KB: I can't wait to start it.

Blue Steel: Kathryn Bigelow in Action

Nancy Mills / 1989

From *American Film*, September 1989. Reprinted by permission of Nancy Mills.

Kathryn Bigelow gave up film to be a director and has given her films the distinctive style that she once put on canvas. "I was an abstract expressionist," Bigelow says. "My paintings definitely reflected a sense of light, but they were dark and frenzied." And so are her films.

The Loveless, which introduced Willem Dafoe to film audiences, was about bikers. *Near Dark* was a vampire Western. Critics described both films as "visually thrilling." And New York's Museum of Modern Art added *Near Dark* to its permanent film collection.

Bigelow's latest film, *Blue Steel*, a psychological thriller starring Jamie Lee Curtis, Ron Silver, Louise Fletcher, Philip Bosco, and Clancy Brown, should erase any lingering doubts about her ability to direct action movies. Considering the stereotype of female directors, she says, "I think people expect fairly tame movies from women. I don't know why that should be gender-related, but we have to work against those preconceptions."

Blue Steel pits rookie cop Curtis against psychotic killer Silver, who romances her while she investigates him. The plot of this tough genre film, however, isn't as arresting as its style. The movie, which was co-written by Eric Red, opens with hauntingly beautiful images of blue hills and valleys. Gradually, audiences will realize they are looking at an extreme close-up of a gun. "I tried to reduce the gun to planes and surfaces," Bigelow says, "so that it could be seen as an object of beauty."

"It's a tough piece," she admits. "It's violent, although the violence is not gratuitous. Women who have seen it see Jamie as a role model. There are very few women in films they can identify with, and they like to see women take charge. Whether that alienates men, I don't know. In this movie, there's no male character for men to identify with."

Bigelow, who is engaged to director James Cameron, is partial to action/adventure. She's more apt to notice a shiny orange truck than a row of trendy boutiques and doesn't recall playing with dolls as a child. ("Say, 'she ripped Barbie's head off,'" Bigelow jokes.)

Bigelow, thirty-seven, "dived into" filmmaking when a performance artist asked her to film some inserts for his show. A graduate of the San Francisco Art Institute and the Whitney Independent Study Program, she supported herself "through a million odd jobs."

When Bigelow needed to cut some film she shot, she thought, "Grad school." She won a scholarship to Columbia University's graduate film program and then (in 1980) made *The Loveless*. In 1983, she moved to Los Angeles to teach a class about B-filmmakers at California Institute of Arts. "I thought it would be interesting for students to see you could make a film for $60,000 in six days," she says. Now Bigelow is commissioning her own scripts.

Genre Bender

Kenneth Turan / 1989

From *GQ*, October 1989, 162, 168–69. Reprinted by permission of Kenneth Turan, film critic, *Los Angeles Times*.

Speed may kill, but action, filmed action, is the real drug. Like many nar-
cotics, it is a special taste, and one that is a little suspect in some circles.
Film should enlighten and uplift the race, the spoilsports say. And if all
that high-mindedness brings with it more than its fair share of snores,
it's a small price to pay for the putative benefits of culture. As Gene Kelly
says mockingly in *Singin' in the Rain*, "Dignity, always dignity."

Action junkies have a different, more operatic motto: a direct steal,
in fact, from Puccini's *Turandot*: "*Nessun dorma*," they insist, "Nobody
shall sleep!" True aficionados are not tempted by bogus protestations of
culture nor by the pale imitations of action films, such as the *Rambo* regi-
ment, that feature lots of huffing and puffing and hurtling bodies but no
visible skill.

Rather, their eyes light up when they talk about the grails of their
quest: exceptional, often underappreciated efforts such as Don Siegel's
Madigan and *Coogan's Bluff*, Sam Peckinpah's *The Wild Bunch*, Walter
Hill's *The Warriors*, George Miller's *The Road Warrior*, and James Cameron's *The Terminator*. They—I—insist that if you don't understand what
makes these pictures spectacular, you just don't understand what makes
film joyously itself.

Kathryn Bigelow understands. "It's pure cinema, where the medium
departs from theater," she says, her voice rising in excitement. "You can
perform, flex your muscles in a way you can do with no other medium.
You can stretch the medium, make associations you never thought you
could make." A pause for breath and a grin. "I think there will be a little
adrenaline in anything I do."

Bigelow does more than talk a good game. Her last film, 1987's *Near Dark*, stunned critics with its stylish, bravura flair for movement and engagement, and her newest one, the just-released *Blue Steel*, starring Jamie Lee Curtis and Ron Silver, will pop more than a few eyeballs. At thirty-seven, tall, strikingly attractive, and articulate, Bigelow is emerging as one of the peerless action/suspense directors of her generation. As Edward R. Pressman, one of *Steel*'s co-producers, has said, "It's provocative that she's a woman doing genre, but it's only interesting because her films work."

And work they certainly do. *Near Dark*, for instance, the story of a roving band of the undead in the Oklahoma outback, was a fascinating transfusion, if you will, of vampire mythology into the ethos of the Western. With a nod to Anne Rice's novels and the help of lead actors Jenny Wright and Adrian Pasdar, it heightened the erotic implications of blood-sharing and still found time—while the Cramps' version of "Fever" played on the sound track—to stage a splendid blood feast-cum-Walpurgis Night in a redneck bar. And I do mean red.

Another key Red, Eric by name, was Bigelow's co-writer on *Near Dark*, and they collaborated again on what came to be *Blue Steel*. "It started with an abstract notion, the idea of an action film from a woman's point of view," Bigelow says. "Gradually, it took shape; it became about a woman cop, a rookie, who goes through a trial by fire."

The first sound heard in *Blue Steel* is a woman's screams, and the first action you see is New York City cop Megan Turner (Curtis) inching down a hallway to break up what seems to be a nasty domestic argument. It turns out, however, not to be reality but merely an exercise in Turner's police-academy training, and one that she is not totally successful in coping with. "In the field," her instructor tells her, "you have to have eyes in the back of your head."

Once in the field, Turner loves her work, but we all know that problems lurk ahead. Almost immediately, she is called upon to single-handedly stop a supermarket robbery, and though, in a heart-stopping sequence, she succeeds, the miscreant's gun is surreptitiously lifted by Eugene Hunt (Silver), a suave and successful commodities broker who was one of the witnesses to the holdup. As the film progresses, Hunt pursues Turner romantically at the same time as her involvement in a series of grim serial murders turns Megan's life into, yes, a living hell.

The robbery scene is one of *Blue Steel*'s several well-constructed action sequences, segments that work as well as they do because Bigelow takes tremendous care with them. "I [story-] board all those sequences," she says. "Every shot is drawn out; I cut it on paper. It really is well worked out before the camera starts turning. Once you get into the cutting room to knit it together, you can see some options: a leap, a juxtaposition, an association you can make that gets you from *a* to *e* quicker than going through *b*, *c*, and *d*. That's where the magic comes in."

Casting is also critical in a film such as this, and Bigelow says that, "when we wrote it, Jamie was a prototype without our ever thinking it could really happen. That was a pipe dream. We thought we would have to cast an unknown. But through a stroke of luck, a casting director sent her the script, we met, and from that point on, that was it. Megan is a tough character to play. There's not a lot of glamour. She has to be incredibly strong but not hard; her beauty has to come from within and has to be androgynous. She has to be an Everyman; I wanted both men and women to identify."

Blue Steel's considerable impact is more visceral than rational. Its logic being the logic of nightmare, not that of reality, it will not score high on anyone's probability meter. Yet Bigelow has made it with such a brilliantly stylized technique, you don't care about the plausibility gaps; you are happy to go along with the director through the hairpin turns that the plot presents, and you end up feeling, as she herself does, about Turner's adventures, "I was there on an emotional level. I rode that ride."

The coauthor and director of these terrible rides grew up in the sunny climes of San Carlos in the San Francisco Bay Area, and she was not terribly interested in movies at first. "I absolutely thought I was going to be an artist," she says. "My background in art is fairly extensive; I focused on it fairly seriously, even obsessively." After high school, Bigelow attended the San Francisco Art Institute for two years and then received a scholarship to the prestigious Whitney Independent Study Group in New York.

"I was nineteen years old," she says, perhaps still not quite believing it, "and Susan Sontag, Richard Serra, and Robert Rauschenberg were commenting on my work." It should have been enough, but somehow it wasn't. "The art world was very politicized in the early seventies," she remembers. "It was difficult to work without a political context; the process of making art became a very serious venture. You couldn't make anything without knowing the references."

So, like fellow eclectic directors of the stripe of David Lynch and Yahoo Serious, Bigelow made the transition from static images to moving ones—with a vengeance. "I was so excited to discover a whole new world that didn't come so heavily analyzed that I wanted to drown myself in film," she says. "So I approached it with child-like exuberance."

That exuberance, even back then, tied into violence, as in Bigelow's first film, a short called *Set-Up*, which the director describes as a street fight dissected both visually and verbally. "I was interested in what worked, what got your adrenaline going." Bigelow was also interested, once her funds ran out, in getting *Set-Up* finished, so she looked around for a film school "that had more equipment per student." That turned out to be Columbia, where Bigelow not only got her master's but was able to take classes with Edward Said and help edit the avant-garde journal *Semiotext(e)*.

Bigelow's first feature, co-directed by Monty Montgomery, was called *The Loveless* and starred fellow New York avant-gardist Willem Dafoe. This nihilistic biker pic laced with melodrama seemed fated, like *Set-Up* before it, to do nothing more than play the international festival circuit, but something else happened.

"By great fortune," Bigelow says, "a casting director showed it to Walter Hill, who cast Willem in *Streets of Fire*." But Hill not only started that actor's mainstream career, he took an interest in Bigelow's as well. He agreed to produce, and helped her get a studio deal for, a contemporary Latino-gang version of *Romeo and Juliet* she wrote called *Spanish Harlem*, but though the project ended up in "development hell," the horror of the experience convinced her that she had to write on speculation to preserve her options. "You tell people, if the good news is they want to make the script, the bad news is they've got to take me as well," she says. "You have to become a gladiator for eight months"—which is, in fact, how *Near Dark* got made.

Though the making of genre pictures doesn't have the cachet of other, more bloated kinds of filmmaking, the very success Bigelow has had in being inventive within its boundaries, in finding genre's possibilities liberating rather than enclosing, is helping change all that.

"If you touch on something that's familiar—touchstones like cops, Westerns, horror films—turn it on its head and when you're about to go too far, pull back and remind the audience of what is familiar," she says with the satisfaction of a job well done. "That's when you're pushing the envelope."

Kathryn Bigelow's Disturbing Vision

Gerald Peary / 1990

From the *Toronto Globe and Mail*, March 30, 1990. Reprinted by permission of Gerald Peary.

"I keep saying I should go into psychoanalysis to see why I am attracted to showing violence," says Kathryn Bigelow. She is the director of *Near Dark*, a blood-soaked 1987 vampire movie, and now, *Blue Steel*, a volatile cop movie featuring a pistol-packing police officer (Jamie Lee Curtis) after a serial killer (Ron Silver) who is shooting up New York City.

Bigelow insists that "film genres are not gender-specific," and that men should be able to direct gentle romances, and women gory shoot-'em-ups. Still, she can't help puzzling about how significantly her ultra-violent obsessions diverge from the pacifist concerns of women of her acquaintance, including women filmmakers. "I wish I could find an explanation in some resonance from my childhood," the filmmaker jokes, when interviewed after *Blue Steel*'s first European screening at the Berlin Film Festival.

An avid filmgoer, Bigelow, thirty-eight, veers toward action-packed genre pictures, including westerns, cops-and-robbers standoffs, and bloody films noir. *Blue Steel* is particularly influenced by two such movies she admires, *Fatal Attraction* and *Dirty Harry*. Of the latter, Bigelow says that being a female doesn't stop her from relating to Clint Eastwood's hotheaded police officer. And if her films are compared to the brutal, hardboiled-to-heartless works of director Walter Hill (*Streets of Fire, The Warriors*) Bigelow happily agrees. "I love Walter Hill! I don't deny trying to emulate him."

Bigelow does look favorably on the filmmaking of two women directors in Hollywood—Randa Haines (*Children of a Lesser God*) and Penny Marshall (*Big*). However, she acknowledges that her real director heroes are all male: Hill, John Ford, Howard Hawks, Sam Peckinpah, Akira Kurosawa, Oliver Stone, James Cameron, Martin Scorsese. "They're high-impact filmmakers, and they draw characters with whom one can have strong emotional investment." Simply, Bigelow says, "The male voice is valuable. I don't think a male voice is an evil voice."

But there's a need for women to be heard also, and Hollywood remains, Bigelow admits, "a male-dominated hierarchy where a woman has to prove herself 200 per cent. I didn't write *Blue Steel* as a personal piece, though it's a picture of a woman fighting for her voice."

Jamie Lee Curtis's Officer Megan Turner is determined to succeed among New York's finest, despite the objections of her unsupportive father, and despite a rebuke for her job performance by male higher-ups in the force. Refusing to have her hands tied by the intractable police hierarchy, the rookie female officer makes like Dirty Harry Callahan and goes one-on-one with psycho murderer Eugene Hunt (Silver).

Bigelow says, "Why should guy directors have all the fun? My interest was in making a women's action film, but one which men could also identify with. Jamie Lee has the right androgynous look, tough but vulnerable, and not glamorously feminine."

Is *Blue Steel* a feminist work?

Bigelow pauses, trying to find the comfortable answer.

"I subscribe to feminism emotionally," she says, "and I sympathize with the struggles for equity. But I think there's a point where the ideology is dogmatic. So I'm not saying that *Blue Steel* is a feminist tract, per se. But there's a political conscience behind it. The story was responsibly researched. I spent time with judges, and with male and female defenders of the law trying to apprehend criminals. And I try not to exploit my characters or the situations they're in."

However, there are few feminists who would endorse what Bigelow terms Officer Turner's "liberation and self-revelation" through "literally strapping on her guns" and facing off against Hunt. Bigelow explains: "Hunt has said to her, 'You and I are alike. You'll realize that.' Megan, the executioner, has to become him in order to stop him. With calm, cool precision, and with a reserve of inner strength far greater than she imagined, Megan fulfills her contract. She becomes a person."

But isn't this initiation into adulthood through violence the traditional "macho" rite of passage?

"If defending herself is macho, then it's macho," Bigelow answers. "It's having to survive in a high-stakes game."

The native California filmmaker—tall, long-limbed, and quite undeniably striking in appearance—was born in San Carlos, below San Francisco, the daughter of the manager of a paint factory. Wall paint led Bigelow to oils and acrylics, and she started out as a visual artist, attending the San Francisco Art Institute and winning a scholarship to the Whitney Independent Study Program. In New York, she became involved with a group of conceptual artists and writers who went by the imposing name, Art and Language. "Then Vito Acconci hired me to film some material to be projected behind his performance piece. For me it was a revelation. I said, 'Ah hah! Movies!'"

Bigelow earned another scholarship, this time to Columbia University's graduate school of film, headed by Czech film director Milos Forman. "I knew the technology already, but wanted to study the scholarship and criticism." She had a revelatory course with then *Village Voice* critic Andrew Sarris, who lectured passionately on the "auteur" theory of cinema—that the greatest films are made by directors with strong personal visions. Bigelow's first film, *Set-Up*, was a short made at Columbia, and shown in the New American Film Series.

Leaving Columbia in 1979 with an MA in film, she began work in a "microscopic-budgeted" feature, *The Loveless*. It was co-directed by Monty Montgomery and starred, in his first movie, Willem Dafoe, then an uncompromisingly avant-garde stage actor.

Released in 1981, pre–Jim Jarmusch's *Stranger Than Paradise* [1984], *The Loveless* was regarded then as too self-conscious and conceptual for the general public, though it became a mainstay of international film festivals.

But it was with *Near Dark* in 1987, widely acclaimed as a horror movie of arresting poetic power and visual elegance, that Kathryn Bigelow became noticed by film critics and cultists. For her tale of a family of vampires on a rampage, she was crowned an "auteurist" herself.

While making *Near Dark*, she learned to shoot a gun. "It was for pragmatic reasons, not enjoyment," she says. "I needed to learn what live ammunition is like, so I could find out about recoil, and that there's a kick."

In *Blue Steel*, a gun becomes a central character in the movie, what Bigelow describes as "A fetishized element . . . the libidinal extension of Hunt's psychosis." Hunt steals the robber's Magnum .44 and, after carving Megan's name on bullets, begins to use it to kill people. "I can justify rifles," Bigelow says, "but I am mystified by people with handguns. They are weapons with grave ramifications."

Near Dark played originally in art houses and gradually gained a popular audience on video. *Blue Steel*, released through MGM/UA, opened in a wide distribution across North America, and Bigelow couldn't be happier.

"When I made art, it was a very isolating and elitist process. A showing required expertise, to understand, for example, the value of a white-on-white painting. Eventually, what became exciting to me was the visceral, the stream-of-consciousness. I now want to make high-impact films which transcend education and class structure, which are impossible to feel ambivalent about, and which inspire a cathartic reaction."

James Cameron and Kathryn Bigelow

Tom Johnson / 1990

From *American Film*, July 1991, 42–46. © 1991 American Film Institute. Reprinted by permission.

James Cameron, self-described "king of the sequel" has built his career on the intelligent action-adventure flick. After supporting himself as a truck driver while writing screenplays, he landed in the industry with a job at Roger Corman's New World Pictures as a miniature-set builder and art director. Cameron came into his own as a director with *The Terminator*, which he co-wrote with Gale Anne Hurd. With its inventive special effects, sophisticated plot twists, and feminist undertones, it set new standards for the genre. Now Cameron must clear his own hurdles with the release of *Terminator 2: Judgment Day*.

It should come as no surprise that Kathryn Bigelow began as a painter: Her work is set apart by its stunning visual nature. She has brought a poetic style and a shot of feminine insight where it has rarely been seen before—to movies like *Near Dark*, a quirky vampire yarn, and *Blue Steel*, an action thriller.

The two directors agreed to let us eavesdrop as they discussed their craft over dinner in a Los Angeles restaurant. The fact that they are husband and wife played only a small part in the conversation.

Bigelow: I think it's interesting that we both have movies coming out within a four-week period of each other.

Cameron: Well, it will be interesting to stay married after the grosses come in.

Bigelow: [Laughs] Respond professionally.

Cameron: You mean we have to be professional with this interview? For the last two movies, we've both been shooting at almost the same time. The difference is you're a little ahead of me on both films. On *Blue Steel* and *Point Break*, you've been about a month ahead on both films. So I get to see every horror looming before it actually happened to me. The horrors of wrapping and not having all the shots you need, the horrors of looping, the horrors of . . . you go through everything a beat before I do.

Bigelow: What joy.

Cameron: Which I suppose, in a way, is good because . . .

Bigelow: [Laughs] It gets you prepared.

Cameron: It gets me prepared, but on the other hand, I have to live through it twice. How do you think actors perceive you? On a spectrum where you have Eric von Stroheim at one end and Woody Allen on the other—you know what I mean, between dictatorial and supportive— how do you place yourself in that spectrum?

Bigelow: Well, with every actor it's different. You have to find a vocabulary that works best for them and understand their process. So with every actor there's a different methodology. With some you need to be very straightforward, deliberate, reveal your needs for a particular scene. With others you involve them in the process, get them to invest emotionally by making it *theirs*. For me the rehearsal period is the invaluable search for communication. It had less to do with perfecting a scene and reevaluating the script than it had to do with communication with a particular actor, examining their process, enabling them to view yours.

Cameron: That's a very smart answer. You know, you read about directors or you hear other directors talking about the manipulative tricks that they use with actors, as if these things can be generalized, and they can't.

Bigelow: Everyone works differently. Everybody has different expectations, different strengths, weaknesses. Because acting, as you know, is a very fragile process, and it's a very fragile bond that occurs between actor and director. I think if you view the director-actor relationship as a process that is always in a state of evolving and transforming, something fluid, never fixed—so you don't project some intractable grid on an actor—then you allow something entirely unexpected to come through, something unpredictable that is a wonderful surprise.

Cameron: It also depends a lot on how much you trust the actor. If an actor comes to you with an idea that seems to be born of the material in a way that you can relate to, you're going to have a totally different response to that actor than to someone who comes to you with something that's clearly a personal agenda. That's why I like working with Michael Biehn, because he always comes back with ideas that aren't exactly the way I saw it but are within the universe created by the script. There's always this great sense that not only is he pushing me and challenging me, but he's doing it in a way that is constructive. And this is not something that I believe is ever done maliciously by an actor. I think they always think that they're being constructively creative.

Bigelow: Some actors seem to feel they have to push against the yoke of authority just to know their parameters.

Cameron: But you can't pull rank. I mean, at a certain point you have to give the character away and say, Now it's *you*.

Bigelow: But as the writer of the material, the inventor of the character, probably nobody understands that person better than you.

Cameron: Well, it's a completely different process.

Bigelow: No, it's not. It's the same. The same trauma, the same precarious balance between ownership and authorship and a series of negotiations. Constant, perennial negotiations.

Cameron: Everything is a negotiation in filmmaking. The only time you're not negotiating is when you're on the set.

Bigelow: But then you're negotiating with the actors. So as you're inching your way toward postproduction on *Terminator 2*, having extrapolated on the premise with all its inherent permutations, how do you feel?

Cameron: Like I'm going to die. I'm still shooting, so that's not a fair question. You can't be objective when you're in the thick of it. I need to put some stuff together, to stand back from it a little. This is obviously a very different picture. I think it bears a kind of similar relationship to *Terminator* as *Aliens* did to *Alien*, in that it has goals beyond the goals of the first film but it tries to be true to the spirit of the first film as much as possible. It's an extrapolation that, hopefully, the audience will perceive to be very logical once they see it, but they may not have thought of it.

Bigelow: But that's the beauty of it. That's the beauty of *Aliens*. Surprise mixed with . . .

Cameron: Familiarity. It's like a Baked Alaska, you want to do two things that shouldn't be able to coexist. You want to be able to create a positive sense of surprise as opposed to disappointment, which is also a surprise, and yet always create a sense of familiarity.

I feel like I'm the sequel king, you know, having done *Terminator 2*, *Rambo: First Blood Part II*, and *Aliens*, which was *Aliens II*. My first movie was a II, which will remain unnamed. See, the great thing about working with you is that you have such a singular style that I don't feel like you're trying to emulate anyone. You know, you kind of always see the world in your own eyes in a certain way, so when I watch your movies, I'm seeing through a totally different perspective. Like, it would never occur to me in a million years to go across the street and set up the scene on a 300mm lens. Why do you do it that way?

Bigelow: First of all, I see a scene in my mind's eye. I get to a location, I have to make an aesthetic translation of the material, not to say that aesthetic necessarily means *pleasing*. I try to address the particular demands of the scene. In other words, should it be a kind of off-center unbalanced camera that is in constant motion, placing the viewer inside the action, or do I want to distance the viewer, keep the viewer on the outside looking in?

Cameron: But how do you decide between a highly subjective approach to a scene like the bank robberies and a highly objective point like the scene where Keanu Reeves is standing at the take-out stand and the bank robbers show up in the background—the character in the scene is being observed by the audience from a kind of godlike perspective, where they see what's going on and he doesn't? How does that decision get made? Does it come from the script?

Bigelow: Well, that was a decision to let the audience in on a secret that the character is not privy to.

Cameron: Do you think that creates a sense of participation?

Bigelow: Absolutely. And that's the same reason for using point-of-view material. How do *you* visualize a scene or approach a scene?

Cameron: I reread the scene. Never more than, like, the day before I shoot it. I reread it, having not read it in a long time, and I see what the most important element in the scene is. Whether it's the suspense, whether it's a specific character moment, whether it's simply an A-to-B scene where we're getting a sense of environment or geography. The shot has to be designed around that. I think the big mistake is to be seduced by the set or the environment or whatever when it's really a scene about an important character moment. You know, I want to see the set when, really, I should be close in on the actor's face. So that's a decision that needs to be made in advance.

Bigelow: If it doesn't move the story forward, it's irrelevant how extraordinary the shot might be. Everything must be at the service of story and character.

Cameron: Yeah, is it a kinetic scene? Is it basically a passive scene? Don't impose a kinetic style just because it's cool on a scene that really needs to settle down and be very conventional. I think some of the best sense I've ever directed have been extremely conventional from a camera standpoint or from a lighting standpoint.

So how do you reconcile the great directorial dialectic, which is: What's the scene about visually and what's it about dramatically? Your background is art and the visual arts. When did you make that decision as a filmmaker?

Bigelow: When I started to work in a narrative form.

Cameron: Which was when? *The Loveless?*

Bigelow: Not that that was great evidence of it, but . . .

Cameron: It absolutely was.

Bigelow: What is interesting about having a background in visual arts is that aspect of production is very freeing for me. I'm very confident along those lines and I don't worry a shot to death. I know when it's right, when it looks right, when it will serve the needs of the film. I know that the look of the film will be adequate. What it frees me to focus on is story and character, which is what I spend twenty-four hours a day, during a production, thinking about.

Cameron: But that can't be true, because otherwise your films would not have any visual impact at all. Some of your mental process has to be devoted to that.

Bigelow: It's not something I deliberate over. I can find good shot. I can make something look exactly the way I want to in an efficient amount of time. What that does is enable me to focus on everything else.

Cameron: Do you ever find yourself halfway into a scene and you find out it's either not working or you just regret it?

Bigelow: Oh, sure.

Cameron: What do you do?

Bigelow: I am faced with the parameters of the schedule and, if we're in a difficult time frame, I'll live with it and proceed.

Cameron: 'Cause you've thrown that die and it's cast.

Bigelow: Exactly. I've made a decision and I have to commit to it. I can't shoot a scene twice. I'm not Woody Allen. You have one shot. You design a scene a certain way and that's the way it will be. There have been scenes that I have regretted doing at the end of the day, but when I put the film together, they work beautifully. And conversely, scenes that I'm thrilled with—the footage is wonderful, the shots are kinetic—they just take over the screen, and it's too much life for the moment. I mean, I'd like to be more refined in my instincts and have experience educate my decisions . . .

Cameron: I had the experience of starting *Terminator 2*, as a conscious decision, almost identically to the first film, with the intention of misleading the audience as a result of that. I found that [having shot the scene before] didn't help at all. I knew there was a way to shoot Arnold Schwarzenegger that worked for that character. Being waist-level on a 25mm lens looking up had a certain effect on him that made him seem larger and more powerful. So I had an inside track on some things, but I still had to create it from scratch. Which just goes to show that every day you go out there, there's a whole new set of problems.

So what was it like, working with Patrick Swayze? Don't you hate that question? It's the lazy journalist question. The thing that I observed from afar [as executive producer] is that Patrick as an actor had much less respect for the script than most other actors I worked with, which at first I resented. In the long run, I think it annealed what was good about the script, because he challenged everything. Which I think is a good process to go through as a director.

Bigelow: I agree. It refined and honed my attitude toward the material and it forced me to be far more specific than I'd ever been in the past with respect to a particular scene, a particular handling of a scene.

Cameron: Ed Harris, on *The Abyss*, never challenged the words. And I don't know if that was just a particular challenge he sets for himself when he does a part, but it was an interesting experience. It was an almost tacit contract: I'll accept these words but I'll say them my way. And it was an entirely different working process. I don't think one is valid over the other, it was just an interesting experience. With Michael Biehn, it was quite the opposite. He would challenge absolutely every word. Not in a confrontational way but, Is this the best way it can be?

Bigelow: I think, ultimately, through challenging the material, you gain insight into it. I think it was a very positive process, an extremely positive process.

Cameron: Sigourney [Weaver] went through an interesting cycle: She'd challenge the script and then gradually see it refracted back to her in the way she thought she wanted it and then go gradually back to the way it was, almost without exception. What ended up on screen was almost 100 per cent as was originally written. But she had to go through all the excursions in order to validate what was already there.

Bigelow: Well, I mean, that's exactly how I viewed Patrick's examination of the material. It was his method of territorializing the character. It was like an exorcism. And in his case, that was exactly what attracted him to the material.

Cameron: You know, Arnold did *The Terminator* seven years ago, and on the first day of shooting *Terminator 2*, he fell back into the character in a split-second in a way that was kind of awesome to behold. It still requires the presence of a director. I still have to say to him once in a while, too much emotion on that line, you know, turn your head this way, whatever. It's always an interactive process.

I dread meeting up with the actor who thinks that his performance will be a hermetically sealed thing and it's my job to set up the camera. Because to me, ultimately, setting up the camera is the boring part. Creating something that never existed before is the exciting part.

Bigelow: I find biblical or religious references in your films, especially the two *Terminators*. Is that intentional or subconscious?

Cameron: I think it's a combination of subconscious and intentional. I catch myself doing it for subconscious reasons, and then I interpret to myself and decide whether it's acceptable or unacceptable to be kept in.

Bigelow: It's very life-affirming in a metaphysical way.

Cameron: I think it demonstrates the principle that religions fulfill deep-seated psychological needs for people and, if you don't get it from a specific religious doctrine, you'll get it from some other source, whether it's a myth that's been handed down or it's a myth you're creating for the first time. And part of filmmaking—certainly the kind of films I like to make—is the creation of a kind of neo-myth. You know, a lot of these psychological archetypes tend to play from the subconscious.

Bigelow: Yes, it seems that humanity needs myths to transcend their own corporeality.

Cameron: To me that's a slightly separate subject because there's an aspect, especially to a film like *The Terminator*—the first one—which is quite consciously meant to give a sense of empowerment to the individual. And, you know, clearly it was the story of a waitress who saves the world, who essentially becomes the most important person in the world, albeit for a brief moment.

Bigelow: It's about the power of the individual as opposed to the collective.

Cameron: Interestingly, after *The Terminator*, I did *Aliens*, which was the story of an individual in a structured, hierarchical situation who rises through the ranks, from a position of no power, to become the person who is completely in control. And basically, once again it was a story about the empowerment of the individual in the system or the individual operating outside the system becoming dysfunctional and the individual having to take action, having to make decisions to do something.

Bigelow: I think, based on your body of work, it would be impossible for you to work with material that didn't have a conscience. Even though it's frighteningly accessible, your work can operate on several levels simultaneously, can be subliminally subversive.

Cameron: It's a very difficult thing to do, but certainly it should be a goal to try and create a piece of entertainment that can stimulate some kind of intellectual pursuit and, at the same time, satisfy a very straightforward need in the audience to be fulfilled.

Sometimes those two things are at odds. It's a question of finding a specific narrative that allows them to work together successfully. I think you're going through a similar evolution in *Point Break*. You're able to satisfy a lot of literary and conceptual impulses for yourself as an artist but, at the same time, tell a very populist story. And a film that doesn't compromise . . .

Bigelow: That's the beauty of pulp. But it's disguised propaganda, perhaps.

Cameron: Absolutely. It has a strong philosophic spine. It's about an individual at odds with the systems or organizations that don't satisfy the basic needs of the human animal.

Bigelow: I think what's interesting in *Terminator* and *Point Break* is that the system is what the characters are struggling to assimilate or to triumph over and participate in at the same time. Creates some sort of paradox.

Cameron: It's the great, ambivalent impulse of humanity: You want to be free and you want to be an individual, but on the other hand, human beings are builders. At a deep-seated instinctive level, we're ants. We like to build things. We like to see order. And so these two things are always in diametric opposition, always.

Bigelow: We like to see order, and we like to make sense of everything—to codify, to catalogue—to put into historical perspective when there is really all this sort of wonderful chaos or anarchy threatening to tear everything apart. It's really at the core of both pictures.

Cameron: That's the difference between a film like *Aliens*, where Sigourney was clearly an individual right from the beginning and always fighting against a structured view of the world, and *Point Break*. In *Point Break*, Keanu Reeves' character has been seduced by that kind of black-and-white western philosophy.

Bigelow: Until he's seduced by a world and a lifestyle that is in diametric opposition to everything he has known. He kind of gains a soul.

Cameron: He finds out there are places where his black-and-white view of the world just doesn't work.

Bigelow: His involvement in the FBI is very innocent, very naïve in a way.

Cameron: It's the kind of gung-ho naïveté Tom Cruise's character had in *Born on the Fourth of July*.

Bigelow: Keanu Reeves' character perceives the FBI with almost a childlike enthusiasm. And that time of innocence is over at the point when he comes into contact with the character Bodhi. Suddenly, survival is equated with enlightenment. It's a revolutionary thought for the character.

Cameron: The funny thing is, in a way, within the film, you see him reborn into a new world where he has a kind of childlike innocence again, but in a different way, in a primal way, in an emotional way.

Anything else, dear?

Bigelow: Do you have anything else?

Cameron: I can't wait till *Point Break* comes out.

Bigelow: Why?

Cameron: I don't know. Because they'll say, Kathryn Bigelow, that must be some strange Eastern European pseudonym for a man. *Kathryn,* it doesn't sound like a man's name, but it must be. Women don't do action like this. It will be very interesting to see the response as the world catches up with you.

From Style to Steel

Nick James / 1990

From *City Limits*, November 29–December 6, 1990, 26. Reprinted by permission of
Nick James.

In 1982, London clubs were almost entirely patronized by people who
had dumped their New Romantic sash cords for the frisson of torn jeans
and a perfect flattop. When it came to music, those hedonists were all
soul fans, but in looks they plumped for the downhome classicism of
fifties rebel style. The previous year, Kathryn Bigelow's debut feature *The
Loveless* had opened, mostly to critical abuse. Complaints followed the
line that Bigelow's tale of the disruption of an American small town by
a gang of marauding bikers was slow, pretentious, and too much in love
with its period. Watching it in '82, in a cinema full of rockabilly night
owls, all I heard was laughter and delight. From the opening, which first
introduced us to Willem Dafoe—astride a Harley, wearing black shades,
black leather, and perfectly greased hair—*The Loveless* belied its dumb
surface and even dumber reputation. It was a delicious, tongue-in-cheek
wallow in sexual iconography whose images were soaked in a lingering
ecstasy of form, at once reverent and irreverent.

Eight years on, Bigelow herself is the imposing, black-clad figure
of legend. The one with the "70mm eyes" and the bright new critical
reputation for remorselessly going against the stereotype of a woman
director. This is her reward for daring to tread through the blood, gore,
and jagged metal of boytown in order to make *Blue Steel*, a psycho-killer
thriller dipped in blood with a female cop at the center. If anything, Bigelow's camera is even more fetishistic now. Apart from the unique credits sequence which features a fiber-optically lit .38 Smith and Wesson
revolver blown up to unimaginable hugeness, there's an equivalent to
the caressing pans across bikes, boots, and zippers of *The Loveless* in the

considerable attention paid to the lineament of the New York City Police Department uniform.

"I don't know if this fetishization of the technology of power is completely conscious," says Bigelow. "Perhaps it's something to do with the social climate today. People feel so powerless and there's great vanity in power. There's something very attractive about iconography of power, in certain rituals of identification in dress. Also there's an instantaneous response to somebody who is very beautiful and there's no point in denying it. You're massaging that imagery and trying to examine, explore, and understand it."

The investigation of uniforms, buildings, and other sculptural manifestations of power was very popular among art critics and structuralists in the late seventies. Magazines like *ZG* carried articles on Nazi iconography and the deconstruction bible *Semiotext(e)* ran a "Poly-sexuality" issue with a leather-clad clone on the cover. In the editorial credits for that edition was none other than Bigelow who, at the time, was active in the Art and Language group of avant-garde art practitioners. Much has been made of Bigelow's switch from the New York art scene to mainstream filmmaking (and her subsequent marriage to Hollywood blockbuster director James Cameron), yet her concern with the texturing of a language, particularly one of power, follows a consistent line.

"I made the change to film because I love the medium," she told me. "I felt that art world audience was very elitist. This came from my work with Art and Language. Their exquisite, painful expression—art as the modification of the social fabric as it exists—I just extrapolated from that into film where the audience is anybody. It doesn't require a certain knowledge to appreciate it."

The move to the overrground hasn't exactly been swift. Bigelow has completed only three movies in the time, with the 1987 cult vampire/western *Near Dark* bridging the gap between boy bikers and woman cops. *Near Dark* played hell with both genres to wonderful comic effect, with its bunch of superhuman hayseed-vampires delighting in their blood-hungry on-the-road lifestyle, and if there's anything about the Bigelow style that's missing from *Blue Steel* it's the knowing bulge in the cheek. "Maybe it's a less humorous subject," she says. "It wasn't as fantastic as *Near Dark*. This was more grave."

Just as critical interest in codes of dress was interpreted and watered down for the eighties in the phrase "power dressing," so Bigelow's fetishistic interest in the surface of things has been lifted and reapplied by scores of ad directors. If you're looking for the progenitor of all those

Levis ads you need to look no further than *The Loveless*. That seems a much more serious offense than the idea that Bigelow's films revel in bloodletting for purely sensational effect—*Taxi Driver* and *The Seven Samurai*, to name but two, are equally aware of the dramatic power of ketchup. But the ad men retained that sense of self-mocking humor which makes *The Loveless* and *Near Dark* so delightful (and Bigelow collaborator Eric Red's *The Hitcher* for that matter).

What's worrying is that Bigelow may start to take herself too seriously. Asked if she might make a film that didn't play around with genre, she says, "Absolutely, because what really drives me is story and character." Somehow that just doesn't sound like Kathryn Bigelow.

Hollywood's Macho Woman

Mark Salisbury / 1991

From the *Guardian*, November 21, 1991, 27. Copyright Guardian News & Media Ltd 1991. Reprinted by permission.

Kathryn Bigelow has been asked this particular question a lot. No matter how delicately you phrase it, how much you skirt around the issue, it comes down to the same thing: why does she make the kind of movie she makes? As the sole woman director regularly working in the traditionally male-dominated action movie arena, Bigelow has had to contend with her critics ill-at-ease with her proficiency with the medium. Moreover, she does it better than most of her male counterparts.

"I don't think of filmmaking as a gender-related occupation or skill," Bigelow recites in response. It's an answer she must have given many times before. "I think a filmmaker is a filmmaker is a filmmaker. That's not to say you don't bring your own either masculine or feminine tendencies to any particular body of work. Men can handle, for instance, emotional material beautifully, just as a woman might. It's a question of perception, of how a woman might handle something that might be perceived as masculine; but then you have to ask yourself, why is it perceived as masculine? Action is action."

By her own admission Bigelow makes "high-impact films that get in your face"; gut-wrenchingly kinetic, explosively visceral, poetically violent; like a female Walter Hill crossed with Sam Peckinpah. While fellow directors Peggy Marshall and Martha Coolidge are content to scour the emotional battlefields, Bigelow goes for a rush response: all fast edits, up-front camerawork, and an almost fetish-like respect for weaponry.

Oliver Stone, producer of her last film *Blue Steel*, says she possesses a relentlessness he describes as masculine. Bigelow laughs at the suggestion, again questioning the need to assign gender. Though she does her best to disguise it, there's a twinge of irritation in her voice.

Point Break, out this week, is Bigelow's highly enjoyable fourth feature. A visually stunning, if intellectually shallow, surfing/sky diving romp, it stars the talented Keanu Reeves as a fresh-faced FBI agent on the trail of a gang of bank robbers who disguise themselves as former U.S. presidents—Reagan, Nixon, and Carter. Tracking them to the beach he falls under the beguiling influence of surfing guru Patrick Swayze. So far, so spectacular.

Yet having formerly succeeded in wringing new twists from well-worn mythologies—bikers, vampires, and cops—with her first three efforts you'd expect more than wipeouts and macho-bonding from Bigelow. "It's not about good guys and bad guys," she contends. "It's a little more complicated when your good guy—your hero—is seduced by the darkness inside him and your 'villain' is no villain whatsoever, he's more of an anti-hero."

Nor, she insists, is it a film simply about surfing. "The ocean in this particular context serves as a crucible for the main characters through which they define, test, and challenge themselves. It's a film about self-realization; they could have been doing anything. The unique thing about surfing is that it kind of exists outside the system, the people that embody it are of their own mind set, they have their own language, dress code, conduct, behavior, and its very primal, very tribal. I tried to use the surfing as a landscape that could offer a subversive mentality."

Californian-born Bigelow regularly connects the subversive surfer thieves of her latest work with the anarchists of her first film, the art-house biker film *The Loveless*, and the nomadic vampires of her second, the inspired *Near Dark*. "Movies can be cathartic," she says. "I think they can transform you, they're kind of windows onto another universe that you can't experience in any other context. I think the most important thing is to work in an accessible format but with a conscience—that's the overriding motivator for me."

Given her position as queen of the action picture, does Bigelow believe her work will encourage women to follow her lead and make tougher, grittier films? "I think they should just be encouraged to work in an as uncompromised a form as possible, be that tougher or softer," she responds. "It's really a question of being true to their vision." Bigelow's own, she says, is reflective of her surroundings. "There's an element of reality . . . certainly *Blue Steel* was inspired by having lived in New York and being aware of a number of women on the police force and imagining what their life and experiences might be like and how they might differ from their male colleagues."

While *Blue Steel*, with its gun-toting female protagonist (Jamie Lee Curtis), can lay claim to initiating the whole women-with-guns trend that peaked this summer with *Thelma and Louise* and Linda Hamilton in *Terminator 2*, Bigelow shies away from acknowledging the connection. "It's just a reality. As the violence in our society escalates I think it's a symptom more of a kind of social disease than a filmmaking trend."

She will, however concede that accepted female dominance on screen hasn't necessarily translated to any great transference of power to women off it. "It's difficult for any emerging filmmaker, be they male or female, because it's such a competitive arena and only a few films are made each year. But I think it's changing. It's a process that can only get better."

Kathryn Bigelow

Ana Maria Bahiana / 1992

From *Cinema Papers*, January 1992, 32–34. Reprinted by permission of Ana Maria Bahiana.

Born in 1951 and raised in San Francisco, Bigelow was trained in the arts; first in the San Francisco Art Institute and then at the Whitney Museum in New York. She found herself bored with what she called the "elitist limitations" of traditional visual arts, so with a group of other avant-garde painters and sculptors Bigelow started dabbling in film as an expressive medium.

The passion struck immediately and lasted. Bigelow enrolled in Columbia University's Graduate School of Film, where she studied under Milos Forman. In 1978 she completed her first project, *Set-Up*, a much-praised short film chronicling a violent street gang confrontation. Three years later Bigelow directed her first feature, *The Loveless*, a stylish biker movie starring Willem Dafoe.

Bigelow's next film, *Near Dark*, had a troubled postproduction. "The company that made it lost its distribution [deal] while we were cutting the movie," recalls Bigelow. "They sold it to Dino de Laurentiis, but DEG went bankrupt while it was releasing the picture. So it happened twice on the one film! That's terrifying for a filmmaker." Still, when the film finally hit the major markets in 1987, it firmly established Bigelow as one of the most promising and interesting American filmmakers—"non-gender specific," she adds with a mischievous grin.

Blue Steel (1990), a gripping thriller starring Jamie Lee Curtis and Ron Silver, and this year's surfers-on-a-crime-rampage, *Point Break* (starring Patrick Swayze, in his first post-*Ghost* role, and Keanu Reeves), further expanded her clout as an action director who, of course, also happens to be a woman, and is married to another master of the genre, James

Cameron. "It's funny," she says. "No one approaches Walter Hill and says, 'Walter, because you're a man, how do you make such and such a movie?'"

Q: After making *Blue Steel*, where the female character is the driving force, you chose to do *Point Break*, which is essentially a male-bonding picture. What attracted you to this project?
A: It had everything: characters with really great psychological dimensions and an environment and setting which I thought offered a lot of possibilities. It is a world that hasn't been seen before. You might think you know a lot about surfing, but when you analyze it under a microscope, it becomes very surprising: primal, tribal, mythical, and romantic.

Q: Did you do a lot of research into the California surfing community?
A: I met and talked to some of them. They have a really strange spirit and are very spiritual, but in a crude, inarticulate way. They don't communicate verbally and are very Zen—there is no other way to describe it. It is like they have evolved to a higher state of consciousness.

Q: Did you uncover any violent strain in the community, such as the one you portray in *Point Break*?
A: No, no, no. They're not violent. In the film Bodhi [Patrick Swayze] says, "I hate violence," and that's very important for his character [a mystical mastermind who shows Johnny (Keanu Reeves), an FBI agent, a whole new way of looking at the world and himself].

Surfers are not violent people unless they're pushed into a situation. There is certainly a lot of aggression out on the water, but surfing is a singular quest and a personal challenge. They put themselves in life-threatening situations every single day because they love it. They are very surprising.

Q: You certainly portray them with an almost mythological dimension.
A: I look at things not in the specific but metaphorically. Politically, it's really interesting to keep those myths alive, to not buy that grid, that system, without challenging it. Maybe they don't articulate it, but surfers do challenge the system. There's a myth here, an American Spirit; they're like cowboys.

Q: Did you get a lot of feedback that you, a female director, were shooting a macho-action film?
A: I had people saying that the audience would never know that this was written and directed by a woman [laughs].

I don't think directing is a gender related job. Perceptions that women are better suited to certain types of material are just stereotypes, they're merely limitations.

Q: Would you say then that there is a stereotype that women can only direct "soft" material?
A: I don't really know if that stereotype exists, because so few women direct! I can't buy into clichés. I think the other way around: Why aren't more women making this kind of action movie? I'm curious.

Q: What was the starting point for your previous film, *Blue Steel*?
A: It all began with the idea of doing a woman action film. Not only has no woman ever done an action thriller, no woman has ever been at the center of one as the central character. Obviously I was fascinated by that because I'm a woman watching all these action films and there's always a man at the center. You begin to identify with this man, with the most powerful character.

From that takeoff—deciding to put a woman in the center—we worked out what the ramifications would be: How was it the same? How was it different? Obviously, when a person is fighting for her life, for survival, there are universal aspects that transcend gender. To what extent is it germane to the fact that she's a woman?

We then put in a serial killer, gave her an obstacle, and also made it a twisted, strange love story.

Q: And for *Near Dark*?
A: *Near Dark* started because we wanted to do a Western. But as no one will finance a Western, we thought, "Okay, how can we subvert the genre? Let's do a Western but disguise it in such a way that it gets sold as something else." Then we thought, "Ha, a vampire Western!"

So it became a wonderful meld of two mythologies: the Western and the vampire movie. One reinforced the other. That sort of clicked.

Again, we came up with some characters and then put them in horrible structures to see what happened.

Q: Were Anne Rice's vampire books a big influence in your writing?

A: We were aware of them, but when we were writing we went straight to Bram Stoker's *Dracula*. The transfusion in the end comes straight from *Dracula*.

Then our effort became: How can we redefine and reinvent this vampire mythology in a way that hasn't been done in writing or in the movies? So first of all we decided not to call them vampires and, second, we took away all the Gothic aspects—castles, bats, crosses, stakes in the heart. Ours are modern vampires, American vampires, on the road. I don't know what they are. They're creatures of the night who must drink blood to survive. They are . . . curious.

Q: What prompted you to make the transition from painting to film?

A: I felt painting was isolating and a bit elitist, whereas film has the potential to become an incredible social tool with which you can reach a mass audience. Some painting requires a certain amount of knowledge or education on the part of the viewer to be appreciated. Film is not like that. It *must* be accessible to work within a cinematic context.

Given that, the transition made a lot of sense. Film is accessible, challenging, and very stylistic, very visual. It works as a narrative and I saw it as a kind of modern literature. It's a very complex medium and I love it.

Q: Were you always attracted to directing?

A: I never thought of it as "directing," but as a different way of making art. I was doing painting, then I was making movies. Later I realized that what I was doing was writing and directing, being a filmmaker. But I really saw it as just switching mediums, from the world of art to mainstream movie-making.

Q: Does your art training help in the visual stylization of your films?

A: It is important, but I am drawn mainly to story and characters. That's the most important thing; the visuals come easily.

With my training, I can obsess on the visuals forever. But I focus more on the story and the character, because that is what needs the work. No matter how beautiful a film looks, the most important thing is that an audience connects with the characters. You can make the picture too nice and distract people from the emotions it has.

Q: Your films show a certain fascination with the subject of violence. Is that a personal interest of yours?

A: I don't know. It's not necessarily a personal fascination, though I do like intensity in movies. I like high-impact movie-making. It's challenging, provocative. It makes you think. It upsets you a little.

I'm just not drawn to material that makes you feel good constantly. I don't know why. I just love to see action films by George Miller, Sam Peckinpah, Martin Scorsese, [James] Cameron, Walter Hill. These are great filmmakers. It's high impact with emotional involvement.

I'm also drawn to strong, dark characters that you believe in and care about. I like putting characters in very intense situations, which are an organic extension of those characters and that story. Take the roadhouse scene of *Near Dark*: I know it is a very violent scene, but I couldn't imagine portraying those characters without that scene, without showing how they live. That is the truth of their life. I thought it was critical to the picture.

In *Blue Steel* the guy is a serial killer. He's not someone who just waves his gun around. He is a seriously deranged human being. You need the truth of his character, his psychosis.

So I guess I believe in violence as a way to portray a character or a story faithfully. That doesn't preclude soft, emotional material that has no violence. It's just that the particular stories I've chosen are very intense.

Q: Do you believe there is a feminine way of expressing violence in film?
A: I don't think there is feminine way of expressing violence or dealing with it. There is only just the filmmaker's approach. I don't think it's gender specific. Violence is violence. Survival is survival. I don't think there is a feminine eye or a feminine voice. You have two eyes, and you look in three dimensions and in a full range of color. So can everybody. What about a woman's background would make that vision different?

In all my films, my characters, male and female, are fighting for their lives. That's a human thing.

Q: As you said, women are still a minority when it comes to directing—especially their own scripts. But there have been a few changes this year, with important films like *Thelma and Louise*, *The Doctor*, and *Rambling Rose* being written or directed by women. What, in your opinion, would be necessary for a major change in Hollywood's gender bias?
A: More women have to want to make movies. Maybe the desire is not there, because I have always believed that where there is a will, there's a way. I don't believe in tokenism. It's not a matter of the industry saying, "Okay, we want more women directors." A woman and a man should

work under the same degree of resistance. In other words, it should be based on their projects and what they have to show behind them.

Women have to realize very early on that every conceivable occupation is open to them. I can't think of anything that would not be open to a woman. So, it's an educational thing. As babies, girls are given certain toys, boys are given certain toys, and certain instincts are developed and become encoded. If you just realize that anything is possible . . . it is!

Momentum and Design: Kathryn Bigelow Interviewed

Gavin Smith / 1995

From *Film Comment* 31, no. 5 (September 1995): 46–50. Reprinted by permission of Film Society of Lincoln Center.

"Everything's already been done," someone observes early in the fever dream of noir dread, yearning desire, and euphoric millennial convulsion that is *Strange Days*. It's New Year's Eve 1999, and in Kathryn Bigelow's alternately brooding and pulverizing new film, Entertainment has, for all intents and purposes, become the medium for a jaded nation's ever more spectral political life. By extension, the film frames the End of History as the End of Cinema as we know it. We're in a Los Angeles of confetti and riot helmets, where the sun never rises and Hollywood is obsolete. In this ultimate police state, the limos are all bullet-proof, supermodels mug Xmas Santas, and a rap star is Black America's foremost statesman. Until now, this paranoid L.A. has never made it to the screen—it only looks this way in real life.

As the year 2K looms, there's a new kind of kick—getting wired on the ultimate high: SQUID, the movies' technological nemesis, a forbidden virtual-reality expressway to our skull. The pleasure community of audiences and actors has been replaced by a world of solitary users and, on the production end, wearers of devices that record sensory and emotional experience for replaying via clips. The wearer becomes the ultimate viewer-surrogate, living out the user's fantasies of sex and violence. The moral economy of creative imagination—of both producer and consumer—has been eliminated from the transaction. Is the end result rapture, or rupture?

Bigelow's protagonist is former cop turned blackjack clip hustler

Lenny Nero (Ralph Fiennes), a man who makes a living fixing clients up with the kind of playbacks Blockbuster probably won't be carrying. Lenny's a decent guy gone to sleaze and, as in all good noir, it's because of a woman. He's hooked on a personal collection of memory clips of his ex, Faith, rising rock star and prime candidate for casualty status (Juliette Lewis in a performance that plumbs astonishing emotional depths). Stumbling into a murky conspiracy of unknown dimensions, Lenny finds himself out of his league. Enter Mace (Angela Bassett), a chauffeur/ security specialist weary of Lenny's hustles but ready and able to back up her friend. (In Bigelow's characteristic androgynous casting, Fiennes's feminine aspect is accentuated while Bassett—magnificent—is the muscle, all tight-lipped self-containment.)

Entertainment is in the eye of the beholder all right: the film's first image is a frantic eye. *Strange Days* seems named for its end times setting, yet "estranged daze" might best evoke the condition of spectatorship that the film envisions—when surveillance and entertainment become indistinguishable, when escapism can be a deathtrip, when microchip-assisted empathy is more likely to appeal to the worst in us than enhance our sense of humanity.

Bigelow's increasingly state-of-the-art films are dependably visceral, compelling genre exercises, visualized with a high-art sense of complex form and acute design and a knack for hyperreal, eroticized, charged visuals. But above all they're metacinema of the first rank, freely interrogating the imperatives of action movie thrill seeking by incarnating them in out-for-kicks outlaws—bikers in *The Loveless* ('81), vampires in *Near Dark* ('87), a serial killer in *Blue Steel* ('89), surfers in *Point Break* ('91)—who seek apotheosis through transgression. *Point Break*'s Bodhi (Patrick Swayze) goes so far as to rationalize that, by defying the law, he and his gang act as benign surrogates for the oppressed masses ("We show them that the human spirit is still alive!") . . . including, perhaps, audiences.

The Fear of Movies, and of seeing, that pervades *Strange Days* is finally overcome by a reaffirmation of cinema as an imaginative space. Alienating spectacle is relieved through social catharsis, and the film declares the primacy of imaginative emotional identification between viewer and characters as, in a delicate point-of-view shift during the final moments, Mace's unrequited love displaces Lenny's at the film's emotional center. *Strange Days* is a disturbing picture of our times that enlists the morbid fascination and terrible beauty of the movies to uphold a vision of passionate, embattled humanity.

Q: How did *Strange Days* come about?
A: Jim Cameron had been thinking of and working on it for about nine years. He presented it to me around 1991 and I thought it was a fabulous, mesmerizing story. At that point nothing was really written, so he wrote a treatment and then we developed it together into a script. Everything I've done I've had input into the writing.

Q: What was your way into it?
A: The politics was very important: the landscape of a society, a flash-point society maybe on the brink of civil war, the tensions that were permeating every crevice. It's not an incredible stretch of the imagination. Anybody who was in L.A. at the time of the riots will acknowledge that. I went down to help with the cleanup, and it gave me a lot of the visuals. You'd be on a street corner with these shells of buildings that once were, with tanks and National Guard cruising by.

Q: How did Jay Cocks become involved?
A: Jay and I had worked on a script, together, after *Point Break*, on *Joan of Arc*, a piece that's near and dear to my heart. It was a masterful script. I thought he would be a real complement to Jim.

Q: Were there any notable elements that came from you specifically?
A: Jeriko [Glenn Plummer] was very important to me, what he stood for and the broader ramifications. There are two simultaneous tracks: the character story, which is the heart and soul of the project, and then the landscape against which the story takes place, that is a kind of narrative in and of itself, a charged political arena. But there's a deep, fundamental need for humanity against that landscape—the fact that a Lenny Nero exists against that landscape, and his ability to be vulnerable, his emotionality, really is his redemption. It's the interface of the two that makes it work; if they were separate, one may be too familiar, the other too didactic. You keep bouncing back and forth from the microcosm to the macrocosm.

Q: His agony is a metaphor for the agony of a divided society—or vice versa. You don't know which is a metaphor for the other.
A: They're reflecting pools—one is not there without the reflection of the other. And as the environment gets more oppressive, the desire for genuine experience, for the SQUID [Superconducting Quantum Interference Device] technology, increases.

Q: And it's a vicious circle.

A: Constantly feeding itself. Part of why cinema is so attractive is what Roland Barthes said about it's being a tear in the fabric of society, a widow onto another universe. The desire to see and watch is part of the human condition. I guess it's called scopophilia—to fetishize watching.

Q: Is this your most personal film?

A: It's a synthesis of all the different tracks I've been exploring, either deliberately or unconsciously, ever since I started making art. Of reflexive ideology, something that comments on itself; a kind of political framework; a narrative that uses classical forms. At the heart of it, it's a love story. And then you have the architecture of a thriller or noir. So it follows every track and yet creates a cohesion out of all that—not that necessarily there's a simple answer, that you can neatly tie up all these threads at the end. Because the tensions still exist: it's an ongoing process, a conversation as opposed to something finite. And there's something very beautiful or serene at the heart of the film that's antithetical to the environment, which is grim, brutal, disturbing, and the hideous creativity of the killer.

Q: All your films deal with elite, closed groups that set themselves above society in order to pursue a private vision of transcendence and exaltation. You could say *Strange Days* takes the idea of escapism to an ultimate state of being.

A: It's a kind of transgression: the desire to escape through watching, to cross over, can be insidious, and comes with its own price—just like the price that's paid in *Point Break*, or the price [Megan (Jamie Lee Curtis)] pays in *Blue Steel*, or the price you pay for immortality in *Near Dark*. There's a connection there, an alternate universe that folds back on the world as we know it. But there's no state that's absolute. It's mutable; it might move through exaltation to utter destruction back to exaltation. *Strange Days* is a movie where we are led to believe that it's the end of the world at the stroke of midnight, and all the forces of destiny seem to suggest you're converging to that point.

Q: *Strange Days* is above all a film that is profoundly troubled about the business of mass entertainment.

A: [Laughs.] It's sort of at war with itself. You can't come out of the art world without tremendous ambivalence. It's part of the process, you question everything.

Q: You're not supposed to do that in Hollywood.

A: Well, what are you supposed to do? You're supposed to entertain.

To simply entertain: is there such thing as a neutral text? I don't think so.

Q: So in *Point Break* you gave us a profoundly satirical and politically literal spectacle of Ronald Reagan using a petrol pump as an improvised flamethrower, laying waste a gas station, then rampaging through the backyards and living rooms of America, pursued by Keanu Reeves of all people—the most blatant critique of the eighties I can think of.

A: [Laughs.] That's what's so fabulous about the medium. It enables you to work on so many different levels. If you were simply to do a critique of the last decade, it'd be so didactic it'd be painful. Satire is such a potent tool. It can be ignored and the piece still works; it can be enjoyed and the piece might work more. *Strange Days* is the ultimate Rorschach.

One difference that's very interesting is the difference between objective and subjective violence, which by the nature of the [point-of-view technology] puts the viewer into a very unusual position—as culpable for the first time. (I shouldn't say first time: in *Peeping Tom* there's a complicity.) And it's not consensual. Or maybe it is because you bought the ticket. And why'd you buy the ticket? The reason the clip of the murder of Iris is so disturbing is that it's so unflinching. There is a kind of purity about it, it's not sensationalized. There's no seductive lighting, it's just flat, cold, harsh bathroom light. There are no interesting angles. It's all dictated by the medium and the apparatus.

Q: It denies the idea of the mediated image.

A: The possibilities are infinite. In a way Lenny Nero is like a film director. He directs the participants. At the climax he's watching someone who he thinks has been killed, who's experiencing that event for pleasure, and yet he's experiencing his revulsion, his terror, and at the same time the killer's pleasure.

Q: It's like a feedback loop.

A: It's such a compression—like sound waves reverberating off reflective surfaces. You have this continuous reflection.

Q: Very conceptual.

A: Right! That's the script. Ralph and I talked a lot about Lenny as a director/producer/writer—and in some ways I found him studying me. So it was really an amazing opportunity to work within the medium, comment on the medium, treat it as subject and yet have all that at the service of a love story. The emotional centerpiece of the film for me is the scene where Lenny explains that it has nothing to do with Faith, or even the fact that he loved her and cared for her. It's that he made this promise and that's all he has left, this commitment to this person.

Q: And his interior world has no correlation with the reality of Faith. His denial and loss are the psychological equivalents of the "false" experiences of the clips. He doesn't even need the clips.
A: When Mace says, "Memories are meant to fade, they're designed that way for a reason," that's the matrix around which the whole movie revolves. Talk about feedback loop—Lenny is caught like a gerbil on a wheel [as Max (Tom Sizemore) says].

Q: Your stressing the importance of the love story as the core of the film makes me think of *Near Dark*, where the love story between Caleb (Adrian Pasdar) and Mae (Jenny Wright) drives the story and the lyrical opening sequence between them establishes an authentic sense of humanity.
A: Without that stuff, it's an exercise in futility. You just go from one explosion to another, you create a wall of sound in which a single character moves from peak experience to peak experience and you have no opportunity for that which engages you—the moments of human contact and character development: things that don't seem like momentum, and so they often have a tendency to get lost at the script or cutting stage.

Q: When you design and execute a complex action sequence, how do you maintain a balance between elements and keep them alive? There's one in *Point Break* where you have multiple areas of attention that have to be kept in motion.
A: You're talking about the surf Nazi shootout. I think geography is so important in action sequences. I see a lot of films in which geography is sacrificed, it's just a lot of fast cutting, a lot of noise, a lot of impacts—and I have no idea where I am, or who's coming from the left or right. So I start with storyboards. I usually have a foam core model built and work the pieces; sometimes I'll do video animatics to see the angles and see how it works—and then I keep compressing and compressing it in the boards, pulling shots out to see how tight I can make it yet be completely oriented.

Q: But it's also possible to use disorientation strategically.

A: Right, I cross lines; I'm not talking about keeping religiously to axes, but just keeping a fundamental sense of geography.

Q: But when you cover a scene like that shootout, or the opening bank robbery, do you cover each character's movements from start to finish so that you have all those options?

A: It depends on what I need. At the end, in the big heist, the two cops lying on the floor—you don't cover them until you need them to figure in the story. So it's based on where you need the focus of attention to be at each particular moment. It's all about fragments. When push comes to shove, I'll always go for an additional setup as opposed to an additional take. I'll get another angle. You need coverage to make something like that work.

Q: Are reverse angles more important in those scenes?

A: Reverses and tie-ins. There's nothing more golden than a tie-in. If you're shooting a gun at me, there's the obligatory single, then me, the reaction, getting shot. But what I think is as important—and I'll always have two or three cameras working simultaneously—is to get the tie-in, so I'll go behind the subject with another camera so you see the geography of the two people. Even if you just use it for six, eight frames, you have an instantaneous sense of, Oh, they're there.

Q: What about the camera movement in the chase at the end of that POV?

A: Basically it's a modified Steadicam that gives you the fluidity of Steadicam but the realism of handheld, without the limitations of either.

Q: So you sort of retuned the Steadicam.

A: Right, there's a gyro-stabilizer you can detune or tune in, depending upon how much life you want in the camera. For when she runs into the train yard and in front of a speeding freight train, well, no insurance company or train yard would ever authorize that. Carrying a camera crew behind you with a train going at eighty miles an hour—I don't think so! So we did that backwards; the train was backing up and we reversed the footage.

For all the POVs we tried to find ways of handling them so that it just looks like that's what happened. There's no real contaminating or adulterating the image so that it looks artificially created or too overly manipulated. Those are my favorite effects.

Q: In the supermarket holdup in *Blue Steel* you intercut different moving camera styles: formal, distanced tracking, subjective handheld, and what I'd call sympathetic choreographed Steadicam movement somewhere in between.

A: I really only started to work compatibly with the Steadicam and trust it in *Point Break*. You can create an edit-free situation, yet it has the pace and sense of a quickly cut sequence. People move in and out of their coverage, and the actor and camera can move counter to one another. I love the purity of an unbroken shot, and I love that juxtaposed with a sequence that has tremendous editorial intrusion.

Q: It's musical.

A: Exactly, there are rest notes and then there are flurries. You need rest moments where the camera is simply covering two people in an unbroken wide shot and you see the body language. It's a cinematic exhale. That's why we have punctuation. Peak experience only exists in relation to something that is not. It's all context.

Q: Were the demands of the chase sequence in *Point Break* very different from the robbery sequences?

A: They're actually very similar. Both need a tremendous amount of coverage. The chase as scripted was this incredible, relentless piece, and it's really what gave me the confidence that I could do these POVs in *Strange Days*. That was my first glimmer of an unbroken sequence: even though there are cuts, it was almost constructed as if there were none.

Q: What were the most complicated shots technically in *Strange Days*?

A: The POVs, because they had to be continuous and unbroken. I shot all the POVs to be unbroken if I wanted them to be. We would choreograph for days in preproduction. In the opening POV, we're putting everybody into the refrigerator and we realize the cops are there and we have to exit, so we look this way and we see the other robber going up the stairs, and we look behind us and see there are cops out the window. . . . You have a whole crew that's equally choreographed: you pan and everybody drops, eighteen people, then you pan back and they all pop up again.

Q: What went into the visual style of the POV sequences?

A: We had to build a camera to do the POVs, a stripped-down Arri that weighed much less than even the smallest EYMO and yet would take all the prime lenses. And I also needed remote follow-focus capacity—your eye is so light and quick and mobile, whereas with a forty-pound Pana-glide, everything is wiping and blurring because of the sheer weight of the camera; so we needed a lightness to give it the flexibility of the eye. Working with cameras that are that flexible, I think, is going to revolu-tionize action photography, because you can do so much more.

But these scenes required additional equipment, and we had to or-ganize hidden cuts within the sequences to get in and out of the equip-ment. For instance, to do the jump across the roof: that's with a helmet camera, and you can't use that for the run up the stairs. I would go out with my Steadicam operator, Jimmy Muro, with a video camera and fig-ure out where all the cuts would be; then I had to organize the action to enable me to make those cuts. To get into the helmet camera, I had to create a whip. You don't want to create an arbitrary whip, so: I hear the cops behind me, I look back, there they are, I come back and now I'm in the helmet rig, I jump. Now I'm on the other side, I look up and down, and then it's a descender fall with the helmet on. It has to make sense. It's fun—it's the ultimate chess game.

Q: What about the Jeriko clip?
A: It was logistically very complicated because Iris [Brigitte Bako] is wit-nessing this event, which had a lot of dialogue, no coverage, no outs, a four-hundred-foot magazine so you have a little bit of latitude, and we could switch equipment when we needed to for the dialogue. You couldn't record dialogue with this little camera, it's too noisy, so we had to switch to Steadicam.

Q: On *Point Break*, how hands-on was your directing of the surfing and skydiving scenes? Is that kind of thing usually left to a second-unit direc-tor/stunt coordinator?
A: With second unit it's all boarded and I make clear what the shots are, what the composition is, what time of day it is, what lens and stock are being used. Anything involving Patrick [Swayze] jumping out of a plane, I was there with a parachute on, strapped in.

Q: But from an insurance point of view you couldn't jump.
A: No—and technically neither could he. . . . But he might have, yeah. For the water work, I was in the water, on a boat, as close as I could be

without getting in the shot or making it logistically problematic for any-body. Sitting on a surfboard, yelling action and cut, then falling off the board. I actually had many units on that working simultaneously. We had a stretch of beach on the North Shore of Oahu, and there were a lot of different breaks, and I just set up stages at each break, literally a hun-dred feet apart. I'd have an underwater unit at stage one, Keanu doubles for the learning-how-to-surf scene at stage two, a wipeout scene at stage three, and four surfers doing a Four-Horsemen-at-dawn shot on stage four, to which I added some optical fog afterwards. So you just work with [walkie-talkies] going back and forth. You gotta always be parallel-pro-cessing. I like to have at least two things going at once, one setup here, one setup there.

Q: So your DP is always setting up the next shot while your operator ex-ecutes the present one.
A: Always, always.

Q: One of the best action sequences you've done is ironically very mod-est in scale and complexity—the final sequence of your episode of *Wild Palms*.
A: That's Jimmy Muro, my Steadicam guy. It's in the choreography, and I staged the action so that just as one event is starting to wind down, an-other one will be coming up in the corner of his frame that will stimulate the camera and it whips around. It goes back to painting. On that one, we're running to the door of the van, he is put in the back and we whip back up to the characters on the balcony getting shot, and they come down to the scene down below. And countermoves—moving the action and the camera in opposing ways. There's an organic quality that lends itself to those sequences as you're blocking it, and it's like you leapfrog the action one step ahead of the camera, and then the camera leads the next piece of action. That's what that piece was a perfect example of. We basically did that in only a few hours.

Q: Was The Animals' "House of the Rising Sun" already written in?
A: No, I put the music on.

Q: The power of that conjunction of visuals and music rises to an almost transcendent emotional level, much the way Michael Mann sometimes does.
A: Kind of like a fugue state. I had fun. I did it really for Oliver [Stone, the

executive producer]. It was an interesting challenge to work at that pace. We did eight to ten pages a day. There's something kind of freeing about it, once you break through to that other side.

Q: On features like yours it's more like two or two-and-a-half-page days.
A: Yeah. It sounds luxurious when compared to the other, but not when the level of complexity and the photographic requirements are so much greater. You just need to be constantly changing angles and images. You have to satisfy the appetite of the viewer's attention span and work within the dictates of that appetite, if you want to stay a step ahead of the viewer, constantly cycling images. Back to the old adage: Material dictates. At a script stage you know how far you can sustain or suspend something. A narrative is a momentum in and of itself. It's like you're skiing down a hill and there's this avalanche behind you. How long do you want to pause? If the piece has inherent momentum, you have to be careful about your pauses. But you can't have momentum without pause. The value of cutting has been painfully abbreviated in some of the bigger contemporary films that are cut in six weeks. You can make a good film that way. You can't make a great film.

Q: A great example of that control of momentum and suspension is the unusually long, ten-and-a-half-minute scene in the middle of *Near Dark* at the bar. I'm fascinated by how you structured it around four contrasting songs on the jukebox. It's a scene in four acts.
A: It's written that way, too. It's an entire reel. In a way it's a film within a film, with a beginning, middle, and end. It's very lyrical in a way, its rhythm. Its strength is its patience. It's ultimately about turning a bar into an abattoir, but it's turning that process into a state of art. Hard to shoot. I always knew I was going to use the George Strait song at the end; I didn't know what the other material was going to be when I shot it, but I knew I would find them. "Fever" by The Cramps I just stumbled on, put it in, and it was uncanny how it worked with Lance Henriksen's performance and the way the light and the fan above his head worked, and how evocative it was of how seductive that world might be. The real challenge in that film was that at a certain point you have to identify with the antagonists and want to take that ride.

Q: That's true of all of your films.
A: I guess so. They become strange ad hoc heroes in a perverse way. At a fundamental level, they are just alternate family structures struggling

to stay intact, the two fathers fighting over the same son. There's always a sequence like that, like the surf Nazis shootout in *Point Break*. In both cases it's the moment where the main character goes through the looking glass and can never return. In *Strange Days* it's when Mace sees the Jeriko video or Lenny witnesses the Iris kill. It's the end of innocence.

Q: Just as there is an interplay of momentum and suspension in your films, there's also an interplay of visual control and visual abandon. Your most tightly controlled film visually is *Blue Steel*, yet certain moments don't follow customary visual patterns. I'm thinking of the scene in the deli when Megan sees the supermarket holdup across the street and you employ three shots that are emphatic, interlocking pirouettes: 1) Turner spinning around to face the cash register; spilling the coffee; 2) her head turning; and 3) a shaky 180-degree pan from the deli's TOILET sign where her partner is, around through the window to the SLOAN supermarket sign across the street. It's an interesting formal repetition-with-variation. It has an odd freedom.

A: I know. I'd probably cut it very differently today. I had that pretty planned out. I don't want to give you the impression that everything is planned to within an inch of its life, but within that framework it's much more freeing than just arriving at a set and figuring out how you're going to do it. You can cover something an infinite number of ways, but I think if you're really intimate with the piece, there's only one way it could ever be done. The best kind of photography and the best kind of filmmaking is when it seems like it's inevitable.

 Blue Steel represents a kind of control I've tended to move away from. It's in a way too restrained. *Blue Steel* is very stylized, intentionally so, but I think I've been interested in a slightly less stylized approach to material. There is an elegance to *Blue Steel*, but [it's like] a series of still frames; there's a stillness in that film that seemed appropriate. When I wrote it I kept seeing it in a slightly removed state.

Q: Its style has a very interiorized quality.

A: I was really just discovering long focal lengths, and that had a lot to do with it. Loving the compression, and the lack of depth of field, that had a tendency to create a kind of claustrophobia. I came through that and out the other side. *Point Break* is virtually the opposite. I'd still use long focal lengths at times, but I'd use an 85mm [lens] instead of a 300mm. I would do masters with a 300 on *Blue Steel*. You had to find locations that could accommodate those focal lengths, and focus was really difficult. *Near*

Dark had a lot of practical locations, and our longest lens was probably an 85. In *Point Break* I started to work with wider lenses and started discovering the 35, which is an extraordinary, beautiful focal length. And I moved the camera more. As you gravitate towards more camera movement, you tend to get wider because the sense of fluidity is magnified.

Q: Your action sequences conform classical principles of attenuation and elaboration of action, arresting or expanding time. In real life, violence is often over in the blink of an eye.

A: Yes and no. You can take the liberty of a moment of suspension, when something puts you in shock or is cathartic. Time stands still. It's perception, obviously. There's two ways of looking at a moment and they're both cinematic: Either suspend it and examine it as if under a magnifying glass, with great detail, or have it be instantaneous, blink and you've missed it—which is more realistic, but in the perception of reality. Suspension of time for me is by cinematic choice and what I would imagine an event to be like.

I was in a tremendous near car accident once. The driver started to doze at the wheel at 5:00 A.M. on the freeway at eighty miles per hour. In seconds we went off the freeway, and we were heading for the side of an overpass, and I said something and then he overcorrected it and we did a complete 360 across six lanes of traffic in one direction and down the meridian and across the oncoming six lanes, and ended up going straight ahead. You saw these semis going by you, they were just blurs of light and sound and horns. It seemed to me an eternity in what was fifteen seconds. There's just this sense of forever in a second. A collision of thoughts. I think it's because your system is flooded with adrenalin and everything is on hyper speed. So it's an aestheticization, a stylistic choice.

Q: You've talked in the past about violence in terms of its inherent cinematic, kinetic qualities, and it's clear that it's useful to you as an expression of a certain kind of passion. But what kind of personal need does its representation satisfy in you?

A: It goes back to the voyeuristic need to watch and the Freudian idea that you want to view what you've been denied. You don't want to watch what you can always see—you want to see something that is transporting in some way, either frightening or some other reaction. And that's the idea of the SQUID in *Strange Days*. They're accessible fantasies and it's fundamentally human.

Q: There's a very strong graphic quality to your compositions, but also a very tactile, sculpted dimensionality them.

A: Probably because I love to shoot on location, which you pay the price for when you're mixing, because there's sound you can't get rid of and performance lines you're reluctant to loop. But I don't know—it could be in the sense that I'm interested in trying to make it replicate something to the extent that you humanly can, rather than go completely into a fantastic fictional space.

Q: The shot in *Point Break* with the camera looking down on Keanu Reeves and Lori Petty lying in bed, with the contrast of black sheets and flesh tone combined with the very precise arrangement of limbs and shoulders, creates an almost sculpted image.

A: What you're commenting on is perhaps how it's lit, the kind of modeling of the light. If cinema is the art form of the twentieth century, lighting in some ways is your brush. That's how you create the tones and densities and dictate where your eye does and doesn't go and how it travels, how shape is defined and formed. And with that image, the starkness of it. If you were to over-light that, it would be much less interesting because it would just be a graphic silhouette. The challenge was trying to get the flesh tones to pop out from the sheets and not become one single shape.

Q: Did you arrange the actors' physical postures?

A: Rather than have a preordained idea of how they should lie, what I love to do is see how an actor organically works a scene or works in a space, and then freeze it, shape it. So it isn't like you're imposing something that might not be organic to them or to that moment.

Q: Where were you born?

A: Right below San Francisco, a town called San Carlos. My father managed a paint factory in South San Francisco, which I guess seems like an obvious influence. As long as I can remember, I was drawing and painting—not much imagination there! My mother was a librarian. It was a fairly normal environment. When I first started painting, I loved the Old Masters. When I was thirteen or fourteen I was doing details of Old Masters, blowing up a corner of a Raphael. I loved doing that, taking a detail and turning it into twelve by twelve feet.

Q: It's interesting that you did something mediated.

A: I got very interested later on when I became more sophisticated about art, with Duchamp and the idea of found objects, which in a way is what filmmaking is. You're taking a lot of elements that already exist, and it's the context you're putting those pre-existent elements into, the associations that you're creating.

Q: Especially genre films.

A: When we wrote *Near Dark* we were very conscious of taking a genre and turning it upside down, subverting it in some way—taking the vampire mythology and putting it in the West. You could say the same with *Strange Days*: it's science fiction, but it's also total noir. I always thought of it as a film noir thriller that takes place on the eve of the millennium, the turn of the century, and perhaps the end of the world [laughs]—in one sentence!

Q: Before you made *The Loveless* you spent the seventies in the New York art world.

A: I've sort of had many incarnations! I came to New York through the Whitney Museum in the early seventies. At that time they gave fifteen people scholarships every year to come to New York and get your own studio. I had been going to school at the San Francisco Art Institute for a year and a half. I didn't realize that my teacher, Sam Tchakalian, had put me up for the Whitney. All of a sudden he came to me and said, "If you want to go to New York and be matriculated at the Art Institute, and work within the Whitney Museum where people like Susan Sontag and Richard Serra talk about your work with you, you can." I was nineteen and I was like, Excuse me? So I did that for a year and a half. At the end you had a piece of your work shown in the Whitney. Which was amazing. The art world at the time became very politicized, conceptual art moved into a political arena, so the work was more and more aggressive. I started working with Art and Language, a British-based group of conceptual artists, and we had a piece at the Venice Biennale one year.

Q: I read that you worked with (video and performance artist) Vito Acconci.

A: I was doing a million odd jobs just to stay alive. One of them was helping Vito Acconci on an installation he was doing. He did these great, very assaultive performance pieces, and needed these slogans and phrases on film loops that would play on the wall behind him during a performance piece he did at [the] Sonnabend [gallery] in a rubber bondage room he created. The job was to film these slogans. I'd never worked with a camera. I was starving to death. If I hadn't been at the brink of economic disaster, I think I never would have had all these detours.

Q: Were you in one of his videos?
A: I was in a Richard Serra video for about five seconds, and a couple of Lawrence Weiner videos, *Done To* and *Green As Well As Red As Well As Blue*. I would by no means consider myself a performance artist, I'm too self-conscious, it's something I could never do. Lawrence's work is less about performance in a classical sense—it's kind of the gestalt of the moment. He puts you in a context and lets you run with the ball, and that's the piece. There's no script. They're very fascinating wordplay pieces. In one I was trying to talk Italian with somebody. It was such a community, almost like a repertory without any kind of structure whatsoever. During that time I don't think I saw a movie that wasn't subtitled. I was really unaware of Hollywood per se, which may kind of protect me today. I think I'm still discovering it.

Q: You were more associated with the New York underground film scene in the late seventies. You also appeared in Lizzie Borden's *Born in Flames*.
A: You know, I've never seen it, although I'm very good friends with Lizzie. We always laugh about this. I played one of three somewhat militant girls in a scene. Art and film were not separated whatsoever—you were working in the same context using different mediums. It was never really thought of filmmaking per se, it was art.

Q: At what point did you gravitate towards film?
A: I did this short film called *Set-Up*. I shot it before I went to Columbia. I went to Columbia because I had run out of money and I needed a cutting room, so I thought, Aha, Graduate School [laughs]! I loved the process, it was intoxicating, so I just dived into film, all periods. I just opened up Pandora's box. I'd see everything, from going to 42nd Street to see a Bruce Lee movie to *Magnificent Ambersons* in Andrew Sarris's class to Fassbinder at Lincoln Center. That would be a day. *Year of 13 Moons*—I thought I'd died and gone to heaven when I saw that film.

Q: What was *Set-Up* about?
A: This was the late seventies when conceptual art mutated through a political phase into a French structuralist phase. There was a kind of natural evolution if I think back on it. It was really a very overtly political piece, a bit incendiary in its own small context. On the surface it's these

two guys who beat each other up [laughs]—maybe nothing's changed! The *Village Voice* called it the first skinhead movie. One guy was calling another a fascist, the other's calling him a commie. It was very politically literal. And then the same images are deconstructed in voiceover by these two philosophers, Sylvère Lotringer and Marshall Blonsky, both teaching at Columbia, discussing the material while you're watching it. So there's this kind of reflexive ideology thing going on. It sounds so kind of young and pretentious . . . but it's only twenty minutes, so it's pretty harmless. And the piece ends with Sylvère talking about the fact that in the sixties you think of the enemy as outside yourself, in other words a police officer, the government, the system, but that that's not really the case at all, fascism is very insidious, we reproduce it all the time.

Q: That's part of what's going on inside *Strange Days*—an interrogation of the need for and dangers of spectacle.
A: The thing that's so interesting is that it's really a reflexive ideology, because you're trapped in the spectacle just as the characters are trapped with their own spectacles (SQUID). We're a watched society and a society of watchers. *Strange Days* [is linked to *Set-Up*] in some ways more than [my other films], because it's really about understanding power structures.

Again, I wasn't really thinking about making a film, even though it was at night and beautifully lit. It was more of a text. But I drew it out, which is one thing that I still constantly go back to—I have to board a whole show. I have to see it and cut it first, every scene. And then I shoot it. Then it's all right, I've put it into my head. In *Set-Up* I didn't know anything about stunt coordinators, and I needed different angles. It had a very strange, kind of crude sense of where the camera should be and how it should be constructed. I knew exactly what I wanted, but I didn't understand that you fake shots and fake hits and put sound effects in. I started shooting at about 9:00 P.M. and finished at 7:00 A.M., it was in an alley off White Street downtown, and it started to snow—and these guys were getting bloodier and bloodier. They were in bed for like two weeks after. I almost killed them. And then on the soundtrack they talk about the fact that they felt kind of exploited in the piece. So the film is constantly folding in on itself like a Moebius strip.

Q: What was the nature of your collaboration with Monty Montgomery, who co-directed *The Loveless* with you?
A: Well, we wrote it together. Coming out of the art world, which is so ad hoc, I didn't really know what directing was. But it was a very easy,

effortless process because we were really thinking on the same page and finishing each other's sentences, so the directing was very fluid. It wasn't like, You do camera and I'll do the actors. There wasn't even any consultation. It was an interesting process, but I don't recommend it, because you become too solipsistic, too protective of the material.

I hadn't embraced narrative at that point; I was still completely conceptual, and narrative was antithetical to anything in the art world. That was the big juncture, when you're thinking of plastic or visual arts, you're using the non-narrative part of your brain. So the thinking behind *The Loveless* was to suspend the narrative and create this visual tapestry with enough narrative to give you the illusion of a story percolating, kind of there but not there, held by gossamer threads.

Q: The whole film feels like one long interlude, like material left over from a larger narrative.
A: It was very perverse. That film has one foot in the art world and half a finger in the film world. It was neither fish nor fowl, and I had no idea of making this as a calling card for the industry. What I was really interested in was a Kenneth Anger *Scorpio Rising* kind of thing—images of power and a skewed perspective of it . . .

Q: *The Loveless* is somewhere between a Warhol aesthetic and stylized narrative. The way the actors function . . .
A: I was very interested in his material. Some of the more aggressive pieces like *Vinyl*, which is wonderful. I think of art as a somewhat elitist medium because it does require a little bit of understanding to appreciate a white-on-white square or Ad Reinhardt's black-on-black paintings. You can't come to it cold—but you can with a film. And in a way, Warhol's use of pop subjects—you could come to that completely cold, too. Everybody could have a different association. You would be mystified, but you wouldn't be completely alienated by it. There would be recognition.

I think my journey West, so to speak, has really been one that I think of as the pursuit of the Narrative. *The Loveless* was all about the rejection of it. I felt sort of sorry for the distributor, who tried to cut a trailer to make it seem like this action-packed motorcycle movie, and I just kept saying, "You've got to use truth in advertising!" I remember going to the Beverly Center when it was released in L.A. and there weren't even posters on display. I went to the manager with a copy of the poster and said, My film's playing here, would you please put a poster up?"

Kathryn Bigelow: Vicarious Thrills

Sheila Johnston / 1995

From *Index on Censorship*, November 1995, 41–45. Reprinted by permission of Sheila Johnston.

Kathryn Bigelow's second feature was reviewed by the trade magazine *Variety* as "undoubtedly the most hard-edged, violent actioner by an American woman," but she must have long since smashed her own record. That film—*Near Dark*, a "vampire western"—had cannibalism, child sex, and blood. *Blue Steel*, in which Jamie Lee Curtis's novice cop is stalked by a psychotic killer, had gun fetishes, rape, wife-beating, and blood. *Point Break* had bloody shoot-outs and Keanu Reeves's face in close proximity to the whirring blades of a lawn-mower. "When Rembrandt died, he gathered everyone around him and said, '*Mehr Licht, mehr Licht*' [more light, more light]," joked Ron Silver, the murderer in *Blue Steel*. When Kathryn dies, she'll be saying '*Mehr Blut, mehr Blut*'— 'more blood, more blood.'"

Four years after *Point Break*, Bigelow has finally completed a new film; *Strange Days*, a futuristic thriller set in Los Angeles at the turn of the millennium. The city is dark, decaying, crime-ridden, wracked by racial tensions. And, skulking through the wreckage is the charming Lenny Nero (Ralph Fiennes), a former cop who has gone to seed and now peddles black-market "SQUID clips," electronic memories that are recorded directly in people's brains and enable buyers to relive, in playback on a small headpiece, a slice of someone else's life. We see a good deal of these SQUIDs in the course of the movie, vividly presented through the dizzy subjective camerawork. Hence the film's long genesis, since it meant building a camera that could replicate the movement of the eye. "You take for granted how effortless that movement is," Bigelow says, "but you can't duplicate it with a forty-pound Panaglide."

Human nature being what it is, the vicarious thrills in keenest demand are sex, rape, burglary, murder, and above all, "snuff'" scenarios in which the original person dies. And Lenny has the sales pitch down pat to hook new users—the choice of term is deliberate—of the highly addictive clips. "I'm the Santa Claus of the subconscious," he likes to purr.

It's a confident and unusual film—and a bloody one. This time *Variety*'s verdict was "a technical tour de force . . . conceptually daring and viscerally powerful." But the reviewer also found the sensationalist content of the SQUID clips "morally questionable," and predicted that "more than a few women will have problems with these scenes."

Bigelow vigorously defends her movie. "There's a sort of hunger that we all seem to share: a need to see, to live a life vicariously, even if for only one or two hours," she says. "It's something I explored back in 1978 in a short film called *Set-Up*. It was about violence, scopophilia, and why we desire this intensity. *Strange Days* is also about watching and its consequences. So there is a common thread between them. But in *Strange Days* I wanted, at the same time, to embed that idea shrewdly within the narrative, so that it's not a diatribe imposed upon it as perhaps I was doing in 1978."

Bigelow began her career as a painter—an "abstract expressionist" as she describes it—immersed in the avant-garde New York scene of the early 1970s. Her name appeared on the masthead of the high-theory culture journal *Semiotext[e]*—in an issue devoted, characteristically, to polysexuality—and she said she thought she'd died and gone to heaven on seeing Rainer Werner Fassbinder's somber gay psychodrama *In a Year with 13 Moons*.

"Working along those lines you become very analytical about what you're doing, about the commodification of culture. Ever since art stopped being at the service of church and state, it has been in constant search of meaning and identity. But at the same time I never lost the desire to communicate. Cinema is *the* art form of the twentieth century."

From her first feature, *The Loveless*, a languid, gorgeously designed biker movie, Bigelow has been nudging more and more toward the commercial mainstream: her films are now less likely to play at the Museum of Modern Art, New York, than a multiplex near you. Today she will name as her favorite directors not Fassbinder, but Walter Hill, Oliver Stone, James Cameron, with all of whom she has been associated and, in the third case, briefly married. Cameron co-wrote the screenplay for *Strange Days*. But she still believes it possible to make "captivating" crowd-pleasers while maintaining critical distance.

"In *Strange Days* the SQUID clips are filtered through the character of Lenny Nero. And he, I think, helps us with our own reactions; he directs us, so to speak. His reaction, for instance, to the killing of Iris [one of the women] is to one of absolute shock, horror, and revulsion. In other words he mediates it for us." So, she adds, does Nero's best friend, played by Angela Bassett, when she witnesses with horror a black singer and political leader being slain by police in a Rodney King–type incident.

To support this claim Bigelow cites her film's first scene: a long, long, apparently unbroken, subjective point-of-view shot of a robbery seen through the eyes of one of the criminals. The camera races through a house and across a roof as the police give chase; and then as the thief leaps to another building and doesn't quite make it, he, and we, plunge to death.

"When I was in the cutting room, friends would come over and I would show them that footage. They stared at this tiny little screen, with no sound. They would sit back at first but, as we progressed along the sequence, I noticed them sitting forward and finally as the camera runs up the stairs, their legs would be moving. So even in that small, crude format they are caught, they are participants in the experience. Now, in that opening sequence you don't yet have a person to identify with. But I do believe the events are mediated through an emotional investment in the characters once you've been introduced to them."

She argues strongly against the notion that we might be "victims" of progress: that, as film and the other mass media, including virtual reality technology, become more sophisticated, the audience becomes more and more sucked into the viewing process. "The history of anything has been based on attempting to push the envelope and as filmmakers we tend to want to use all the tools available. That exploration is always valid because it can create new images and new ways of thinking.

"Obviously now, with computer generated imagery, it's possible to do almost anything; your only limitation is your imagination. And it probably does promote a more visceral response in the audience. On the other hand, I also think that the viewer is *responding* to that response at the same time. It's a relationship that is constantly ratcheting up the stakes."

Strange Days includes a graphic and extended rape scene (as did *Blue Steel*). Oliver Stone would certainly have been sent to the doghouse for showing such material. And I wondered whether Bigelow, as a woman, felt she was able to get away with more than a male director would. "There's violence against women in our culture; there's truth to that existing in our lives. It's not like it's being made up.

"In *Strange Days* it's the dramatic event that propels the rest of the story forward, not unlike the shower scene in *Psycho*. I boarded it very carefully. I walked through it shot by shot with the actors. Everybody was part of the process; we all shared in its necessity. It is not there for any kind of titillation or exploitation, but as an awful fact of our existence. So it really depends on how it's handled. Whether that is influenced by gender, I don't know, although I'm sure it has something to do with it.

"And we also had another woman who's a nice contrast. If Iris were the only woman in the picture I would say 'you're giving me no options, no other potential reality.' But since Angela Bassett, who is all-empowering, who is the moral center of the film, who is completely self-possessed, is there it gives you a spectrum of identities to explore."

Political correctness is only one of the pressures on U.S. filmmakers; on their flank are right-wingers like Bob Dole, Dan Quayle, and Michael Medved who hold Hollywood responsible for a multitude of sins. "They're using the movie industry in a political game. Rather than turning their attention to the cause of the social ills that are being represented in a film they fault the errand-boy," Bigelow says. "It does make life more difficult but the struggle for freedom of speech is so on-going and so important that it probably entrenches you all the more."

Reality Bytes

Andrew Hultkrans / 1995

From *Artforum*, November 1995. © Artforum. Reprinted by permission of *Artforum* and Andrew Hultkrans.

A painter who enrolled in the Whitney Program before migrating to Columbia Film School, Kathryn Bigelow is something of an anomaly in Planet Hollywood. Combining an affinity for the frenetic rhythms of the thriller with a taste for subversive genre-bending that recalls her "high art" beginnings, Bigelow is a consummate technician whose balletic action sequences remind us how cinematically pure the language of violence can be. Her latest film, *Strange Days*, is a tech-noir set in a Los Angeles on the brink of the millennium, where conflicting visions of rapture and revolution divide the collective psyche, and the apolitical insulate themselves by getting high on other people's lives.

With a script by director James Cameron (*True Lies*) and writer Jay Cocks (*The Age of Innocence; The Last Temptation of Christ*), *Strange Days*—a cyberpunk extrapolation of the archetypal noir—recasts Chandler's mean streets as paramilitarized zones where tanks roll by impassively while wasted youth bludgeon Santa Claus on the curb. Scurrying through the back alleys of a decadent underground like an oiled rat, Lenny Nero (Ralph Fiennes) peddles other people's realities preserved on MiniDiscs through the magic of SQUID (Superconducting Quantum Interference Device), a technology that records and plays back human experience "straight from the cerebral cortex," allowing the user to be anyone this time around, for a price.

Nero has broken the first commandment of the Dealer's Credo—"never get high off your own supply"—and has become a memory addict, hooked on a feedback loop of happier times with a femme fatale who has gutted his life by the time the film begins. When he gets a snuff clip of his friend's murder, he reluctantly assumes the mantle of Philip Marlowe, and enlisting the aid of Mace (Angela Bassett), an Amazon Warrior moonlighting as a chauffeur, becomes embroiled in a conspiratorial web with enough red herrings to rival *The Big Sleep*.

Like Polanski's *Chinatown*, *Strange Days* is no less noir for being in color. Bigelow's blacks are black, and her light, what there is of it, is dark cyan, a visual correlative to the creeping rot eating away at her characters. And, as in her last three studio releases (*Near Dark*, 1987; *Blue Steel*, 1989; *Point Break*, 1991), Bigelow is no slave to the fast cut. *Strange Days*, her best film to date, closes with a sequence that leaves us rattled long after the credits roll. The camera lingers on the bloody face of a racist cop. Gun drawn, he drags his suicided partner along by his own handcuffs, attempting, one last time, to effect his Final Solution as confetti falls from the night sky like acid snow.

Andrew Hultkrans: It's quite a leap from Conceptual art to the culture industry.

Kathryn Bigelow: It does seem like a departure. I was studying painting at the San Francisco Art Institute and one of my teachers put me up for the Whitney Program, so I went. This was '73 or '74, when Conceptual art really came to the fore. And I became dissatisfied with the art world—the fact that it requires a certain amount of knowledge to appreciate abstract material.

Film, of course, does not demand this kind of knowledge. Film was this incredible social tool that required nothing of you besides twenty minutes to two hours of your time. So I shot this short piece called *Set-Up* [1978]. I was matriculating in film history and criticism. I was reading Freud, which led me to the philosophy department. I was working on *Semiotext(e)*. I had Peter Wollen as a teacher, and Edward Said—extraordinary thinkers. So, naturally I was influenced by them, which ironically pulled me back into the art world. Structuralist thought is hopelessly out of fashion now, but it's what led me to *The Loveless* [1981], my first feature-length narrative film. I was still resisting narrative; that film is more like a meditation.

Then I ran out of money again and got a teaching job at CalArts, out here. I was forced to move for economic reasons; I had no intention of *The Loveless* being a calling card to the industry. Working in the art world, of course, you have nothing but disdain for Hollywood.

AH: *The Loveless* is a series of period tableaux; there are scenes where there's hardly any sound, certainly no dialogue. Most of your films contain visceral action sequences, but also these contemplative pauses to examine the mise-en-scene. Is this something you retain from your intellectual roots, or is it your natural rhythm?

KB: Well, I don't see *Strange Days* as a pure action genre piece. I think of it as a character-driven piece. It's got a tremendous amount of dialogue and story—at one point we thought of it as science fiction as if written by David Mamet. The pauses in *Strange Days* are motivated more by story and character than by the need to linger on the mise-en-scene. That's not to say we don't fill every frame; your eye wanders outward to this complex environment that the principal characters don't bother to acknowledge. They take it for granted that there's an ad hoc revolution taking place, a civil war.

AH: A police state.

KB: Exactly, yet life still goes on, the hustle is still happening, the clubs are still open, and you gotta eat dinner.

AH: Though the social ills extrapolated in *Strange Days* are all too real in today's L.A., your version of the city is also an interzone between the L.A. of the present and the future L.A. of Ridley Scott's *Blade Runner*. What is it about this town that makes it such a primary source text for pre- and post- apocalyptic urban environments?

KB: It's the template, isn't it? Perhaps because there's so little history here, there's a fragile balance, an inherent tension. Also, it's not a city. There is no center. And in its lack of identity it has a kind of poly-identity: it's whatever you project onto it, a faceless place that harbors a multitude of identities, all blurred into one. That's not to say the city isn't a microcosm for the rest of the country. L.A.'s culturally polyglot society is critical to the flashpoint world of *Strange Days*, but I don't think it's atypical of the U.S. It's just in sharper relief here.

AH: Prowling the grim precincts of L.A. 1999, *Strange Days* gives us a damaged antihero, Lenny Nero [Ralph Fiennes], who is fiddling—jacking off, or in, as the case may be—while L.A. burns. He caters to a populace that has given up on changing social reality; instead, it withdraws into solipsism through his SQUID disks—slices of people's personal experience recorded through a new technology and offered for sale. More than a satire on escapist entertainment, your SQUID idea involves a commentary on cinema, on scopophilia, on addiction to the image, on the notion of a truly "captive" audience.

KB: Yes, and Jim Cameron, the piece's originator, has been thinking about those ideas for a long time too. The desire to watch, to experience vicariously—as our environment is increasingly mediated, so are all of our experiences. There's a tremendous gluttony for images right now; that hunger to experience somebody else's life instead of our own is so palpable. It's pure escapism, but it seems fundamental. What else is the appetite for cinema?

AH: But in *Strange Days*, the environment is getting too real, and really brutal. You'd think that people living in such an environment wouldn't want experience, they'd want cinema as we know it today: true escapism, in which nothing can affect you viscerally, at least not literally. The disks, though, deliver the real thing—real experience.

KB: The disks deliver pure sensation, but it's risk-free sensation. You're allowed to have the experience without the experience's potential limitations and dangers. Cinema audiences are demanding increasingly more intense experiences, so it's a necessary extrapolation to make: to break that fourth wall, to go that extra step to the truly experiential. The direction is well paved. We're obviously not there yet, but once you have it, what is the future of cinema? Ultimately it becomes—

AH: Experience.

KB: Then cinema becomes obsolete.

AH: Although, as Faith [Juliette Lewis] says in *Strange Days*, movies are better because you know when they're over. Except that you do know when the disks are over, and that's the problem: they pixilate out and you're back in your grim apartment.

KB: But they offer you this window into another world, this tear in society's fabric, which cinema also offers. That's what's so attractive, because, as you say, our own realities seem so grim or pedestrian by comparison. We're all looking for out-of-body experiences, which is what the disks provide.

AH: But a lot of the disks the film shows us are not typical Hollywood fantasies. They're set in the kind of urban milieu that people generally try to escape.

KB: You go from one grim reality to another grim reality, but one of them is safer. And the disks don't have to be grim; it's just in the nature of the thriller genre that grimness is what we focus on. Certainly whatever you ask Lenny for, he will provide.

AH: Except death.

KB: Except death, because he doesn't deal in death. Death is a way out, and Lenny's mired in his past, he's caught in a feedback loop.

AH: "Like a gerbil on a wheel," as Max [Tom Sizemore] says. The ultimate noir fall guy.

KB: But the noir fall guy is an inexorable downward spiral. Lenny's stuck in a loop. And unlike the noir hero, he taps into a redemption motif, with the help of Mace [Angela Bassett].

AH: You don't ridicule the media in *Strange Days*—there are no parodies of ads or news. You're critiquing not a society of the spectacle but a post-spectacular society that places a primacy on real experience. Yet the film's crucial SQUID disc—the record of a slaying—takes us back to the power of mass broadcast, because there is the threat of riots if it is released to the public.

KB: The SQUID disks offer pure experience, unmediated. They're pure and uncut, "straight from the cerebral cortex"; you can't get more unmediated than that. It's important how they're used; there's no such thing as neutral technology; it's all in its application. But that still brings us back to the individual, as opposed to the media. Ultimately *Strange Days* addresses the question of responsibility to the truth. I'm sure five years from the time frame of the movie there would be a technology by which you could adulterate the contents of a disk and have anything happen, but certainly the murder disk is a smoking gun, and it's critical how that information is disseminated. It's pure and truthful information, and as such it reveals the inadequacies of the media and the news.

AH: So do the disks make the media irrelevant.? The media are marginal in *Strange Days*. There's a little talk radio, a couple of TV news clips, but they seem like today's news and talk shows.

KB: Except for the information they're talking about. Bear in mind, it's only four years from now. Think back four years, what's different? Your computer has gotten smaller and more people have cellular phones. You think that in the year 2000 there'll be this radical transformation, but the most that will happen is your computer will sit in the palm of your hand and you'll be able to speak to it.

On the other hand, I do think the turn of the millennium is going to be a huge cultural event, a merchandising and media extravaganza of nightmarish proportions. I also think there'll be a spiritual component, because you'll have a lot of people expecting the Rapture. You'll have this need to embrace the unknown.

AH: What's the history of *Strange Days*?
KB: Jim Cameron had been working on the idea for nine or ten years. He presented it to me almost four years ago, and I thought it was tremendous. These two characters on the eve of the millennium, with one character trying to get the woman who loves him to help him save the woman he loves. It's this great emotional matrix. And then, through a series of dialogues, we developed the political element, this particular society. The edginess, the grit, was something I kept striving for; ironically, Jim's thrust was the romantic element and mine was the harder edge, so it was kind of reverse gender. Jim wrote a treatment as a result of our dialogues, and then he and Jay Cocks turned it into a script.

AH: You incorporated the Rodney King incident, through both the subplot of racist cops and a beating that quotes the King video.
KB: That story was unfolding as we were working on the treatment, and I thought it was part of the cultural history of the landscape here. So there's a character in the film who's brought down not by what he says but by the misuse of power and a traffic stop—a purely random event that causes a catastrophe. Also, the riots were a real emotional time for anybody living here, and I participated in the cleanup. Being on the streets with burned-out shells of buildings and the National Guard milling around suggested a lot of the film's visual basis. You became inured to it very quickly.

AH: Both Mace and Lenny have personal tragedy in their pasts. How does Mace resist the urge to withdraw into solipsism, to use the disks?
KB: Mace is the narrative's moral center, so she's simply capable of resisting. Whereas Lenny, being morally de-centered, is floundering in his own narcissistic tide pool, which he doesn't seem able to escape. It's not

until two-thirds of the way through the movie that we realize his potential for change. Mace is the film's unblemished hero; Lenny is an anti-
hero. That's interesting in an action context, where the heroes are often
inarticulate but glib. It's different to have a hero who evinces feeling and
is therefore construed as weak. These are clichés that desperately need
subverting.

AH: Race is heavily coded in the film; of the two main characters, one
is black and one is white. And disk abuse seems to be largely a white
pursuit; African Americans aren't into it. Does this have anything to do
with the way the African American community often bears the burden
of representing the "real" in American culture? The discourse of the real
is incredibly overdetermined in hip-hop, for instance. In the film, black
characters advocate reality, while the white community represented by
Lenny and Max signifies—
KB: Escape and fantasy and duplicity and hidden agendas. The racial
component was conscious in the film, and Mace's earthbound tendency
was fundamental to it, and a nice sharp contrast to Lenny. She does represent a hard-edged, reality-based component, whereas Lenny is in fantasy. You could look at it from a gender viewpoint as well, because the
SQUID disks tend to highlight male fantasies, not female ones.

AH: Another race-based issue: the white characters seem stuck in the
past, like Lenny, or nihilistically concerned with the present, like Max.
But the African Americans are concerned with a revolution in the future. We hear a black talk-radio caller who's saying "2K [the year 2000]
is coming, it's going to be revolution." So you get opposing views of the
millennium: all the black voices are saying 2K is a new beginning, and all
the white voices are saying it's the end of the world, the Rapture, Judgment Day.
KB: The white characters aren't forward-looking like Jeriko [Glenn
Plummer]. Jeriko and Max are the film's ad hoc philosophers. Max's
philosophy is nihilistic and cynical and present-day; Jeriko's rhetoric
is black revolutionary. That was certainly intentional but it was by no
means intended as an indictment of American white males.

AH: We see thrill-seeking adrenaline addicts in all your films.
KB: Thrill-seeking adrenaline addicts have always fascinated me. The
idea seems to be that it's not until you risk your humanness that you feel
most human. Not until you risk all awareness do you gain awareness. It's

about peak experience. For me, also, it's about cinema as a cathartic medium. In order for cinema to be cathartic, you need to create a crucible by which a character comes to define himself. In *Point Break* [1991], trial by fire became part of the subject.

AH: Anther trope you use is the infantilized male who depends on a woman for emotional, psychological, and, in the case of Caleb in *Near Dark* [1987], even physical sustenance. One of the subtexts of your films, I think, is the weaning process.
KB: In order to have self-realization. It's weaning, but it's also searching for androgyny. Man and woman become fused.

AH: The man takes the woman into himself?
KB: Exactly. Or the strength that the relationship provides. I think of it as a fusion, a taking advantage of the catharsis that union provides, quite literally in *Near Dark* and psychologically in *Strange Days*, where, as opposed to having Mace's blood coursing through Lenny's veins, she helps him realize that he lives in real time, not playback.

AH: Do you see *Strange Days* as a genre film?
KB: Playing with genre is both conscious and unconscious, because I don't think you're ever immune to genre. Even if you choose not to use it, that's a loaded decision in and of itself. But I have a desire to subvert and redefine. Genre exists for that purpose. It's a great interlocutor with the audience, a way in, a language they understand and that makes them comfortable. Once you touch base in a genre you can go in any direction. It's interesting to do a vampire western like *Near Dark*, to create a hybrid, but I'm not always cross-pollinating genres strategically.

AH: It's not, "I'm going to do a tech noir today?"
KB: [Laughter] Ironically, as we started to develop *Strange Days*, we did talk about it as a tech noir.

AH: So you're a fan of film noir?
KB: Are you kidding? Film noir is probably my favorite genre. That's how I moved from art to film, so to speak: I went through Fassbinder on my way to noir.

Strange Days Probes Import of Vicarious Living

David Sterritt / 1995

Reprinted with permission from the November 20, 1995, issue of the *Christian Science Monitor.* © 1995 The Christian Science Monitor (www.CSMonitor.com).

"I think it's about time a movie coming out of the studio system had some content," says Kathryn Bigelow about *Strange Days*, her latest film. "I know it's disturbing. I know it's provocative. But it's about something. And that, in and of itself, is a step in the right direction."

Many who disagree about the merits of *Strange Days* would agree with Bigelow on that point. Although the movie has not stirred major waves at the box office, to the disappointment of 20th Century Fox, it has stirred major discussion among critics and audiences. It also earned the distinction of an American premiere at the New York Film Festival, one of the most selective and prestigious events of its kind.

Love it or hate it, most moviegoers have a hard time dismissing it—and that's unusual in an age when Hollywood would rather duck difficult issues than risk a slump in ticket sales. Supporters of the movie cite its technical brilliance and its cautionary view of so-called entertainment that wallows in vicarious sex and violence. Detractors say *Strange Days* does some wallowing of its own, and note that the movie's finale wishes away its social issues by pointing fingers at a couple of rogue cops rather than the system that spawned them.

The story takes place on the eve of the twenty-first century. The main character is Lenny Nero, a former cop who now peddles software for an illegal entertainment device that pumps images and feelings directly into the user's brain. His latest "clips" contain clues to the murder of a popular rap singer, whose death threatens to spark the most destructive race riot of all time. Other characters include Lenny's former lover, a rock star with bad habits, and a friend who uses her street-smarts to steer Lenny toward a more constructive life.

Ralph Fiennes plays the hero, supported by Juliette Lewis and Angela Bassett as the women in his life. Bigelow wrote the screenplay with Jay Cocks, based on a story by James Cameron, whose high-tech adventures include hits like *Aliens* and the Terminator movies.

One of very few women to build a sustained career as a Hollywood director, Bigelow started work on *Strange Days* soon after the Los Angeles riots that followed the Rodney King verdict. "I was involved in the downtown cleanup," she told me in a recent interview, "and I was very moved by that experience. You got a palpable sense of the anger and frustration and economic disparity in which we live."

This sense of urgency found its way into Bigelow's movie. "It was important to me to hold a mirror to society," she says, calling the film "an environment, a canvas, a landscape that speaks about issues which should never be forgotten."

Among these issues are racial tension and the misuse of official power. But another subject of the film is "the need to watch, the need to see," Bigelow says.

"What is this need we have to experience life vicariously?" she asks. "Does it mean we find our own lives so mundane we have to escape them? Does this create a kind of passivity . . . a 'distanciation,' a constantly mediated view of the world through television, the press, or cinematic experience as opposed to genuine experience?"

Perhaps the most controversial scene in *Strange Days* is a vicious murder vicariously witnessed by the hero—and by us—as recorded on a sensory "clip" by the killer himself. Bigelow acknowledges it's a horrifying episode, but insists it serves a positive purpose. "My challenge was to approach it in as cold and honest a light as I could," she says.

Then why include such a segment at all? "Because knowledge is power," the filmmaker replies. "The answer is not to shield one's vision and cut oneself off from awareness. There's nothing more dangerous than lack of awareness."

In the end, Bigelow says, the movie means to make an optimistic statement. "I wanted to treat 'the system' fairly," she says, "because if it's the enemy, then we're the enemy, since by not changing it we're reproducing it. . . . The film ends in a strong insistence on hope. Ultimately it's humanity—not technology—that takes us into the next century and the next millennium."

Happy New Millennium

Roald Rynning / 1996

From *Film Review* (London), April 1996, 22–24. Reprinted by permission of International Feature Agency, Amsterdam.

Tall, dark, and beautiful, Kathryn Bigelow looks more like a Hollywood actress than a film director. And she looks *nothing* like the other creators of the action movie genre—all Hollywood tough guys.

Nor is the forty-three-year-old painter-turned-director known for doing the expected. What other woman ever made films about bikers (*The Loveless*), vampires (*Near Dark*), surfers (*Point Break*) and cops (*Blue Steel*)? And in March Bigelow is serving up a controversial blend of violent sci-fi in *Strange Days*, a film starring Ralph Fiennes, Angela Bassett, and Juliette Lewis. In America, this shocking vision of pre-apocalyptic Los Angeles at the turn of the century has already been met by both enthusiastic acclaim, boos, and much talk for a need for censorship.

"The movie isn't only about violence. It's a love story and it emphasizes characters," defends Bigelow of her often intensely overwhelming film.

Bigelow makes genre pictures, she says, because they offer her the opportunity to explore the visceral dynamic she loves.

It also offers accessibility. It gives the audience a familiarity to draw them in. "What I intend is to transform the action genre and ultimately speak on character."

Set at New Year's Eve 1999, *Strange Days* deals with the illegal trafficking of a virtual reality technology that replicates any and all sensation.

"The streets are a war zone and sex can kill you, so the hunger for vicarious experience is very great," tells Bigelow of her vision of the L.A. future. "Complications arise when a voyeuristic sadist uses the new technology to record himself raping and strangling a prostitute. He then delights in showing this clip."

There is a lengthy, detailed, and very disturbing account of a rape and strangulation that has caused women to criticize the director for being anti-women.

"It should be uncomfortable to watch," argues Bigelow. "And aren't women lucky that these voyeuristic fantasies are not usually fantasies shared by women? I find this particular scene important because it shows how the darker nature of the cinematic process can seduce you and pull you into the abyss. Like the brilliant *Peeping Tom* [the 1960 film featuring the killer cameraman's point of view]. *Strange Days* utilizes the medium to comment on the medium."

The Los Angeles Police's killing of the film's rapper-activist has also been seen as an exploitation of the Rodney King beating. "The storyline was presented to me during the King incident. As I developed it further, I realized that the incident would in the year 2000 have become L.A. cultural history. So I decided to honor that event.

"But I wasn't interested in tearing an institution apart. The two loose-cannon cops act outside any authority and misuse their power. And ultimately justice prevails. Art does imitate life and any kind of reexamination of the King beating is positive."

The original script of *Strange Days* was written by James Cameron, the writer director of the *Terminator* films and Bigelow's former husband (they divorced in 1991 after a two-year marriage). Cameron's company, Lightstorm, produced the film.

"I loved the script, which I developed with James and writer Jay Cocks, and I brought it to the screen with a conscience," insists Bigelow, who cast Ralph Fiennes as Lenny Nero, a black market dealer in "playback," the technology that lets one have another person's experiences.

"I wanted a male lead that wasn't glib," she says of the British actor. "I had seen him in *Schindler's List* and watched a couple of scenes from *Quiz Show*, then in postproduction. I needed an actor of his caliber to bring off the emotional complexity of Lenny.

"Also, I could not have actors or a crew who were not passionate about the movie. We had seventy-seven nights filming and that is too demanding for people who aren't passionate about their work."

As for Fiennes's British accent, the no-nonsense Bigelow insists, "The accent works or I wouldn't have had it there. Anyway, it's irrelevant where he comes from."

Lewis plays a Courtney Love type of singer and performs her own songs in the film. "I cast Juliette with the intention of dubbing her, but she insisted she could sing and that she'd always dreamt of becoming a rock star. This, she said, was her chance. So we did some tests and discovered that she *was* a good singer. Now she's considering recording."

Strange Days was difficult to prepare for and shoot. "For the point-of-view we needed to build a special camera to move from room-to-room, showing off 180 degrees of them."

She adds, "Then we went to war for five and a half months. Shooting the point-of-view scenes involved a lot of choreography and rehearsals. It was filmed at night and we had great difficulty hiding the lights. But we were up for the challenge."

Growing up in San Carlos, California, wasn't less challenging, according to Bigelow. She always felt like an outsider.

"Everyone else seemed so much more normal," says the director of her childhood. "I began drawing in order to create my own universe. I still have a tendency to withdraw into my own world. Directing films requires communications with hundreds of people, and it has made me open up."

Before movies, Bigelow studied painting for two years at the San Francisco Art Institute. Then she won a scholarship to the Whitney Museum's Independent Study Program in New York. Here she began using film as another tool, showing shorts behind performance pieces.

A twenty-minute short followed (*Set-Up*) in which two men beat each other while someone reads aloud an essay on violence. Seeing it, the Columbia University's Graduate School of Film offered her a place.

Seeing Sam Peckinpah's classic Western *The Wild Bunch* was a turning point for her as a filmmaker. "I realized it wasn't a film about violence per se; Peckinpah just used violence as a language to discuss honor and as a means of catharsis. That's what I myself respond to."

After graduating film school, she co-directed *The Loveless*, starring Willem Dafoe, and headed for Hollywood. It took her four years to find a producer to let her direct her vampire film, *Near Dark* (1987).

She has always been an unusual entity in Tinseltown. Female directors usually make modest, sensitive, and small art house films.

"To ghettoize men and women is unproductive," sighs Bigelow. "When I arrived in Hollywood, I only received high school comedies—that seemed to be the only avenue for women directors in the eighties. I wanted to make it clear that I wanted to do something else."

Like her favorite filmmakers—Stone, Scorsese, and Kurosawa—Bigelow makes edgy and complex films. Does she think being a woman makes it more difficult for her to make men's movies?

"It would be impossible for me to know because I don't know what kind of resistance or not a male counterpart would have," answers the director whose next project is *Company of Angels*, the story of Joan of Arc. "It's a great, inspiring story about one of the few heroines in history who have legendary status. Joan was a sixteen-year-old girl who lived at a time when teenaged girls had less status than cattle. But she manages to change the course of history because she believed in something strongly enough."

It could be a metaphor for Bigelow's life as well.

Action Figure

Johanna Schneller / 1999–2002

From *Premiere* (USA) 15, no. 12 (August 2002): 62–65, 88. Reprinted by permission of Johanna Schneller.

Kathryn Bigelow is whipping up a storm. The stunning, six-feet-tall director is on a barge lashed to a dock in the maritime village of Chester, Nova Scotia, shooting the climactic scene of *The Weight of Water*. At her call of action, huge wind and rain machines whir to life. Orange Zodiac boats and green Sea-Doo jet skis skip back and forth, churning up waves. A crew of firemen shoot high-pressure hoses straight up to create a slashing rain, and fifteen burly men in yellow rubberwear overalls run up and down the length of the dock, heave-hoing a thick rope that is tethered to a yacht's mask making it pitch and buck. The noise is incredible. Bigelow, in her element, beams.

Through the wind and rain, she keeps a close eye on the monitor. When the scene ends and hoses go flat, she steps nimbly onto the yacht to confer with two actors, Catherine McCormack (*Spy Game*) and Josh Lucas (*The Deep End*), who lie soaked and breathless on its deck. Lucas's character had just hauled McCormack's from the sea, and he's trying desperately to revive her. Bigelow whispers something in his ear. He looks at her quizzically. They confer a bit more. Finally Bigelow steps back onto the barge, and the storm begins again.

"Kathryn told me to touch Catherine's face," Lucas says later. "She said, 'And keep touching her face, because you need to connect with her.' I was like, 'The boat's about to fall over, I'm trying to revive her, that's the last thing in the world I would do.' But Kathryn will tweak you. She'll bring you ideas that you don't understand, but, okay, you try them. I did one take like that and it blew me away; it was a revelation. Kathryn sees things you don't see."

That's the essence of a Bigelow film: As jazzed as she gets staging chaos, she loves small, human moments more. In the midst of a melee, Bigelow always trains her camera on something intimate. As a result, her films tend to linger longer in viewers' minds than the slam-bang hyper-activity of most action fare. Based on the novel by Anita Shreve, *Weight* is Bigelow's sixth feature film; she developed it for five years, snagging the rights while the book was still in galleys. Although the film was shot in 1999, it was delayed in distribution and will be released this fall. In the meantime she made her seventh film, this month's *K-19: The Widowmaker*, starring Harrison Ford and Liam Neeson in the true story of a dangerously disabled Russian nuclear submarine at the height of the Cold War.

"Kathryn develops and co-writes her movies, and she comes at them from two directions, from the visuals and from character," says director James Cameron (*Titanic, The Terminator*), who was married to Bigelow for two years and produced two of her films, *Point Break* (1991) and *Strange Days* (1995). "She's a painter, so she gets the poetic image she wants, but she also shows you everything her characters are feeling."

Because her films feature vivid action scenes, and because she is practically the only woman working regularly in that genre, Bigelow, fifty, is often summed up as a female action director. She rejects the label. "I try to distance myself from gender distinctions. They seem arcane to me," she says. "I suppose [being a woman director] is seen as a novelty, but it's also a ghettoization."

"Kathryn is the first woman director I've worked with, but I wouldn't have done it if I thought of her as a woman director," Ford says, sounding irritated at the very question. "She's a director. She's proven that."

Striking and strong, Bigelow resembles Katharine Ross. She craves demanding physical activity (yoga, mountain biking, deep-sea diving), wears her shiny brown hair long and straight, and favors low-rise jeans and tiny tank tops. She has a soft musical voice and a full-throated laugh, and she speaks in dense, clause-filled sentences that are at once carefully grammatical (she never splits infinitives), lushly evocative, and often vague.

"Kathryn's language is very coded," says Willem Dafoe, who's been a close friend since he starred in *The Loveless* (his first film as well as hers). "She's not the most direct person, and that's by design. My wife is a director, too, in theater. I constantly see walls put up around gender. The boys' network still operates pretty strongly in L.A. Then throw in the fact that Kathryn cuts a striking figure—in a town where appearance can be valued more than accomplishment—and that makes it even kinkier."

Paramount head Sherry Lansing, whose company will distribute *K-19*, is a woman who knows about gender labeling. "Kathryn had chosen to work in a traditionally male-dominated area, so she's had to break down barriers," Lansing says. "But she's simply a great director, as obsessed with her work as all great directors are." Lansing offered Bigelow directing gigs twice before, "but she turned me down. She's choosy." Both were action films, "but she could do anything," Lansing says.

Bigelow won't be able to avoid labels on *K-19*, however: At a budget of $90 million, it's the most expensive film ever directed by a woman (and the costliest independently financed film). And it is action-packed. Ford and Neeson play co-captains of a Soviet nuclear submarine that in 1961 traveled to Iceland to fire a test missile, to let the U.S. know where the U.S.S.R. stood in the arms race. But the cooling system failed and the nuclear reactor came within minutes of burning through the hull, which would have triggered an explosion several times greater than Hiroshima. The captain played by Ford faced a chilling choice: Send men into the core to repair it, exposing them to lethal radiation; or let the ship explode, which may well have led to all-out nuclear war.

At the end of April, in a bustling editing suite in a Hollywood production facility called the Lot, Bigelow is putting the final touches on *K-19* with Walter Murch, the renowned sound designer and film editor of *Apocalypse Now*, *The Conversation*, and *The English Patient*. One wall is covered in note cards, each of which bears a *K-19* story point: "#151, Interior missile bay. Darkness, hissing, grinding." "#301, Whistling jet of steam. Vadim sees it in horror." The opposite wall is papered with small stills.

"Walter takes a frame from each scene and puts them on wall board, to use as an emotional touchstone," Bigelow says. When they consider reordering scenes or beats, they try it on the boards before they cut the film. He works at one end of her office, standing up at an editing bay complete with a wide-screen TV monitor, while she sits on a couch at the other end, fielding phone calls and watching a monitor of her own (enabling them to work closely without driving each other crazy). On his editing machine, a joke dial in the lower right hand corner is labeled "Better," with an arrow pointing clockwise. "So when we get stuck on something, we just turn the dial and, poof, it's better," Bigelow says, laughing. "This is the kind of secret you learn when you work with a pro like Walter."

Bigelow first heard about *K-19* from Christine Whitaker, the head of *National Geographic*'s fledgling feature films division, who'd acquired a documentary about the sub and decided it should be *Geographic*'s maiden feature. "I knew Kathryn would bring a level of compassion, as well as deliver the action," Whitaker says. "She shows you the raw emotion just beneath a character's skin. She immediately understood what the story needed to be."

Bigelow threw herself into the project, as always. She traveled to Russia several times, pored over reams of military documents that were recently declassified, and spent hours with both a Russian duty officer and a nuclear fusion expert at MIT. Suggest that research is usually the screenwriter's job, and Bigelow strongly disagrees. "How do you design a shot if you don't understand the underlying mechanics?" she asks. "How can you convey the information that needs to be conveyed, without knowing it yourself?"

Her devotion to each phase of a film is the reason she's made only seven in her twenty-year career. "I think Scorsese once made this distinction: There are filmmakers, and there are directors," Bigelow says. "Filmmakers develop their own projects, which mean doing the research, shaping the script. I need to know my subject through and through, rip it apart. Whereas if you receive a script already in go mode, it would be like being handed a finished painting that only needed a frame. I don't know how you'd find yourself in it."

As part of her *K-19* research, she was the first American to set foot on a remote Russian sub base, where she stood on the deck of the actual *K-19*, now scrapped. She met with surviving crew members, and with the widow of the captain played by Ford. Suspicious at first—could an American film do justice to a Russian story?—the widow came to trust Bigelow, presenting her with a photo of her husband in uniform, which now hangs on the edit room wall.

When it came time to build the submarine set, Bigelow insisted it be to scale, even though that meant working in cramped conditions with low ceilings. "She sacrificed a comfortable work environment to gain authenticity," Whitaker says. "It had a ripple effect for the actors; it put them in the right mind-set."

"She can be forceful in pursuing goals," Murch says. "Early on, there were some conflicts between her and the financiers. Someone less resilient and persistent would have capitulated, but she didn't. If something comes to a head, her words can sting. But her storms blow over quickly. Those who stay are able to take it."

Bigelow had always been forceful. She started painting at six, "because my piano teacher hit my hand at my first recital." Bigelow got up, turned to her mother, and said, "I don't think so."

"My mom was a wonderful woman, a stoic Norwegian, an educator [a high school English teacher, she later became a librarian] who graduated valedictorian from Stanford. So, all right, but I had to do something else. My father managed a paint factory, how about painting? I loved it. Loved it. I could have drowned."

The only child of liberal-minded, middle-class parents in the small, northern California town of San Carlos, Bigelow was always "fiercely independent." From an early age she was taken to museums and concerts and encouraged to make her own decisions. She and a pack of friends ran freely through the neighborhood. At ten, she came home with a horse and convinced her animal-loving parents to let her keep it in a neighbor's backyard.

Both her parents are now deceased, as is her half-sister, ten years her senior, from her father's first marriage; Bigelow met her only later in life. "I became really close with her in the last five years, when she was struggling with cancer," Bigelow says. "The nineties was an interesting decade for me, full of the disappearance of family members. That's a great metaphor for life: Not until you're ready to lose something do you realize how absolutely vital it is to you. Why is that? I can't stand that!"

At seventeen, she enrolled in the San Francisco Art Institute, then followed up with postgraduate work at New York University and Columbia. "When I was painting, nothing I did didn't have a reference. Not even a pencil mark upon a piece of paper. I'd kind of over-informed myself. But when I began to make the transition to film, there was a kind of pure, raw joy in what I was watching and doing."

Her first film, *Set-Up*, was a twenty-minute short made with a two-thousand-dollar grant from the National Endowment for the Arts. It depicted super-violent acts while philosophers discussed in voiceovers the role of cinematic violence in society. "We shot it in an alley near Canal Street, just put some lights, and did it," Bigelow says. "I was never daunted by challenges. I think there's something off in my psyche—I'm sure years of therapy could take care of it, but I don't have time for that." She laughs.

Bigelow came to L.A. at the behest of an artist friend, John Baldessari, to teach a six-month class on B-movie makers of the thirties, forties, and fifties at CalArts. Then she met Walter Hill (*The Warriors, Streets of Fire*), who offered Bigelow a writer-director job, and she never left.

"Painting can be elitist, while film crosses all class and cultural lines," she says. "My goal is to make material as accessible as possible, but with a conscience. So I include some genre elements, which gives you a comfort level, and then I add other dimensions, which you don't see coming, to make you walk out of the theater and think. But it can't be pedagogical; it's not, 'I know more than you, and I'm teaching you.' You have to keep the material subversive, so it doesn't reveal itself. I'll crawl through fire for that."

In *K-19*, for example, she starts with a genre idea: a submarine movie. She adds a strong antinuclear message. And she puts a human face on a culture that's been demonized—the iconic face of Harrison Ford, no less. "I'm trying to take the looking glass of heroism and refract it, to take the quote unquote enemy, and make him whom I identify with and cry for," Bigelow says. "I'm asking the audience to go on a fairly exotic ride, to make you believe that you are them [the Russian submariners], and that we are the same, that geopolitical borders aren't real. And then, I hope, to make you think that while what we're doing in the world today—well, if only we could count to ten."

"Kathryn sees this film, and I think all her films, as a benign virus she uses to spread ideas where she can," Murch says.

Not all of those ideas have been successful. *The Loveless* (codirected by Monty Montgomery), in which a bunch of bikers travel to the Daytona races, was stunning to look at but basically plotless. In one scene, Dafoe slowly pours an entire bottle of ketchup over his fries. "Kathryn was this brainy, beautiful semiotician making a stylish, arch biker movie," Dafoe says. "It was a strange combination, and I was quite taken with her. We had a tight schedule, no money, and she had the nerve to be a perfectionist, God bless her. I remember toward the end that we shot thirty-six hours straight. I was riding a bike in this field on black beauties. I was young and foolish then."

In *Near Dark* (1987), Bigelow came closer to satisfying her subversive impulses. She wanted to make a western, to share the infinite vistas of her youthful horseback. Westerns were out of favor, she says, "but I thought, 'How can I turn that disadvantage into an advantage? How about a vampire western?'"

Bigelow and a cast of hot-blooded newcomers—Bill Paxton, Lance Henriksen, Adrian Pasdar, James LeGros—shot for forty nights in a row.

"The cast and crew developed a symbiotic relationship with the story," Bigelow says. "We became vampires. But I wanted to show that no matter how arcane their life was, even vampires are encoded to gravitate toward conventional nuclear family structures."

"I loved performing for her," says Bill Paxton, the wild-card vampire. "And her laugh was infectious. If Kathryn ran the world, there would be no problems. I think *Near Dark* is a classic, man. I just did *Spy Kids 2* for director Robert Rodriguez, and all he wanted to talk about was *Near Dark*. He knew every line."

Bigelow met James Cameron in 1986, when he was directing *The Abyss* and she was writing and directing *Blue Steel* (1990), in which a female cop played by Jamie Lee Curtis is stalked by her lover. They fell in love and were married on Martha's Vineyard. Dafoe stood up with them; Paxton was there. Later, Cameron shot a video for Paxton's band, Martini Ranch, which depicted a post-apocalyptic, all-female Magnificent Seven. Bigelow played a Clint Eastwood type in a serape and sombrero. "You have to see the way she flicks away her cheroot—it's so sweet," Paxton says. "Tough but feminine."

She and Cameron rewrote *Point Break* together, which he produced. "She went to the mat for Keanu Reeves" to play an FBI agent who goes undercover to infiltrate a gang of surfing bank robbers, Cameron remembers. "We had this meeting where the Fox executives were going, 'Keanu Reeves in an action film? Based on what? *Bill & Ted*?' They were being so insulting. But she insisted he could be an action star. This was long before *Speed* or *The Matrix*. I didn't see it either, frankly. I supported her in the meeting, but when we walked out, I was going, 'Based on what?'" Cameron laughs. "But she worked on his wardrobe, she showed him how to walk, she made him work out. She was his Olympic coach. He should send her a bottle of champagne every year, to thank her."

Bigelow and Cameron divorced in 1991 but went on to make *Strange Days* together. "Our working relationship was always close and friendly," Cameron says. "I think she had to distance herself from me a little. People gossip; there was a nasty perception that I was sneaking onto her sets and telling her where to put the camera," he snorts. "When anybody who knows anything about filmmaking can see we have totally different styles. The shortest lens she uses is the longest lens I use"—which means her close-ups are set against a blurred background—"because she's more selective about what she makes you watch. I'd love to work with her again. For one thing, she always brings her films in on time, on schedule, and on budget. Which I've heard can be difficult." He laughs.

Bigelow won't talk about Cameron, however, in any capacity. "That's all ancient history," she says. "And personal." Nor will she discuss her current significant other, with whom she lives in an airy, sparsely furnished house in the Hollywood Hills with two dogs. "I think it's best if we stick to the work," she demurs.

Very seldom have all the subversive and philosophical pieces come together in her films, she admits. But there's honor in the attempt. "For a movie to be great, it has to engage your mind," she says. "There is no such thing as a mindless entertainment. Because if you're truly transported, all neurons are firing. Without meaning and content, you'd be bored."

"Whenever I come to town, Kathryn and I go to the biggest, grossest, most commercial film we can find," Dafoe says. "She recognizes that pop culture can be high culture, that it has its fingers on a pulse."

Bigelow doesn't make paintings anymore. She still sketches the initial storyboards for her films, rough takes in thick pencil or pastel, which she calls "gesture drawings. They get the emotion of a sequence or character, then I give it to somebody to do a more detailed translation. But I can't paint as a hobby," she says. "It's a state of mind. It isn't something soothing and relaxing for me. I have to be passionately committed, all or nothing, and for me, that's films." She pauses. "What would happen if that burning desire—which is what gets me up in the morning—suddenly ceased? It would be, I don't know." She grins. "I just can't imagine it."

Direct from the Gut

Peter Howell / 2000

From the *Toronto Star*, September 9, 2000. Reprinted by permission of Torstar Syndication Services.

Sexism may be rampant in Hollywood, with female directors all but shut out of the boys' club of moviemaking, but it isn't bothering Kathryn Bigelow.

The striking six-footer who directed tonight's Roy Thomson Hall festival gala presentation *The Weight of Water*, her seventh film, says her biggest work problems have had nothing to do with sex. She hasn't even heard of the current book *Is That a Gun in Your Pocket?*, by *Premiere* writer Rachel Abramowitz, which complains of how decades of feminism have failed to make major changes to the male domination of studio filmmaking.

"To be honest, I can't cite an example of a film (where her gender has been an issue)," Bigelow, forty-eight, said in an interview yesterday, looking like Emma Peel reborn in a chic and sleek black outfit. "I may be naive, perhaps painfully naive, but if anything has been difficult or frustrating, I don't think it's gender related."

"I think it's usually symptomatic of wanting to do projects that are very personal and truthful and challenging. That's not to say the inequities that do exist shouldn't be fought vehemently at every juncture. But I feel very comfortable."

Bigelow is not convinced by the oft-expressed argument that women make movies differently from men.

"I think life experience gives us all unique perspectives. There's a component, which is perhaps gigantic, where gender does inform perspective. But is there a women's aesthetic or just a personal aesthetic? I'm not sure."

The Weight of Water, based on the best-selling novel of the same name by Anita Shreve, fit her stringent criteria, especially on the personal front. The book is centered around the murders in 1873 of two Norwegian immigrant women on a remote island off New Hampshire. (A grotto near Nova Scotia's scenic Peggy's Cove was used for filming.) Bigelow's mother came from Norway.

"I read this book in manuscript form while I was shooting *Strange Days* (in 1994) and sadly, she passed away at that time. Her side of the family was all Norwegian, so I grew up with these incredible stories of coming to America and trying to make a life here, what they were leaving behind and how difficult that was for them. Their hunger for a new reality kind of overrode everything.

"These stories haunted my extreme youth, and so quite honestly when I read this in manuscript form it was kind of a way to bring Mom back to life. It was very personal to me."

The movie seems a bit of a departure from her more action-oriented films of the past decade: *Strange Days* (which starred Ralph Fiennes as a cybersleuth), *Point Break* (with Keanu Reeves as an FBI agent chasing surfer felons), and *Blue Steel* (Jamie Lee Curtis as a rookie cop sexing and stalking a serial killer).

The Weight of Water has ample opportunities for sex and thrills, particularly with Sean Penn and Elizabeth Hurley amongst the leads.

But Bigelow avoids taking obvious dramatic or sexual turns. *Weight* is more of a psycho-thriller, weaving between concurrent stories set in the 1800s and today. She doesn't see *Weight* as any kind of departure for her. "I never work from the set piece back, which is an action methodology. I don't look at it in categories. I'm just attracted to character, and I always work from the character out. It really is dictated by the character and by the story.

"With any film I've done, I always start from a very visceral standpoint. It's just a gut response. For *The Weight of Water*, I read the manuscript and I could see the movie immediately."

It did take some doing though, to go back and forth between the Penn-Hurley intrigue of modern times to the travails of Sarah Polley's character of more than one hundred years ago.

"It was a little bit of a high-wire act. It was one of those pieces you tend to tear apart and rebuild many, many times."

She chose Sarah Polley for the role of Norwegian immigrant wife Maren after seeing her in Atom Egoyan's *The Sweet Hereafter*. "I just think she's someone of staggering talent."

The Weight of Water demands close attention, and not just because of its tricky twin-narrative structure. A lot of information is inferred rather than stated or shown openly.

Will today's impatient audiences, perhaps the same ones who thrilled to *Point Break* or *Strange Days*, be able to handle a more layered work from Bigelow? "Everyone who has seen it seems to have been able to," she said firmly. "I certainly think enough films have been dumbed down and it's very refreshing to have one that actually engages your mind."

K-19: The Widowmaker:
A Film by Kathryn Bigelow

Ted Elick / 2002

From *DGA Magazine* 27, no. 2 (July 2002): 24–32. Permission to reprint courtesy of
the Director's Guild of America, Inc.

In 1961, at the height of the Cold War, the Soviet Union was eager to
display its ability to launch nuclear missiles within striking distance of
the United States. With arms-race tensions at fever pitch, the Soviets believed it essential to demonstrate to American intelligence that they had
the capability to strike back.

Their newest sub, the *K-19*, was rushed from the shipyard for sea trials
and missile-test firing. Unfortunately for the crew, at depth in the North
Atlantic, the atomic reactor's cooling system sprung a leak. The reactor
core began to heat up, threatening a reactor meltdown—all with the potential of causing the sub's nuclear missile warheads to accidentally explode which in turn could destroy a nearby NATO base and set off World
War III.

The dramatic details of this event remained secret for decades, and
the captain and crew's heroism and sacrifices were not recognized by
their own government until well after the fall of communism.

Enter director/producer Kathryn Bigelow, who has always had a passion for history. More than five years ago, Ken Stovitz, her agent at Creative Artists Agency, suggested she meet with several organizations that
were considering producing feature films on historical subjects—among
them, *National Geographic* producer Hank Palmieri.

Palmieri and Bigelow discussed a number of stories, but the one that
would grab and consume her for the next five years began with the viewing of a Russian documentary that *National Geographic* had re-aired for

Western audiences. The story touched on the bare bones of the Soviet atomic submarine *K-19*'s ill-fated maiden voyage. Bigelow immediately saw the potential for a big-screen adaptation of the story, and became personally committed to telling the submariners' story.

"The documentary was rough and cursory, yet still a very fascinating story," Bigelow said. "What occurred to me, as Hank and I discussed this incident, was how little I knew about the Russian psychology during the Cold War or the Russian military mindset. Courage and heroism are, of course, universal. What was intriguing was that it was Russian heroism that had a profound impact upon American lives by preventing a possible nuclear confrontation. I thought the story was not only a vital slice of history, but also an opportunity to excavate the Russian military psyche at that time, which would give us an opportunity to look at ourselves through the eyes of the enemy. That is always valuable."

Despite the inherent drama in the piece, the principal obstacle and challenge to getting the film made was that the story was about the Russians, not Americans.

"In mainstream Hollywood, the Russians have not been treated as heroes," she said. "But I felt, if a member of the audience could begin to identify with these submariners and want them to survive, then you crossed the Rubicon, so to speak. That's what set me on my journey."

That journey began with developing a screenplay. Bigelow, whose screenwriting credits include *The Loveless*, *Near Dark*, and *Blue Steel*, takes a very active role in developing a script. First working with writer Louis Nowra (story credit) then Christopher Kyle (screenwriter), whom she discovered through his work as a playwright, she began to fill in the details of the ill-fated voyage of the *K-19*.

The process became a journalistic enterprise, with Bigelow making several trips to Russia to interview survivors and gain access to accounts of an incident that, at one time, the Soviet Union considered a major embarrassment. She recognized an interesting parallel to the end of the Cold War with her attempts to discover the truth within the story.

"There was bias and resistance, very reminiscent of the sixties, on this shore and in Russia," she explained. "I would go to Russia and speak with the survivors. First of all, I'm an American, and I don't know if being a woman played into the bias, but I also don't have a military background. I'm not a submariner; I'm a filmmaker, and I want to tell their story.

"So through an interpreter, because I don't speak Russian, I realized there was a lot of suspicion, a lot of skepticism. Hollywood mainstream films have not portrayed the Russians in a way that they felt was as respectful as it could be. That's putting it mildly. They've felt mocked and ridiculed. 'OK, yet another obstacle.' So I tried to talk them through and show them my commitment and my understanding of the story—how I would shape it, how it was meant to be a tribute, to honor these men and give that event as much meaning as I humanly could. It was a very long process."

Bigelow said that the first person to embrace both the idea of the film and her as the one who could tell the story was the widow of Captain Nikolai Zateyev who commanded the *K-19*. His fictional counterpart, Captain Vostrikov, is portrayed by Harrison Ford in the film.

"I spent hours and hours with her and I knew very well her suspicions" Bigelow said. "We looked at all of her old photographs, and I asked hundreds of questions. I think she finally realized that I was determined and that I had done my homework. At one point, she suddenly put her arms around me and, with her eyes filling with tears, said, 'You must tell the story. You must tell the story.'"

It is the memory of that emotional moment that still affects Bigelow many years later. Mrs. Zateyev then gave a photo of her husband to Bigelow. It is framed in her office and served as a source of inspiration during the production.

Soon, the survivors themselves, many in their eighties and suffering for years with the aftereffects of radiation poisoning, began to trust Bigelow and rewarded her determination with a wealth of details about the incident.

"The screenplay was in a constant state of development," Bigelow explained. "It was connecting the dots. There is also a memoir the captain had written, capturing a beat-by-beat account of the moment when he was awoken at 4:30 A.M. and told the aft reactor was in a potentially catastrophic state. We married that account with the wonderful anecdotes that survivors and various submariners and captains from throughout the international submarine community told us. It was then that Chris Kyle and I decided upon, what we called, the primary reactor to the story."

For Bigelow, the primary reactor was the relationship between Vostrikov (Ford) and Polenin (Liam Neeson). "The survivors told us that Liam's character was the one you wanted to spend time with, you wanted to go drinking with, the one you treated like part of your family. Harrison's was a man you feared, yet, if you were in a life-or-death situation, he was the one you wanted making the decisions about your survival. We made Polenin the former captain of the boat who stood up for his men, warned the Soviet leadership that the *K-19* wasn't ready, and was "rewarded" by being demoted to executive officer under Vostrikov. That was the primary reactor. These two men ultimately were going to be on a collision course. Set that against the literal reactor having a catastrophic malfunction and you have a quantum relationship with those two dynamics.

"So Chris and I are in Moscow, going through the script in copious detail, working every detail about the story, character, subject, the microcosm and macrocosm simultaneously. It was unfolding, like a flower blooming. It's not like everything was instantaneously declassified for us. 'OK, here's the plan for the Russian submarine. Here's how the nuclear reactor worked.' I didn't get the plans for the reactor until moments before we had to go into set fabrication. Little by little, sometimes through nefarious ways, I was able to get the information to make this story as accurate as possible. Each time we were fed with more information, we'd incorporate it into the script. Of course, then you realize, 'Oh, this element is going into sharp relief, but now this one is becoming obscure.' It's like a big jigsaw puzzle and balancing act."

Not only did the survivors begin to open up, but the Russian government did as well. So much so that Bigelow was finally able to achieve her ultimate goal: setting foot on the deck of the actual *K-19* and becoming the first Western civilian to visit the Russian Northern Fleet Naval Base in the Kola Peninsula.

"I felt that I needed to actually meet and touch the *K-19*," Bigelow said. "I couldn't look into the eyes of the captain, he was deceased. I needed to touch the boat. Then I knew that I could make the movie. The government said, 'No Western civilian has been there.' This is just on the heels of the *Kursk* disaster [the Russian submarine that sunk in August 2000 trapping all its crew aboard]. It was a very sensitive time. But I was determined. I just don't take 'no' for an answer. I think your job, as director, is that for every door that closes, you've got to open two more."

On her final research trip, Bigelow brought along her 1st AD Steve Danton (with whom she'd worked on *Strange Days*) and cinematographer Jeff Cronenweth (*Fight Club*).

"I involve my cinematographer and AD in everything," Bigelow said. "That would be ground zero to the extent that we can almost work as a single organism. It keeps everything so smooth and as organized as humanly possible. We're in communication constantly. During production I would start and end every day working with Steve, not only discussing what we'd do the next day, but also discussing four weeks down the road when we'd be shooting on water. Having that kind of preparation and organization sounds like it would be anathema to the creative process, but it isn't. If you have that level of organization, it enables you to have some freedom and spontaneity."

Her quest for accuracy also led Bigelow to a former Russian submarine captain of communications, Igor Kolosov, who conducts tours of and maintains the *Scorpion*, a Soviet diesel-electric sub now a tourist attraction moored next to the Queen Mary in Long Beach, California. Armed with her digital video camera, Bigelow made a film she calls, "A Day in the Life of Igor." "I can easily block a scene with you and me eating lunch," she explained, "but I'm not a submariner. I didn't spend much time studying nuclear physics. I was an art major who also studied biology. I needed to know what the day-to-day life details would be like on a nuclear submarine.

"So I went down there, by myself, and asked Igor all kinds of questions. 'You get up in the morning, what do you do? Where do you brush your teeth? What is your day like?' and Igor walked me through every detail. These are the kinds of details I covet." One of the details that made it into the film is the use of cotton swabs dipped in alcohol. Water is very scarce on a submarine, and, in addition to personal uses, it's used to cool the reactor. With 129 men submerged for months, water is not something they're going to let the crew bathe in every day—thus the little swabs dipped in alcohol.

This attention to detail is something Bigelow demanded of all members of the cast and crew. Before filming began, the bulk of the cast attended a two-week boot camp at the Canadian Naval Training Center in Halifax, Nova Scotia. Originally, efforts were made to secure cooperation from the United States, but—aside from initial technical advice from Vice Admiral Harry Schrader, who was very helpful but unfortunately passed away—the production received little assistance from the U.S. because there was no American aspect to the story.

"The commitment was kind of the unspoken part of the script," Bigelow explained. "A lot of the younger actors had never even been in a film before. One actor left in the middle of his drama year at Juilliard to attend, and suddenly they were putting out one-hundred-foot walls of fire where the heat level is staggering. They were also trained in what to do in the event of a hull rupture and various kinds of survival situations like search and rescue, oxygen deprivation, smoke and fire in a maze situation, you name it. They were trained, and they came through with flying colors.

"You can't really teach that stuff in drama school. You can't say, 'OK, today we're going to work on the first act of *Hamlet*, then we're going to put out a one-hundred-foot wall of fire.' The pressure in those hoses is so great it requires several men to hold on. We had four hoses, and a one-hundred-foot wall of fire. The challenge is to get the fire down quickly and, finally, out. You have to keep inching forward. This kind of training galvanized this crew.

"In the movie, Harrison says, 'I've taken this crew to the edge.' Basically what he's saying is 'I've made these 129 different men into a crew.' And that's what this boot camp did. These boys came from all over—Europe, Iceland, New York, Los Angeles, Canada—all descending on Halifax where the Canadian navy and admiral were kind enough to train my cast. By the end of boot camp, the actors were working as one body, one organism. That to me was the true rehearsal period. They would have killed for each other. Unlike production, where it's literally smoke and mirrors, they were put into legitimate situations. But they walked away friends for life and e-mail me constantly about how this experience has changed their lives."

In addition, every member of the cast, as well as Bigelow, Danton, and Cronenweth, underwent atomic physics training from technical advisers from the Massachusetts Institute of Technology (MIT), who also were on set during the filming. For Bigelow, the MIT advisers were crucial because she couldn't imagine blocking, directing, and talking with actors about a sequence she didn't thoroughly understand.

"If you're on a Russian nuclear submarine, everybody has training in atomic physics," she said. "You have all these different drills. Let's say the first eight compartments of a submarine are disabled. Well, there's so much redundancy that in most cases, from every single compartment, you can drive the entire boat. I don't care if you're the cook or the person in charge of cleaning the head, you know how to drive the boat.

"Also, I wanted everybody to know how to properly use the equipment when we're filming different drills. Even the extras had training so they're not just in the background turning knobs. They know exactly what they have to do whether the boat is diving, maintaining, or surfacing. I see films where extras aren't trained this way and, subconsciously, I think the audience sees it as well. Give them credit. The audience knows something is wrong. They may not be able to point to the extras, but they notice it."

To begin mapping out her visuals, Bigelow, who received art training at the San Francisco Art Institute, began her own storyboards, using stills and movies she had shot on location scouts with her production designer, Kalli Juliusson, at a Russian mining town on Spitzbergen, an island halfway between the northernmost part of Norway and the North Pole. She fed these into Photoshop, then took photos from location shoots in Nova Scotia and overlaid the Spitzbergen material.

Bigelow, who drew her own storyboards on *Near Dark*, then began working with the storyboard artists and set designers so that she could get the kind of coverage she planned to convey the drama of the *K-19*.

Through discussions with Cronenweth, the set was planned to allow for camera platforms at strategic locations as well as a unique overhead truss system that allowed for the camera to be hung from a bungee cord trolley. "This we designed early on so that the camera could be moved 180 degrees and guide it down the bungee to allow for the changes in altitude within the submarine that we wanted. With a Steadicam, we had the gyro stabilization, so that now we could glide along while the crew is running the drills. It's like dance choreography, but to get that kind of freedom you have to have a tremendous amount of organization that had to be thought through before the set was even pencil on paper."

The only real concession Bigelow made between the interior of an actual submarine and her set was in the bulkhead door between compartments. The standard thirty-one inches circumference was widened to thirty-five inches to allow for the various camera rigs and to make it easier for the cast and crew—far less agile than hardcore submariners—to move from one compartment to the next.

The film was shot in Moscow, Canada's Lake Winnipeg standing-in for the Arctic Ocean ice pack, and in the snow-covered Halifax shipyards that also served as a base for shooting in the open North Atlantic.

Again, Bigelow feels that careful preparation helped her to shoot on water. "From working on *Point Break*, I learned that working on water is an area that even a director can't control," she says with a smile. "Once you relegate yourself to that, you realize that you've got to be painfully flexible. You've got to be ready to shoot anything. That means you've got to have multiple call sheets for any given hour of the day because it's all dependent on the weather. That kind of flexibility necessitates the need for improvisation, which is why part of the casting sessions involved improvisations.

"You've got to be flexible for an idea that might suddenly come up on the set. For instance, we could be in the process of a deep dive sequence and a technical adviser suddenly says, 'Wait a minute, this is inaccurate.' You say, 'Well, you read it in the script didn't you?' They say, 'Yes, I did, but seeing it, it just occurred to me . . .' so there is this planned disorder and orderly chaos that is constantly being balanced while you work."

For Bigelow, the final part of juggling the story is in working with the editor, in this case Walter Murch. "He's a legend," Bigelow said. "He is someone with a tremendously strong intellect. So you initially begin with the writers, sifting through this massive amount of information, then the story is refracted through the filmmaker, then further refined working with the hands and eyes of an editor like Walter Murch. It is a life-altering experience."

Later this year, as her next film *The Weight of Water*—which made a strong showing at the 25th Toronto Film Festival—receives wide distribution, Bigelow is planning a screening of *K-19: The Widowmaker* for the survivors as well as one for Russian Federation President Vladimir Putin. Maestro Valery Gergiev of the Kirov Orchestra, who conducted the score for the film, spoke to Putin about the project.

"I think what's happened between our two countries is wonderful," Bigelow said when asked how she felt when watching news footage of President Bush and Putin in Texas last summer. "Myself, growing up in the sixties, I never would have imagined it. Russia is now, to a certain extent a part of NATO. The arms agreement has happened, and I've been able to involve the Nuclear Threat Initiative as part of the benefit associated with the film's premiere.

"I think what is important with this film, is that the younger Russian generations realize that the virtue of their culture and country are not only appreciated within the geographic confines of their own country," Bigelow said. "That, in fact, that appreciation is worldwide. I also know there is a multitude of stories of heroism and bravery, and I hope this film will inspire the many extraordinary Russian filmmakers to get those stories made. That would be the greatest of all possible outcomes."

When asked to define the directing process, Bigelow feels that it's a very elusive one. "It's different from person to person and from situation to situation. There's the director to actor, director to cameraman, director to writer. Each given event has its own set of dynamics that require completely distinct tools and sets of circumstances, calling on life experiences in one's past. It's like a traffic pattern over LAX. You're the person monitoring all those patterns. I think that's why I love it so much. There's the parallel processing of information and multitasking so that no doors are closed that you cannot open. You can never be in a period where there is ever any stagnation whatsoever of any kind. A department might have lost something. You can't stop. It's also like the space shuttle, or commanding a submarine. There are so many built-in redundancies so you're always prepared for what you have not anticipated."

Bigelow, also a producer on *K-19*, wanted to combine her produced and directed by credits in the end titles. However, the Writers Guild contract calls for the writer's credit to be listed no later than the second credit in the end titles. An exception to this is when the director is the sole producer on the project. Bigelow sought a waiver from the WGA but was told it would not be granted unless she gave up her possessory credit onscreen and in paid advertising.

"I didn't realize that it was an either/or situation," Bigelow said. "When you're finishing a film, you're like a horse out of the starting gate with extreme blinders on. My focus was on making sure the film had a beginning, middle, and end, and that it was as solid as it could be. The last thing I was thinking about, sadly, and perhaps erroneously, were my credits. I feel a possessory credit means that without a particular person's drive and commitment, the film probably would not have been made. So it's a bit of an inaccuracy for *K-19* not to have a possessory credit. Of all the things I had planned for during production, this is the one I didn't anticipate. I do not want future filmmakers to share my experience. Knowing this now, I'll approach it differently the next time."

Her Underwater Canvas

Richard Natale / 2002

From the *Los Angeles Times Calendar*, July 14, 2002, 5, 75. Reprinted by permission of the Los Angeles Times Syndicate.

One of Kathryn Bigelow's teachers in art school instructed his students to find their "most productive weakness."

That seemingly contradictory bit of advice remained lodged somewhere in a corner of her mind, and when she began directing movies, Bigelow discovered what her weakness was. "Withstanding pressure," she says. So she set out to conquer it.

"I learned to treat the reality of constant pressure on a movie set abstractly, like it was a mental process," she says.

It's a character trait that was called on during the shooting of *K-19: The Widowmaker.* A $100-million Soviet submarine drama based on a true incident on a nuclear sub in 1961, the film took seven years to complete—but the shoot itself finished on time and on budget.

The credit for that, all agree, rests squarely on Bigelow's shoulders. "It was a huge logistical undertaking," says Harrison Ford, who stars as the sub's Capt. Alexei Vostrikov. "But I don't remember ever facing the feeling of chaos. Directors have to be able to think on their feet when the time isn't there, the light isn't there, when the capacity of an actor to perform isn't there—and they have to find a way to make it work anyway. Kathryn never would have survived if she hadn't been able to do that."

But it's the fifty-year-old director's art school background, rather than her newfound grace under pressure, that comes up repeatedly in an interview. At other times, she compares the work of her B-movie heroes—directors Samuel Fuller and Anthony Mann—to the "pure expression" of Jackson Pollock and Willem de Kooning. She explains her ability to flout conventions about women directing action movies by saying her instincts were honed during her early years as an artist.

"In painting, there are no preconceived notions of what's possible. You're always starting with a blank canvas," she says. "And that's what's given me strength."

K-19 is based on the maiden, disaster-prone voyage of a Soviet nuclear submarine in 1961. The threat of a nuclear meltdown aboard the sub is a harrowing, little-known chapter in the history of the Cold War. It was only through the clear thinking of the sub's captain and the heroism of its crew that a disaster of global significance was averted.

Suppressed for three decades, the story of the *K-19* came to light in the early nineties after the demise of the Soviet Union. Rights to the story were immediately scooped up by *National Geographic*'s film division after executives there saw a British-made documentary on the subject, says Christine Whitaker, the company's executive vice president of production.

A story that focuses on Russian submariners and told from their point of view may have seemed an odd choice for an English-language feature film, but "one of the primary reasons we were attracted to it," Whitaker says, "is that *National Geographic* has been turning the camera on other cultures for 115 years. It fit in with our mission" of expanding into feature films.

Whitaker thought of Bigelow, who had made her name with fast-paced action stories, including the biker-horror film *Near Dark* (1987); the psychological cop thriller *Blue Steel* (1990), starring Jamie Lee Curtis; the action adventure *Point Break* (1991) with Keanu Reeves; and the apocalyptic sci-fi drama *Strange Days* (1995) with Ralph Fiennes and Angela Bassett (her former husband, James Cameron, was a producer and co-writer on that).

"From our first meeting," Whitaker says, Bigelow "understood the humanity behind the story. It wasn't just a submarine thriller. It was about men rising above their circumstances and their politics to do something for the greater good."

The opportunity to illuminate this obscure chapter in history was as much a learning experience for Bigelow as she hopes it will be for the audience. "I had no idea of the Russian psychology at the time. For me, they were horrible people who were going to push a button and destroy the world.

"This was such a great opportunity to put a human face to some incredibly brave individuals without whom our lives would have been changed."

Bigelow developed the script with playwright Christopher Kyle for the British production company Working Title. That was the easy part. The project was stalled when Universal Pictures announced another submarine drama, *U-571*, released in 2000, and Bigelow went off to make a more personal independent project, *The Weight of Water*, starring Sean Penn and Elizabeth Hurley; after several delays, *The Weight of Water* is to be released in November.

After Working Title put *K-19* in turnaround about three years ago, it was shopped to a number of companies. The overseas independent company Intermedia agreed to finance the movie that, by this time, also had an expensive star, Ford, attached. During production, Intermedia contracted with Paramount Pictures to distribute the film in the U.S. and certain key countries abroad.

Just as the deal was finally set, a competing script materialized, which led to litigation that was eventually settled, according to Intermedia principal Nigel Sinclair. He is legally proscribed from discussing the terms of the settlement.

While the film was in preproduction, another real-life submarine disaster occurred. In August 2000, the Russian nuclear sub *Kursk* was lost and all 118 men aboard perished. After debating the propriety of releasing *K-19* at that juncture, Bigelow says, she decided to proceed.

The *Kursk* disaster put to rest any doubts that American audiences would respond to a story about an ill-fated Russian submarine. "Sadly, the horrendous disaster of the *Kursk* had the entire world spellbound, and the myopic idea that Americans only want to see stories about Americans dissolved completely," she says.

There were additional pressures, the most daunting of which was that "we were working against a potential SAG strike and there was no wiggle room in terms of schedule," Whitaker says. "We were shooting in three different countries and the dates were not fungible."

In addition, says Sinclair, all but twenty-two days of the sixteen-week shoot were on water, an element that has wreaked havoc with the best-laid plans (and budgets) of moviemakers in the past. (*Waterworld* being the most calamitous example).

"I flew up to Canada for the first day of the water shoot," Sinclair recalls. "There were twenty-eight vessels, including two subs, two frigates, eighteen to twenty support boats and a naval helicopter. It was easy to imagine a shoot like this going $20 million over budget. But we didn't."

Bigelow was raised in the Northern California city of San Carlos, which she calls "a good place to grow up." As an only child, she says she has been interested in art "for as long as I can remember. Though I had friends, I was an introvert and I expressed myself through art. Next thing I know, I'm at the San Francisco Art Institute and my teacher has submitted my work to the Whitney Museum's independent study program."

She was accepted into the program and moved to New York. Soon thereafter, however, she switched to film, enrolling at Columbia University.

To anyone familiar with her body of work, Bigelow's love of B-movies informs her style. *Near Dark* pays homage to such time-honored B-grade genres as the biker movie, the western, and the horror film. *Blue Steel*, *Point Break*, and even the more epic *Strange Days* are alive with a pulp sensibility. If *K-19* seems incongruous in this mix, she cites B-movie auteur Fuller's 1954 submarine drama *Hell and High Water*, with its masterful camera moves in confined spaces.

"I love B-movies, like Anthony Mann's *Crime Wave*, because the creative muscle [of the filmmaker] hasn't been put through the Hollywood homogenization machine," she says. "There is a wildly chaotic rawness to [B-movies]. And they're not self-important."

From the preparation of *K-19* through its postproduction, she relied heavily on her gut and not her brain. "I work so instinctively that I can't be cerebral too early. It would ruin the spontaneity." Overthinking a film's themes can compromise the drama, and Bigelow says she chose to allow the film to emerge through the accrual of detail, not dissimilar to the way an artist layers paint on a blank canvas.

Besides, on a project of this magnitude, there was no time for musing or second-guessing. The meticulous construction of the *K-19* sets was an intense experience. She catches herself, and laughs, "Oh yeah, as you can see, I really got into it."

The sets were built using photographic studies of the sub's interiors and, just before construction began, the production secured access to the blueprint of the *K-19*.

"We worked on getting that over a period of years through the process of declassification. As you can imagine, given the nature of the history between the military industrial complexes of the U.S. and the USSR and the fact that this was a nuclear submarine, it wasn't something they handed out like a vacation brochure."

The production bought a Russian nuclear sub built two or three years after the *K-19* and cannibalized the interiors. "Because we were able to use all original equipment, we began to understand the architecture of submarines, which are ergonomically designed so that the instruments are all within arm's distance."

The cast and crew underwent two weeks of "boot camp" training with Russian submariners so they understood their duties aboard the *K-19* as well as the demands and procedures of daily life under the sea.

Built to scale, the sets were "extremely, extremely tight," Bigelow says, "no space, no oxygen. After spending months in these incredibly microscopic chambers, you felt you had a legitimate impression of what it would be like to be a submariner. It created a verisimilitude that, I think, was necessary for the piece."

The thought of Bigelow, who is five-feet-eleven, and the film's two leading men, Ford and Liam Neeson, who are even taller, crammed into a small set with a camera and crew produces a rather claustrophobic image. "Claustrophobia is not an option for submariners," says Ford, although he admits "it was a bit of a challenge to find different ways to keep the visual environment alive. One of Kathryn's biggest talents is visualization, and she was very collaborative with the actors in letting us find motivations for the kinds of movement that reinforced the reality of the space."

Bigelow says she devoted as much attention to the characters' inner lives as to their physical environment, interviewing survivors of the *K-19* and Vostrikov's [in real life Capt. Nikolai Vladimirovich Zateyev] widow. "Her ability to accept what I wanted to do and let me in emotionally was extraordinary, especially given that I represent the Hollywood community, which has usually portrayed the Soviets as either sinister or laughable."

Transcending those stereotypes, she continues, was essential to the success of her undertaking. "At the end of the day, in order for the story to have resonance, you have to care about the characters," even if they were, politically, our polar opposites. Her sincerest hope is that American audiences will come away from the film thinking, "They were the enemy and I desperately wanted them to live."

K-19: The Widowmaker: Harrison Ford and Kathryn Bigelow Interview

Scott Huver / 2002

From Hollywood.com, July 19, 2002. Reprinted by permission of Hollywood.com Inc.

"I don't play heroes," insists Harrison Ford. It's a rather remarkable statement from an actor who's portrayed more than his share of iconic big-screen good guys, from cocky interplanetary rogue Han Solo to intrepid adventurer Indiana Jones to crisis-wrangling CIA analyst Jack Ryan. Instead, Ford has a different definition for his film protagonists: "I play guys who behave well under difficult circumstances," he says. "I play people who have particular dilemmas and if it comes off as heroic, then that's a cultural definition of the behavior."

In his latest film, *K-19: The Widowmaker*, Ford gets an ideal opportunity to prove his point—and explore cultural definitions of heroism—by essaying the true story of Russian submarine captain and stern taskmaster Alexei Vostrikov [in real life, Capt. Nikolai Vladimirovich Zateyev—PK], who finds himself at the helm of an experimental nuclear sub on her maiden voyage at the height of the Cold War in 1961. When the vessel's reactor goes awry, Vostrikov finds himself under "difficult circumstances" indeed. He sends his crewmen in to repair the deadly radioactive device despite a potential mutiny led by his more humanistic second-in-command (Liam Neeson), who wants to get help from a nearby American naval ship instead. Unwilling to surrender the latest pride of the Soviet fleet to the U.S. even to save his crew's lives, and faced with the prospect of triggering World War III if his sub explodes, Vostrikov is a character painted in subtle shades of gray who sits on the horns of the thorniest dilemma of his life. Ford found the story all the more

134

compelling because it was true, and he was so intrigued by the challenging role he departed from the hugely successful Jack Ryan franchise to take it on.

"It had to be understood that I was playing a character that would not be sympathetic at first," says Ford, whose last turn at a more overtly unlikable character came in the horror thriller *What Lies Beneath*. "I enjoyed the challenge of that."

The Story Behind the Story

The dramatic events of 1961 and the heroism and sacrifice of the real *K-19* crew were kept secret by the Russian government for three decades until the collapse of the Soviet regime. When director Kathryn Bigelow learned of the incident in a meeting with *National Geographic* (which helped produce the film as well as a documentary on the subject), she was immediately fascinated, but it took five years before her vision became a reality.

Bigelow, one of Hollywood's few female big-budget action-movie directors, admits she had to prove to the *K-19* survivors that she was going to tell the story of their struggles and their spirit accurately.

Attempting to assuage the skeptical Russians' worries led to powerful emotional conversations and connections that further inspired her. "Basically you're asked to give their lives and that experience meaning, and that was a huge request that I did not take lightly." Still, Bigelow knew that despite the tale's natural elements of suspense, alterations would inevitably have to be made to make the film work on-screen and she took a little dramatic license with the historical facts (Ford's character, for example, is a somewhat fictionalized version of the *K-19*'s real captain).

"It's intended as a character piece," she says. "Yes, it's a study of this boat as well, but I was more interested in the human drama."

"They're submariners, they're not filmmakers," offers Ford. "They're Russians, they're living a much different life. I think that their immediate reaction was that we should be telling their stories with their characters, as they understood it. But that's really not the purpose of a theatrical motion picture."

After meeting with survivors in Moscow and St. Petersburg, Ford—who also served as a producer on the film—also noticed how difficult it was to determine exactly what had happened during the crisis. "Because the submarine is so compartmentalized and because the information about what was going on was not necessarily shared by those in command, they all had much different stories about what happened," he says. "They didn't all agree and it was a little confusing to sort it out, but I think finally what we were looking for was a dramatic telling of the story of their sacrifice and their devotion to duty. We were absolutely committed to telling the story of their devotion to duty, their heroism, their selflessness," he adds.

"I was incredibly moved by their story of their struggle," says Ford of meeting the submarine's septuagenarian survivors. "This was the defining event of their lives, and they lived without being able to tell the story for a long time. It was a military secret, and they had a great devotion to each other even thirty years later, although [many of them] hadn't seen each other."

By the end, the *K-19* survivors and the captain's widow were won over by the filmmakers' efforts. "The Russians have seen it now," said Bigelow. "They've wept. They've said, 'You actually treat us too kindly.'"

The Casting Call Goes Out

Once the central conflict between the film's two leading characters (Neeson plays Mikhail Polenin, the ship's original captain, who is replaced by Vostrikov but kept aboard as second-in-command) was established, "finding actors—finding human beings—that could embody those men [was] an extremely difficult task," says Bigelow. "These are incredibly formidable men. Their grace under pressure is, I hope, obvious given the bones of the story."

Casting such powerful presences was a challenge, though Bigelow says she always imagined Neeson in the part of Polenin, and was both thrilled and taken aback when he signed on: she then had to find a worthy adversary for the Oscar-nominated star. "The list was frighteningly short and at the top of it was Harrison. Never thinking that the universe would reward your first [choice]—I mean, it just doesn't work like that," she says.

"Liam's great," says Ford. "He's a very capable, talented actor who devotes himself to the work with real discipline. He's got a good head on his shoulders and a good heart."

When asked if he and Neeson, who share the rare distinction of having starred in different generations of George Lucas's *Star Wars* films and who have both taken direction from Steven Spielberg, ever compared notes about working with the two legendary auteurs, Ford answers simply, "No, we didn't." He thinks about it and repeats himself, as if the notion had never occurred to him on the set. "We're neither of us the kind of actors that want to sit around talking about acting."

Just Say "Nyet"

Ford is willing to talk about one acting conceit in the film: Although all the characters in the film are Russian, they speak English on screen— and yet his character speaks in a Russian accent. "There was some question of whether or not we should be doing an accent, and I thought it would help remind us, always, that we were in a Russian context," he explains. "One of the most important things to do in this film was to maintain a Russian point of view," Ford continues. "Besides which, I had an Irish co-star, real Russians on the crew, actors from England, actors from America—I think it helped unify the whole sound.

"It's always important to reflect on your history and the choices you've made as a nation, to understand what shapes your national will," Ford says. "I think in the context of the Cold War we'd opened a Pandora's Box of nuclear potential. And the whole concept of a balance of power through mutually assured destruction is an idea that we should certainly think about, because it's not necessarily the best way of dealing with things.

"I think one of the things that was interesting to me was to not directly deal with or redress a situation where we demonize the enemy," Ford adds. "It's like Pogo [the opossum star of cartoonist Walt Kelly's satirical comic strip] said—Pogo, one of my favorite political philosophers: 'I've seen the face of my enemy and he is us.'"

"I Like to Be Strong"

Stuart Jeffries / 2002

From the *Guardian*, October 21, 2002. Copyright Guardian News & Media Ltd 2002. Reprinted by permission.

In 1997 James Cameron made *Titanic*, a film about the real-life disastrous maiden voyage of a state-of-the-art ocean liner across the north Atlantic. Five years later, Kathryn Bigelow has got the same sinking feeling as her former husband. She has made *K-19: The Widowmaker*, a film about the real-life disastrous maiden voyage of the first, purportedly state-of-the-art, nuclear Soviet submarine across the north Atlantic.

True, there are huge differences between the two projects: not least that the story of *K-19* is hardly embedded in our collective consciousness, as is the sinking of the *Titanic*. For decades, the events that took place aboard a submarine three hundred miles off the U.S. coast, and the very real risk the world unwittingly ran of nuclear Armageddon as *K-19*'s reactor cooling system malfunctioned, were kept secret by Soviet authorities.

The story of *K-19* deserves a place in our nightmares. It is almost intolerably grim. The film contains a particularly harrowing half hour in which Soviet submariners try to weld a new cooling system around the reactor wearing protective suits that are about as effective at repelling radiation as light raincoats. After ten-minute shifts, each two-man crew of welders emerges from fitting water pipes—vomiting, bleeding, and fatally poisoned by radiation—to be replaced by another set of hitherto unsung heroes. It's a disaster movie, for sure, and one that needed making.

Despite this harrowing material, *K-19* was given a summer release in the U.S., where it was pitted hopelessly against seasonal no-brainers like *Spider-Man* and *Men in Black II*. Bigelow—prim, poised, barefoot, and

138

careful in her answers—concedes: "I think it's not necessarily well-suited for a summer release. It's the kind of film that's going to have a long life. I see it as more of a *Schindler's List* than a *Spider-Man*. Call me crazy."

Kathryn Bigelow may well be crazy. She spent six years on *K-19*, and came up with a film whose failure to do well at the box office (it cost $100 million to make and so far has only recouped slightly more than $35 million in the U.S.) could jeopardize her future Hollywood career. This career was already ailing following the puzzling failure of *The Weight of Water*, her 2000 film featuring a nude Liz Hurley rubbing her nipples with ice cubes, to attract a mass audience Stateside, or even a British release.

This time, though, Bigelow is once again in the company of men. Her first short, made when she was a film student, featured two men beating each other to a pulp in a dark alley, while two professors mused in voiceover about why cinematic violence is so seductive. Her first feature film, *The Loveless*, starred Willem Dafoe in a violent biker picture. Later there was the very masculine *Point Break*, a surfer flick with Patrick Swayze and Keanu Reeves, who when they weren't riding the waves were robbing banks. Now *K-19*, that floating men's club.

Whence Bigelow's obsession with setting films in overwhelmingly male milieux? One theory is that it's hard for an intelligent woman to be brought up watching Hollywood movies and find women depicted there interesting. Much more engaging to identify with one of the male protagonists in a western or a war movie. And perhaps this engagement with strong men has carried over to making films. Does Bigelow agree? "I'm mystified. This is a piece I saw as being universal."

Perhaps. But it's worth looking at Bigelow's depiction of women to get an insight into a cinematic vision that isn't always gender-free. On the rare occasion Bigelow does women, they are appealingly tough. Take *Blue Steel* (1990), in which gym-buffed Jamie Lee Curtis plays a rookie cop suspended for killing on her first day and then stalked by a psychopath. Curtis's cop is no victim—she fights back against her oppressors with intelligence and physical strength.

And then there's Bigelow's 1995 sci-fi picture *Strange Days* (written by Cameron, then her husband), again a mostly all-male film, but with Angela Bassett as a chauffeur who saves Ralph Fiennes's skinny white ass as the clock counts calamitously down to a new millennium. It's easy, and certainly good fun, to imagine that Bassett—beating the crap out of all-comers in frock and heels in the last reel—is a cinematic projection of Bigelow's self-image. And why not? This is a fifty-year-old woman who loves to tell stories of her own derring-do. She dives: "I lost my weight belt at 115 feet diving in Fiji, which was not fun; your lungs explode if you hit the surface too fast." She rides a mountain bike: "I hurt my knee doing gymnastics, and riding a bike uphill helps my quad." And she climbed Mount Kilimanjaro in subzero temperatures: "I like to be strong."

This strong woman was once a tall, shy girl who in her teens became intrigued by the paintings of Raphael and would enlarge details of them—feet, hands, eyes—into twelve by fourteen foot canvases in the garage. She went on to study art at the San Francisco Art Institute, and then film at Columbia University. She lived in New York from 1971 to 1983, hanging out with what she calls "conceptual-slash-political artists" like Richard Serra, Philip Glass, and Art and Language, the British conceptual art group with whom she did a piece at the Venice Biennale in 1981.

How did she get from conceptual art to making a humanistic movie like *K-19*? "I think I appropriated from those artists a sense of art, if you will, as playing a social role. I began to think of art as elitist, whereas film was not."

From the outset, *K-19* was a difficult commercial proposition. A year before she started work on the picture, Tony Scott had made *Crimson Tide*, in which first officer Denzel Washington stages a mutiny aboard a U.S. nuclear sub to prevent his trigger-happy captain Gene Hackman from launching his missiles. Did we really need another such film, complete with claustrophobic underwater mutiny?

"Yes, I think we do," says Bigelow. "I wanted to make a human film about this real-life story. I wanted this to be accurate, I didn't want it to be a Hollywood version of this Russian submarine in peril." And more than that: "I think that the story of the *K-19* can, if it has a message—I hate that word—reinforce a pride in humanity and the potential in all of us for bravery and courage."

How did she learn of the story of *K-19*? "Someone at *National Geographic* told me about it in 1995. He said that very little was known about it except that there had been an interview in Pravda in 1986 with the captain because he wanted the world to know what his crew went through." And now, the captain dead and the article forgotten, Bigelow has decided to tell the story for a very different audience.

What did the crew go through? In July 1961, *K-19* set off on its maiden voyage. It was all going very well. The crew tested a missile and took up an intentionally intimidating position three hundred miles off the U.S. coast. Then a leak in the cooling system led the reactor to overheat.

Worse yet, the sub was armed with nuclear warheads and any explosion would have destroyed a nearby NATO base. This, the captain feared, would prompt the U.S. to launch strikes against Moscow and Leningrad. The Soviet Union would respond by striking U.S. targets, which would provoke further U.S. retaliation.

"There was so little known about it that the research and development took years. I went straight to the source. I spent a lot of time with the survivors, and with the family of the deceased captain, who Harrison Ford plays. The cold war was shrouded in so much secrecy and my government, in order to justify what was going on, created stereotypical responses. I found it deeply moving to go beyond those and find the Russian individuals. I just got obsessed by the story."

Time's Up

Nick Dawson / 2009

From *Filmmaker Magazine*, Spring 2009. Reprinted by permission of *Filmmaker Magazine* and Nick Dawson.

Leading up to the Oscars on March 7, we will be highlighting the nominated films that have appeared in the magazine or on the Website in the last year. Nick Dawson interviewed *The Hurt Locker* director Kathryn Bigelow for our Spring 2009 issue. *The Hurt Locker* is nominated for Best Picture, Best Director (Bigelow), Best Actor (Jeremy Renner), Original Screenplay (Mark Boal), Best Cinematography (Barry Ackroyd), Best Editing (Bob Murawski and Chris Innis), Best Original Score (Marco Beltrami and Buck Sanders), Best Sound Editing (Paul N. J. Ottosson) and Best Sound Mixing (Paul N. J. Ottosson and Ray Beckett).

Now that the end is in sight for the Iraq war, hopefully the whole cinematic idea of "Iraq War fatigue" will go along with it. The phrase has been thrown around by industry journalists as a catchall term to describe the average American's ostensible lack of desire to watch films set against the Middle East conflict. But if there was ever a director who could turn the tide, it is Kathryn Bigelow, who has returned to features for the first time since 2002 with her new movie *The Hurt Locker*.

The film tells the story of Army bomb disposal expert Sgt. Will James (the superb Jeremy Renner), who must survive the final thirty-eight days of his detail in Iraq if he is to make it home to his wife and child. However, unlike the other two soldiers on his team, Sanborn (Anthony Mackie) and Eldridge (Brian Geraghty), James thrives on the intense risk and danger of having to diffuse roadside bombs and IEDs (improvised explosive devices) in the Baghdad war zone, day in and day out. His gonzo approach to his job makes him, for Sanborn and Eldridge, just as dangerous as the snipers on top of the surrounding rooftops.

Written by investigative journalist-turned-screenwriter Mark Boal, who embedded with a volunteer army bomb disposal squad in Iraq in 2004, *The Hurt Locker* is a riveting movie that vividly conveys what it's like to be on the ground in Iraq. It concerns itself not with the politics of the war, but with the visceral experiences of the soldiers who fight. Bigelow's film opens with a quote from writer Chris Hedges which reads, "The rush of battle is a potent and often lethal addiction, for war is a drug," and Renner's James is the embodiment of that idea, a true thrill-seeking addict, a soldier who can only get his fix from his daily dance with death.

Instead of being about the Iraq war, then, *The Hurt Locker* is simply about war. It's a drama that examines the psychological toll of war on its soldiers and a thriller that eschews fast-cutting and showy visuals for a far more unsettling depiction of combat that is palpably grounded in reality. The film also has the flashes of dark humor and kinetic immediacy of Bigelow's very best work such as *Near Dark* (1987), *Point Break* (1991), and *Strange Days* (1995), and announces that the director has lost none of her sharpness or relevance.

The day after a New York City screening of *The Hurt Locker* that closed out the *Film Comment* Selects series, *Filmmaker* sat down with Bigelow to discuss her long-awaited return to the big screen.

The Hurt Locker will be released on June 26 by Summit Entertainment.

Filmmaker: How did you first meet Mark Boal and how did you two decide to work together on *The Hurt Locker*?

Bigelow: I became familiar with his journalism probably in about 2002. There was an article of his that I developed into a television series for Fox and Imagine. We developed that, and then he went off to Iraq to do an embed. Perhaps like most people, I felt it was a pretty underreported war, so I was extremely curious. He would send me e-mails in country, and it was phenomenally interesting: The psychology of the soldiers, the fact that it's a conflict that's very unique to this particular engagement. It's not a ground war, it's not air-to-ground, it's basically a war of invisible, potentially catastrophic threats, 24/7. There is no place that is off-limits, there is no downtime for the soldiers, or for anybody, including Mark. When he went out with the bomb squad on a daily basis, the entire 360 degree environment was a potential threat, be it a human being, a water bottle, a rice bag filled with unidentified objects, a rubble pile with wires sticking out of the ground, etc. It's just infinite permutations and that's a very specific kind of warfare that has, again, been unexplored and unexamined. Given that it's a volunteer army, these men arguably have the most dangerous job in the world. It became really fascinating to explore the psychology behind the type of soldier who volunteers for this particular conflict and then, because of his or her aptitude, is chosen and given the opportunity to go into bomb disarmament and goes *toward* what everybody else is running from. That became a really rich subject on which to do a film.

Filmmaker: So was it during Mark's time in Iraq that you decided to turn his experiences into a film?

Bigelow: Yeah, the thought mutually occurred to us. He came back rich with firsthand observations, very incredible material: the day in the office of a bomb tech. Then we started developing.

Filmmaker: Mark has the sole screenwriting credit, but I presume that you were heavily involved in shaping the script with him.

Bigelow: I would say that it was a collaboration, but he's definitely the writer. I mean, he's the person with the firsthand observations, and it's from all those observations and reporting that every single sequence in the movie originated. I think as a filmmaker, you're constantly shaping and seeing it in your mind's eye through to its end, no matter how early and embryonic it is in its process. You're constantly looking at it from the macrocosm to the microcosm, and you're oscillating between the two. Whereas Mark, having been in theater, in country, is looking at it from such a granular position.

Filmmaker: Did you quickly formulate the style, look, and feel of the film?

Bigelow: I think that comes always as a process, at least for me, as you begin to get inside the DNA of the material and it begins to reveal itself. Even when we were working on the script, I was beginning to do some preliminary, rough storyboards just to look at the physicality of it. It's very specific to its geography, this particular movie, because bomb disarmament protocol requires a containment area of sometimes one hundred meters to three hundred meters. So understanding that geography and looking at it from a production standpoint, you're like, "Okay, how will we convey that to an audience who obviously has not had an opportunity to go on the ground with a bomb squad?" You want to make it as real and as authentic as possible, to put the audience into the Humvee, into a boots-on-the-ground experience. How do you do that? You do it by finding a look, a feel, and a texture that is very immediate, raw, and vital, and yet also is not aestheticized. I wanted, as a filmmaker, to sort of step aside and let just the rawness and integrity of the subject be as pronounced as possible and not have it feel sort of "cinematic."

Filmmaker: I believe you shot with four discrete camera units. Was that throughout the whole film, or simply for certain sequences?
Bigelow: All the time, unless we were in a contained space that you simply couldn't get that many people in. We shot for forty-four days, and I would say that forty days of that we had four discrete units, sometimes even a couple more. We shot on 16mm, and Barry Ackroyd—who's really profoundly brilliant—was my cinematographer. We were constantly creating a fluid set that was alive and active in 360 degrees from a camera standpoint, a production design standpoint, and a performance standpoint, so we were basically reenacting with each take, from beginning to end, a bomb disarmament. You are looking at it from different perspectives, but it all is cut as a continuous linear whole. It's not broken into different stories from different points of view. You're recreating that entire bomb disarmament from the point they arrive to the containment to the decision: Are they going to blow it in place, are they going to use the robot, or are they actually going to go down and pull out the blasting cap? [The first step] is you've got to figure out what the potential IED or roadside bomb is. Is that a pile of rubble, or is it a 155 round that's going to spread your DNA into the next county?

Filmmaker: Presumably having four different camera units gave you great options in the editing room, but it must have been problematic from a logistical point of view because you don't want crew or other cameramen in the shot.
Bigelow: I never worry about messy or dirty dailies, although actually they were not too bad. There's kind of a choreography [to shooting]. As a filmmaker, you always wonder how other filmmakers work and I have no idea, but for me it's very instinctual. I come from a visual arts background so to take the three-dimensional world and turn it into two dimensions is a process I find I can do automatically and instinctually and instantly. It actually comes very easily. You say, "If the actor's here, one unit's here . . . ," and then you create a sort of movement that is fairly

rational and logical and doesn't get you into trouble. Especially if you've been doing it for a little while.

Filmmaker: Why did you choose to shoot in Jordan, and what was the experience of shooting in there like?

Bigelow: If you want to shoot a movie about the Middle East, you go to the Middle East. I mean, I scouted Morocco, but it just did not look like Baghdad. And also, the extras would have been North African, and not Arabic, and that became *extremely* important to me. Again [I wanted] to keep it as accurate and authentic as possible. I was very trusting and open and eager to embrace the Middle East as a location for a movie that takes place in the Middle East, and my desire was to get as close to the war zone as possible. I would have shot in Baghdad if I could, and in fact at one point we were five kilometers from the border and Barry and I wanted very much [to go there]. It would have been half an hour's drive to get across the border and go in and at least shoot in Iraq. But our security couldn't guarantee our safety—there were too many snipers. But anyway, shooting in Jordan was a great experience. It's very cosmopolitan, they have a very rich film school, and in fact I created a trainee program because the film infrastructure there is young. We shot in a Palestinian refugee camp at 2:00 in the morning for the alleyway sequence, and the elder of the camp brought me tea, which gives you a sense of the warmth and hospitality of the Jordanians. Even though our art department came in and worked with the locations, you could look 360 degrees on any given day of the shoot and it would be perfect. And the other great gift was the Iraqi extras, two million of them in Jordan, in Amman. Before the invasion, there was a thriving theatrical community in Baghdad so in those refugees were tremendous actors, for instance Suhail [Aldabbach], who plays the suicide bomber. I think it's a devastatingly wonderful performance that he gives in a small but poignant moment of the film. He's apparently a very well-known actor in Iraq who we had the benefit of working with, sadly, because he had to leave the country for political reasons.

Filmmaker: I want to briefly touch on the issue of so-called "Iraq War fatigue" which resulted, supposedly, in the underperformance of Iraq war movies. Did that issue impact you during the fundraising process?

Bigelow: We actually raised our money independently through foreign finance and didn't feel the pulse of the marketplace until we had completed it, so we were able to work with virtually zero compromise or zero hesitation. And then, luckily enough, when we premiered it, we sold it immediately. It's a combat movie and there hasn't been one about this particular conflict, so I see it having more in common with *Platoon*, *Apocalypse Now*, *Saving Private Ryan*, or *Full Metal Jacket*. It's a war film, it's in theater.

Filmmaker: My personal perspective is that it's a psychological drama set against the backdrop of a war, which happens to be in Iraq. I feel like this is the only Iraq-themed movie not to offer judgment or commentary on the conflict but to simply portray it.

Bigelow: Just like you'd look at *Full Metal Jacket* or *Platoon*, certainly you could argue that that commentary is innate within the very fact of its existence. However it isn't there necessarily to judge but to provide information and give you as honest, accurate, and authentic a portrait of the boots-on-the-ground [experience of] this particular conflict. One of the great comments that has come back to me, again and again and again—and I take it as just an extraordinary compliment—is somebody saying, "I had no idea what it was like, and now I have an awareness of it." You've opened a door, but without judging or taking a pedagogical position. You say, "Here it is." I really look at it as a character study and also as an observation of the day in the life of a bomb squad—what that's like, what the psychology of heroism, courage, and bravery, making instantaneous decisions under extreme, extreme pressure and stress on a daily basis, and what the price of that heroism is. In the case of Sergeant James, it's a flight from intimacy.

Filmmaker: I think you use actors very smartly in the film: The performances of Guy Pearce and Ralph Fiennes make a big impact, and the rest of the cast is made up of relatively unfamiliar faces. Jeremy Renner, in particular, is a revelation.

Bigelow: I just think he's a profound talent. You know, when you're working on a script, you not only shoot it, cut it, and mix it and do the sound design in your head before you've found the locations, but you also know [characters like] James. You know him like he's sitting in front of you—you can see him, you can see his mannerisms, you can see the way he turns his head—so there's an incredible familiarity with the character, and this is always my process. I know the person the minute I see them, so you just begin to canvas all [the potential actors]. I also was determined to use emerging talent. I really feel there's a point where I personally don't want to see a movie with the same four actors; as brilliant as they may be, it's just nice to widen that pool. How else do you make the opportunity for a breakout actor than forcing the hand? So I made it a mission parameter to find breakout actors and emerging talent, and also I think it underscored the tension because with the lack of familiarity also comes a sense of unpredictability, as we find from the beginning: "Wait a minute, now anything can happen . . . I thought it was one thing, now it's something else." Every day is a game changer, and I also felt that lack of stability is what the soldier feels in the field. There is no safe zone, not even back at the base, because a mortar round can hit you while you're sleeping. The soldiers that Mark went out with, the bomb techs, they sleep in flak vests. You never know what's going to happen.

Filmmaker: Your films are known for the energy and immediacy of their action. I'd be interested to hear about methods that you use to construct that feeling when building your scenes, either in shooting or in post.

Bigelow: Well, it all starts from character. It's not like I work from the set piece in; it's from the character out. Every shot, every action, every staging or blocking has to be a credible and logical move and physical response for that character. One of my pet peeves in action is when you lose a sense of geography and there's just frenetic cutting to give you an illusion of freneticism. But it doesn't work that way. It really has to be built, piece by piece, from the inside out. I think it's really important to never let the audience lose a sense of geography, so I'm very geography-centric in my photography. Probably that's why [I use] the multiple cameras, which I've been doing since *Point Break*. They allow me to look at any particular set piece from every possible perspective. Even though the camera's moving, even though the shot might be very short, if there's a lack of orientation, it's instantaneous and you recover from it, or you never lose it. I don't want to ask the audience to recover their footing and reorient themselves. I want to never lose them. In fact, I want to draw them further and further into this vortex of information. Then I feel like I've succeeded in at least presenting an event in as experiential a way as possible. I love it when photography and cinema can be experiential. I think that's its great gift. I think literature can be reflective, but film can be experiential. It's the gift of traveling you from [here] to . . . wherever. That's the great gift we can offer, so I never want to lose that opportunity.

Filmmaker: You've established a strong reputation for yourself as well as a distinctive style, but nevertheless it's been a long time since your last film. How do you view your place in today's Hollywood?

Bigelow: I'd certainly like to be a lot more prolific, but because the types of projects that I choose tend to be somewhat uncompromising therefore, out of necessity, I kind of tend to work "off the reservation." I mean, had a movie like *The Hurt Locker* been done in a studio context, you would never have been able to shoot in the Middle East, for instance. And because of the necessity of [shooting there] you're backed into taking a truly uncompromised approach. I don't know, it's hard to step back and take a look at an overview of one's position, but that's where you come in. [*laughs*]

Filmmaker: From a personal perspective, I'm just very glad that you have a new movie out.

Bigelow: Oh, thank you, and I am too, but you know it's definitely a process that can require a certain amount of time. I mean, perhaps not this much time, but then I did do a television series as well. My hope would be to, without sacrificing content and substance, be a little more prolific. But then, at the same time, wanting to be topical and relevant, the bar that I've set for myself is at such a place that very little satisfies those parameters that I place on myself. So that's what makes it difficult to be as prolific as I'd like to be. That's where it's tricky. If I can somehow figure that one out . . . [*laughs*]

Filmmaker: At the end of the day, what you'll be judged on are your films, so I think you have to be like that.

Bigelow: Yeah, that's kind of the bottom line, which is what makes them potentially timeless and matter. And if they don't, then it's back to that art precept and the necessity to push the medium a bit. And if they're not doing that, then it's another process, and that's one I guess I'm less interested in. [*laughs*]

An Interview with *Hurt Locker*'s Kathryn Bigelow

Robert Horton / 2009

From the *Everett Herald*, July 10, 2009. Interview conducted May 29. Reprinted by permission of Robert Horton.

Kathryn Bigelow held the local premiere of her new film *The Hurt Locker* at the Seattle International Film Festival in May. Bigelow has a reputation as a director of male-oriented cult films such as *Point Break* and *Near Dark* but hasn't made a feature since the financially disappointing *K-19*.

I interviewed her in a gigantic conference room at a Seattle hotel, and in person she seems far from the cliché of an action-movie maven: willowy, thoughtful, and quick to laugh, she gives off the air of someone with defined ideas about how she sees the world.

The Hurt Locker rivetingly follows an Explosive Ordnance Disposal [unit] in the Iraq War. Mark Boal, a reporter who spent time embedded with combat units in Iraq, wrote the screenplay. I began by asking Bigelow about her crystal-clear staging of tense action scenes, which give the viewer the chance to actually understand the geography of war.

Kathryn Bigelow: It was very important to provide a very clear map of the landscape and the process of bomb disarmament. It took me a while, spending time with EOD techs, to really understand that the ground troops—a large part of what they're doing is they're on the alert for anything suspicious: a pair of wires, a new patch of asphalt, a paper bag fluttering. Something they didn't see the day before or on their rotation that morning. They call in the coordinates and the EOD guys go out. There's another team that then stops the war for these guys, to create approximately three hundred meters of containment.

Now, how do you translate that to an audience, who haven't gone to bomb protocol school? In terms of how it's shot, we have a multitude of angles. So you're in tight, in an emotionally intimate way with the character, but at the same time you've also got to place that character in the big picture. Then the audience can be as emotionally invested as possible.

Q: So many action movies today—
KB: You lose geography. It's just kineticism. It's an artificial emphasis when something is fundamentally lacking. The key is to start with really great material—call me crazy! I think I'm very fortunate here because these men [in *The Hurt Locker*] arguably have the most dangerous job in the world, so what they're doing is inherently, incredibly dramatic and intense. So I don't need to make what they're doing more dramatic. I can't imagine anything more dangerous or courageous.

Q: The central character, Sergeant James, is both reckless and heroic. You don't simplify him into one thing or the other.
KB: This is something that came out of Mark Boal's observations of some of the men he spent time with in Iraq—if you composited and fictionalized them, you'd see a really interesting psychological portrait. When you're lying on your belly and you're five inches away from the bomb, there's no blast suit or helmet that's going to protect you. There's no margin for error. And so you have this personality that gives you a kind of hubris and recklessness—and yet a profound skill set. Those were the kinds of ideas that culminated in how we see Sergeant William James.

This is somebody whose heroism has cost him a great deal: in family, and fatherhood, in the terms that we revere. But those things are not where his heart is. At the same time that he is extraordinarily heroic and courageous, it's also a flight from intimacy. It's come at a big price, his bravado, but it saved him, it saved his men, it's given him a charge that is unlike anything else.

Q: There have been other non-documentary Iraq War films—did you want this to be the first to capture the ground war as it is?
KB: I saw this from the beginning, as soon as Mark came back from his embed, as a combat film, not a reintegration to the home front, not an overt commentary on the war. It's really meant to be reportorial. And to put you where the journalist was. And however you're feeling

ideologically, politically, about it, I think it gives you the opportunity to appreciate these men in this job.

Q: What's the reaction been from veterans?

KB: It's been extremely positive. Some vets have said they can't wait to show it to their families when it comes out. Because it gives them a glimpse at what they've been doing for the last year. And I don't mean just EOD, but kind of the whole mise-en-scene—the heat and the feel and bringing something to life in a way that I think has been admired for its accuracy and authenticity.

Q: Do you like this thing of going off somewhere difficult to shoot?

KB: I love it, I love it, I love every second of it. We shot a million feet of film in forty days in the Middle East. That's something real and immersive and transporting for me, and I think that's really inspiring. It quickens the senses. That's what we look for in anything—in prose, in poetry, in a canvas, in a film—you want to have your senses quickened. I mean you don't want them dulled! If it's challenging, I'm usually pretty interested in it. I don't like easy rides.

Interview: Kathryn Bigelow

Scott Tobias / 2009

Originally appeared at AVClub.com, June 24, 2009. Used by permission of Onion, Inc.

Drawn into filmmaking after earlier creative endeavors as a painter—first at the San Francisco Art Institute, and later as a fellow at the Whitney Museum—director Kathryn Bigelow made her feature debut with the 1982 biker movie *The Loveless*, but her real breakthrough was 1987's *Near Dark*, a superb vampire Western that showcased a graphic intensity and a love of genre cinema. Those same qualities are apparent in her subsequent work, including 1990's *Blue Steel*, 1991's *Point Break*, 1995's *Strange Days*, and 2002's *K-19: The Widowmaker*. Bigelow's résumé also includes directing stints on acclaimed television shows like *Homicide: Life on the Street* and *Wild Palms*, and the less-circulated 2000 ensemble piece *The Weight of Water*.

After a seven-year absence from the big screen, Bigelow has returned with a vengeance with *The Hurt Locker*, a thrilling, nerve-racking Iraq War action film about Army bomb-squad technicians who spend their days defusing improvised explosives. Jeremy Renner (*Dahmer*) stars as a brash, recklessly confident sergeant who plunges his team headlong into harrowing life-or-death situations. Anthony Mackie co-stars as a subordinate who struggles to keep his new superior in check. Bigelow recently spoke to the *A.V. Club* about shooting in 135-degree weather, the psychological profile of people who deal with bombs, and where she's been for the last seven years.

A.V. Club: There was a seven-year gap between *K-19* and this new movie. Were you attempting to get other film projects off the ground during that time? What finally brought you to *The Hurt Locker*?

Kathryn Bigelow: Well, actually, I became familiar with [screenwriter

Mark Boal's] journalism and turned one of his articles into a television series [Fox's *The Inside*]. That took a fair amount of time. And then it was a short-lived series, so it's not one to dwell on. But then at that time—it was 2004, so two years after *K-19*—I realized he was going off to do an embed in Baghdad with a bomb squad. And not unlike the general public, I felt fairly unaware of what was going on in Baghdad. I think it's a war that has been underreported in many respects, so I was extremely curious, and I kind of suspected that, providing he survived, he might come back with some really rich material that would be worthy of a cinematic translation, and that's what happened. So then he came back and we started working on the script in 2005, raised the money in 2006, shot in 2007, cut it, and here we are. These things take time, is all I'm trying to say. I think what people don't realize is how long these things can take in development. I've always developed all my own pieces, and they're time-consumers.

AVC: Mark comes from a journalistic background, too, so was there a learning curve for him as a screenwriter as well?
KB: Yeah, I think so, though he worked with Paul Haggis on *In the Valley of Elah*, because that was also based on an article he did for *Playboy* called "Death and Dishonor." So he began to become familiar with the craft of screenwriting there, and then in my opinion, mastered it on this. But definitely going from fact-based writing to fictionalization—and then creating the kind of architecture for cinematic translation—was a bit of a process. Although he took to it quite naturally.

AVC: Was it always a certainty that the film would have to be made outside the studio system?
KB: We never approached any other financing avenue. I wanted to keep it as independent as humanly possible, and I wanted to shoot in the Middle East. That alone probably would have been a non-starter. And then I anticipated that and didn't pursue. And also, to be honest, I've never made a non-independent movie. No matter what scale it's been, it's always been independent. So I wanted to retain complete creative control, I wanted final cut, I wanted the opportunity to cast breakout, emerging talent, and as I said, shoot in the Middle East.

AVC: Have those been the conditions you've always had? Final cut? Is that something you've had to earn?
KB: Actually, no, I've never had it contractually. This is the first time,

contractually. On the other hand, I have to say I've been very fortunate in that I've worked with very little to no compromise. I mean, there's always a compromise when you're looking at the scale of something. You only have so much money to shoot a movie with. But that's not really a creative compromise.

AVC: Why was it so important for you to shoot in the Middle East? Presumably a studio would have set you up in the California desert.
KB: A studio would have been even adventurous enough to go to Morocco, perhaps, but once I scouted the Middle East, I realized that Morocco, even though it's a beautiful country and often used as a backdrop for the Middle East . . . your extras are North Africans. It may be wonderful for a movie about North Africa, but to an Arab individual, the opportunity to cast Arabs as Arabs became incredibly important. And on top of that, the great bonus of taking the show to Jordan—a great bonus and also a sad fact—is that hundreds of thousands of Iraqi refugees are in the city of Amman as a result of the occupation, some of whom are actors. So you know, not only are you shooting five kilometers from the Iraqi border, and the architecture is perfect, but you can swing the camera 360 degrees, and there's not a bad angle to be had. Your background players and your bit players and your speaking Iraqi parts are Iraqi. So that became my modus operandi.

AVC: How did you go about casting locally, casting refugees?
KB: We had a wonderful casting director, and there is a bit of a film infrastructure in Jordan. I think it will become a fairly thriving film community, but at the time, it was fairly limited. We had a woman who works in theater, and she is very aware of actors, of Jordanian and Iraqi actors who were in Amman at the time.

AVC: What were the physical conditions like, shooting in that area? Was it an arduous production?
KB: We started shooting, just because of the nature of actors' schedules, in July in 2007 in Amman, and Amman has a slight elevation. I had also scouted Kuwait, which at that time of year, is truly punishing. I think the day I was there, it was about 135 degrees. I couldn't even imagine what 135 degrees could feel like. It sort of feels like you're standing in front of an overheated car with the hood up, but you can't get rid of the car; it's just this blast of hot air, and it's very punishing. That was Kuwait. Anyway, we were in Jordan, and there was an average temperature

of about 115 degrees, and the most challenging aspect was putting that bomb suit on Jeremy [Renner] every day. Jeremy is an extraordinarily talented actor, but you're asking him in that kind of climate to put on a piece of wardrobe—it wasn't just wardrobe, but an actual bomb suit—that weighed between 80 and 100 pounds. Every day. You know, spend all day in it. That was really punishing. I was very sensitive to his needs and his oxygen levels, and trying to keep him as comfortable as possible, there's only so much that can be done. That was probably the most difficult physical, logistical aspect of the shoot.

AVC: Were there any cultural sensitivities that had to be observed? Or was that not an issue?

KB: Jordan is a very secular, Westernized country in some respects. In some of the outer neighborhoods we shot in, there was a tremendous amount of support and receptivity. And I actually anticipated some confusion. You try to leave flyers. There is a location department that tries to communicate with everybody in an area, but it's not easy. For example, there's an early scene that takes place in probably a three-hundred-meter area involving a mosque and a daisy train and a taxi cab, and you're talking hundreds and hundreds of people in that containment area. And we arrived in the morning the first day we shot there. You know, the Humvees come in, actors jump out in their digitals and their M4s, and the crew is there with the cameras. I would have thought there would be more confusion, but not at all. They were excited and kind of embraced the experience.

AVC: Regarding the bomb squad, is there a personality profile that makes certain people well-equipped for that job?

KB: Well, a couple things to bear in mind that are fascinating is that when Mark came back from his embed and his observations, I realized that the real responsibility of the filmmaking here was to keep the film reportorial, keep it as honest, realistic, and authentic as possible. And you know, he would describe the psychologies of these men who arguably have the most dangerous job in the world. And yet you then realize that this is a volunteer military, so these are men who have chosen to be there. So there is a kind of interesting psychology at work. Are you familiar with Chris Hedges's book *War Is a Force That Gives Us Meaning*? It's an incredible study of that particular psychology, and I'm not making a generalization of everybody, but certainly there's a kind of allure he speaks of, that combat can provide for some individuals. That was interesting. But at the same time, EOD [Explosive Ordnance Disposal] techs have extremely high IQs. They're invited into EOD after they've passed an aptitude test and scored at an incredibly high level. So not only are you extraordinarily brave and heroic and courageous, but you're very, very smart and you've chosen to do this. You have to make extreme life-or-death decisions in seconds about complicated electronic devices, and in a very short period of time, for which there is no margin of error.

AVC: With his brash, almost reckless confidence, Jeremy Renner's character is reminiscent of Robert Duvall in *Apocalypse Now*. Is that a fair comparison? Does war tend to create these kinds of characters?

KB: I think that's what's interesting about looking at Chris Hedges's interest in unpacking that psychology. Does war create it? Does war attract it? But also, I don't think it's a generalization one can apply to everybody. I think about what would provoke you or I to sign up tomorrow and apply for the bomb squad. It's a very interesting psychology that I find really pretty extraordinary. And I think what the film does, and what the script did so successfully, and hopefully what the film does, is humanize these individuals. They're not necessarily adrenaline junkies. They're also complicated, emotional human beings. There's no easy answer, I guess is what I'm trying to say. It's not like a machine that is programmed one way.

AVC: Because *The Hurt Locker* takes a soldier's-eye view of the war, it really couldn't be called a polemic, but it does suggest the toll of soldiers returning from multiple tours of duty. What does that do to a soldier, not only in the arena of warfare, but also in resettling?

KB: For some individuals—some soldiers, some contractors—combat provides a kind of purpose and meaning beyond which all else potentially pales in comparison. Again, for some individuals, I think it's very interesting to look at that. And you can also say that about firemen, police officers. There are individuals who choose to walk into a burning building to save lives, and that's what these men are doing. I see them as extraordinary portraits, regardless of how you feel about the conflict. I think of the film, in a way, as nonpartisan. It's not commenting, as Mark said when he was working on the script. There's that old saw about how there's no politics in the trenches. And when he went over there, sure enough, there's nobody talking about politics. They're talking about whether they're gonna survive, or "What's your favorite beer?" I think the script successfully looks at the humanity of these men and their courage, and shares with us what a day in the life of a bomb tech is. It's that they save thousands of lives, sometimes at the sacrifice or peril of their own.

AVC: Your films in general are known for their intensity, but *The Hurt Locker* is perhaps even more rough-and-tumble than your previous work. How did that affect the way you went about preparing to shoot it?

KB: When Mark came back and had done such an extraordinary job in the field, we really wanted to protect the reportorial aspect. Keep it as authentic and immediate and raw and visceral as possible. But on the other hand, it is a film, so I wanted to strike a tonal balance between substance and entertainment. And I think the script quite skillfully did that. But I will say, a day in the life of a bomb tech is so inherently dangerous that as a filmmaker, I felt my job, in a way, was to get out of the way, if that makes sense. You don't need to aestheticize that, you just need to present it.

AVC: The script is also pretty chancy, structurally. There's a major subplot that comes into play later in the film, but it's more or less plotless much of the way.

KB: I don't look at it like that. I look at it as reportorial. These guys go out ten, twelve, actually more times a day than the film shows—I guess the film would have to be twenty-four hours long. But they go out several times a day and have experiences like the ones you see seven times in the movie, over the course of thirty-eight days. So that's the nature of a day in the life. Like, you're basically going to the office with this particular individual, only his office happens to be Baghdad, and he's a bomb tech. So that's what dictated it. It wasn't like trying to impose an architecture on it. Whatever the other more conventional format or architecture for a screenplay might be, where you kind of hunt down the bomb-maker, or something, I dunno. I think this was an opportunity to be more reportorial and authentic and responsible to the reporting.

AVC: What's next for you?

KB: What's next? Good question. I hope something soon. Actually, I'm working on a few things. Who knows what will finally materialize? But once you embark on a project that is both topical and relevant, I suppose it sets a new bar. So I'm definitely inclined toward that.

Kathryn Bigelow to *Movieline*: "I Thrive on Production. I Don't Know if I Thrive in Normal Life."

Kyle Buchanan / 2009

From *Movieline*, June 25, 2009. Reprinted by permission of *Movieline* and Kyle Buchanan.

It's long been taken for granted that Kathryn Bigelow is Hollywood's best female action director—and that's a reputation she firmed up before tomorrow's release of *The Hurt Locker*, her best film so far. The Iraq War bomb squad thriller is a shot of adrenaline for not just the audience, but Bigelow's career, which includes classics like *Near Dark*, *Point Break*, and *Strange Days*. The whip-smart director recently sat down with *Movieline* to talk all things *Hurt Locker*, though the conversation soon veered to *Point Break* parodies, wooing the King of Jordan, and a certain vampire franchise she'd been heavily touted for.

Q: Jeremy Renner's character in *The Hurt Locker* thrives on the theater of war, and outside it, he feels like an incomplete person. That's a personality type I could apply to a lot of directors: Only when they're on set do they feel most themselves. Does that describe you at all?

KB: Oh, good question. [long pause] I don't think production comes anywhere close to the theater of war of course, but Chris Hedges writes about that particular psychology so beautifully in *War Is a Force That Gives Us Meaning*. You should check it out—you probably already have—but he talks about the kind of sense of purpose and meaning that peak experience can give you that can never be replicated outside that peak experience. I suppose, personally, from my frame of reference, production is very intense and nothing else comes quite close to that. And yet, as a kind of more meta version of myself at that time . . . I don't know. I'd probably have to be far more self-aware than I am to answer that accurately. I thrive on production. It feels very much like a natural environment for me.

Q: Do you have to re-acclimate after you're done shooting?
KB: Well, I think I do just because of the stamina that's required. The hours are punishing, there's a kind of sleep deprivation and exhaustion that forces you to kind of reframe your existence. When that abruptly stops and you have to be a different type of human being, you kind of redefine yourself all over again, with a less rigorous approach to your life, I suppose. I don't know, that's a very interesting question. I thrive on production. I don't know if I thrive in normal life. [Laughs]

Q: I understand why you don't want to compare a production to war, because there aren't those life-or-death stakes—although some directors may beg to differ on that point. But there are some parallels: you're mobilizing a battalion . . .
KB: Right.

Q: . . . and moving it into this other country like an invading force. And as the director, you're commanding people to take position and execute certain operations. Did you ever feel like you could use that feeling in your film?
KB: Especially in this particular film, I'm really conscious of this being a conflict that's ongoing, and being painfully responsible with respect to that. So I never kind of felt the sort of hubris of entering a completely foreign culture with a few hundred people and making it your own. Because it's an ongoing conflict, it's kind of unique in that sense.

Q: You shot this film in Jordan, and even though that's a relatively liberal country in the Middle East, was it a somewhat culturally dissonant thing for you—as a woman, wearing no burqa—to be in charge of such a major production full of men?
KB: You know, I kind of wondered if that aspect was going to meet with any resistance, and there wasn't any at all. First of all, it's a very sophisticated, very secular, very generous, hospitable environment. And very film-friendly. I had met with the King, and he was extraordinary. A brilliant man, and very supportive of this production going to his country. I

can't look at it in any other hypothetical way, because I didn't experience anything else, but for the most part, it was a really smooth production.

Jordan is a very sophisticated place in that one of its great strengths and also one if its limitations are one and the same, and that's its geographic environment and proximity [to more unstable countries]. So, strategy is very key to this particular country, and they've kind of established themselves as a Switzerland in the Middle East. We were met with a lot of support, especially from the royal family.

Q: I don't suppose you've met with many kings in your career.
KB: No, that was the first. [Laughs] That was definitely the first.

Q: Directors are often in the position of auditioning actors, yet you were now being auditioned by a king!
KB: Right, exactly. "You want to do what with my country?" "Oh, just bring in a few Humvees and tanks . . ."

Q: Did you feel you had to pussyfoot around it at all in your pitch?
KB: No, I was very straightforward. There was no time for hesitation—you have a very specific allotment of time you're allowed to speak with him and state your case and present what your needs are. I sort of felt like the fate of the production rested on the outcome of that particular meeting, yet on the other hand, I didn't want to be anything other than straightforward and honest. Ultimately, I don't know how anything else could serve you, because it's a movie about a bomb squad in Iraq.

Q: Was the king very familiar with your work?
KB: It just so happens that the wife of one of his sons, Prince Ali, is a former CNN reporter. She was very helpful, as they all were. I think that it meant a lot, that [the story] be as accurate as possible.

Q: We haven't seen a feature film from you since 2002's *K19: The Widowmaker.*
KB: Well, I did a television series, and that was actually also based on an article by Mark's for Fox and Imagine. It was based on an article of his called "Jailbait" that he wrote for *Playboy*, and the [show] was titled *Inside.* It was short-lived, but it was an interesting experience nonetheless, dabbling in network. So I came out of that and developed a few pieces, of which [*The Hurt Locker*] was one. This one began in 2005, was shot in the summer of 2007, and is being released in the summer of 2009. That's

pretty fast for an independent film with so many elements, but I wish it was faster. I always develop from scratch—if I could just shoot something that's handed to me, I don't know whether the films would be as interesting, but they'd certainly be more plentiful. [Laughs]

Q: Well, one property that people thought you might be handed was the third *Twilight* movie, *Eclipse*. When they were on the hunt for a director, you were the subject of a lot of speculation: you're a woman, familiar with action, Summit is releasing both *The Hurt Locker* and *Eclipse* . . .
KB: Right. But I've done my vampire film [*Near Dark*].

Q: But did Summit approach you?
KB: [Looking into her lap] I don't want to get into that. Sorry.

Q: Jeff Wells has compared *The Hurt Locker* to *Aliens*. What do you make of that comparison?
KB: Well, I think it's a huge, huge, huge compliment. I love that movie. I think it's a really high watermark for filmmaking. It's incredibly experiential, that film, and to me, that's where the medium really flourishes: when you can provide this experiential canvas for an audience. I think prose is better at being more reflective than a film, but film can put you on the ground or in space, wherever the desired location may be.

Q: I heard that Edgar Wright took you to go see *Point Break Live!* the sort of dinner theater parody of your film where they cast a Keanu Reeves from the audience and throw buckets of water at the actors. At what point did you become aware of that?
KB: I had heard about it maybe a year prior when I was cutting [*The Hurt Locker*] . . . it was in the Bay Area, and then it came to Los Angeles. And when it came, Edgar Wright was in town, and of course, having just done *Hot Fuzz*, he wanted me to go with him to see *Point Break Live!* It was very surreal . . . I mean, having someone play you jumping onto that set with a megaphone going, "Cut! Cut! Cut!" It was a blast. I thought it was great.

Q: I would imagine that when you think of *Point Break*, you associate it with the experience of having made it, but can you divorce yourself from that to get a sense of how it's received pop culturally?
KB: I suppose I can. Maybe I'll always be a little too close to it, I'll always feel the reality of making it, the struggles and triumphs. It's probably a

little too real. But I'm very happy that people still love that film. We just had a retrospective the other night and I introduced it, and the woman who played me at *Point Break Live!* was at that film. It was a very spirited audience.

Interview with Kathryn Bigelow

Ryan Stewart / 2009

From *Slant*, June 26, 2009. Reprinted by permission of *Slant*.

"There's a price for that kind of heroism," Kathryn Bigelow says of *The Hurt Locker*'s lead character, an ingenious Army grunt who stares bombs in the face for his daily bread and who slowly comes to appreciate the immense toll that such death-defying work takes on the psyche. Depictions of men under nerve-melting pressure are frequent in Bigelow's famously kinetic oeuvre, which spans two decades and includes the deliriously inventive cowboy-vampire pastiche *Near Dark* and the darkly spiritual surf saga *Point Break*, but rarely have form and favored subject been so expertly harmonized as in *Hurt Locker*.

Earlier this week, the director called me up to discuss the film and those who inspired it. A master class in experiential action cinema from one of its most learned professors, this barely-fictionalized, ground-level look at the U.S. Army's Explosive Ordnance Disposal technicians is so immersive that it's practically tactile, a work of exhaustive filmic intricacy that required Bigelow to contemplate even "the sound of heat and dust, and the sun," as she tells it.

Slant: I was just reading an old magazine interview you gave for *Strange Days*, in which you said, "As our society progresses, genuine experience becomes riskier and the desire for it increases." The context for that was virtual reality, of course, but doesn't it also sort of explain why someone would volunteer to diffuse bombs?

Kathryn Bigelow: Very, very interesting question, and I would say that it's hard to generalize why a person would choose Explosive Ordnance Disposal. Also, just to back up a bit, one has to be invited into the Explosive Ordnance Disposal unit after you've decided that you're going to pursue the military. My understanding is that there are all these aptitude tests to take first and then, if you've scored extremely highly, you can be invited into the EOD. So, it's a pretty rarified world that these EOD techs exist in, and I'm not sure, but my humble opinion is that it's way more complicated than that. These are men who, as you indicated, have gone into this profession by choice, and it's perhaps the most dangerous job in the world. They have volunteered and every single day they go out there, sometimes at the risk—the peril—of a potential sacrifice of their own, and they are saving thousands of lives by disarming or at least rendering safe these explosive ordnances.

Slant: And they're affected by it in varying degrees, of course. You gave Jeremy Renner's lead bomb tech character this quality of implacable cheeriness, an imperviousness to danger that unnerves his colleagues and keeps them distant from him. Do you think there's some correlation between anti-social tendencies and the job itself, which seemingly no normal person would do?

KB: I don't really have the stats to make that sort of assessment, but I definitely think that it takes a very, very courageous individual, certainly a very brave one, and there was a comment that [screenwriter] Mark Boal made when he came back from his embed; he said that courage is not the absence of fear, it's maintaining your sense of humor in the face of fear. The job itself, this profession, is so inherently dangerous, and yet it does happen to be at the epicenter of this particular conflict, and I think that it takes a pretty extraordinary human being to do it, one who is perhaps a very complicated psychological mix. So, I think it would be hard for me to give you a compact answer. I wouldn't hazard one since I'm not a psychologist. Nonetheless, we did certainly show some other bomb techs; there is a myriad of psychologies and personalities there, and they've all decided to do this job.

Slant: As someone who strives to create immersive cinema, did you find it necessary to get into the headspace of these guys and share their experiences? I heard that you tried to cross the border into Iraq.

KB: Well, the genesis of the piece was Mark Boal's embed, as you know, in Baghdad in 2004, with a bomb squad. So, it began as a piece of reporting and my feeling as a filmmaker was that I really wanted to maintain that reportorial quality. He was sort of parachuted in—I mean figuratively, not literally. He was parachuted into the daily life of a bomb squad tech and I wanted to basically put the audience into the shoes of not only the reporter, but also the soldier on the ground. That really is what I wanted to maintain: the authenticity, the accuracy, the specificity of what Mark brought back from his embed. He wrote and crafted a magnificent script. I also had these three—well, several—extraordinary actors and we were shooting in the Middle East. It's a movie about the Middle East and it's also about that particular conflict. I wanted to get as close to the conflict as possible, and because of the large scale of the sets, I needed to be able to shoot in vast areas. In choosing Amman, Jordan, which is on the border of Iraq—not the city itself, but the country—I was able to turn the camera 360 degrees and have the architecture and the mise-en-scène be as accurate as possible. Nonetheless, it's still a fictionalization of a day in the life of a bomb tech.

Slant: How did you go about marrying that visceral, reportorial style with Marco Beltrami's score? Was he okay with the score being used so sparingly?

KB: Yes, he was okay with it. Marco's a very talented composer, and he and Buck Sanders were two gentlemen who worked together on the piece, but they also worked in concert with my sound designer, Paul Ottosson [won Oscars for Sound Editing and Sound Design for *The Hurt Locker*, ed. note] who is also an extraordinary talent. My interest going into the film, having imagined it to be as immersive as possible, was that I wanted to sort of blur the distinction between sound design and score, and I presented this as an idea to both the sound designer and the composers and they both loved that, as a challenge. They thought that it would be a really interesting creative space in which to work. For instance, Paul Ottosson gave the composers many of his sound design tracks that he was also working with, things like the sounds of helicopters or F-14s flying overhead. It was like, if one could actually qualify the sound of heat and dust and the sun—there were just so many of these beautiful textures that he had and that he was working with. So, the composers were able to actually utilize the components of the sound design and begin to weave together subtly rhythmic and sonic textures that melded beautifully with the design. And it was really intended as that kind of cohesive collaboration right from the beginning.

Slant: In terms of your collaboration with the actors, did you present them with horror stories of things gone wrong on the job to instill that fearful, respect-the-bomb mindset? How did you give them a thousand-yard stare?

KB: [Laughs] Well, they're very smart, talented, creative actors! They took it upon themselves to do a lot of the homework, certainly. Jeremy Renner spent some time with the EOD at Fort Irwin in California, and he was basically inducted into a kind of accelerated version of their training. He ended up being incredibly well-versed in the mechanics and logistics and processes of bomb disarmament, as was Anthony Mackie, who spent time in Fort Bragg, and Brian Geraghty, who was in country once he got to the Middle East and spent time with some of our EOD technical advisors on location. All three of them, by choice, completely immersed themselves so that they would have the benefit of that understanding.

Slant: There's a moment in the film I want to ask you about—it struck me as a sort of prototypical Kathryn Bigelow moment.
KB: Uh-oh. [Laughs]

Slant: No, no, just the grocery store scene. After one character has rotated back to the world, after all he's been through, he's sort of stymied and defeated by a wall of breakfast cereal. You seem to feel that our consumer society takes more from us than it gives, in terms of the human spirit.
KB: I think that's a really smart assessment and an interesting one, although I wouldn't look at it quite so literally. You're not wrong at all, but what I think is—here's a guy who has spent however many days and however many tours of duty, in probably as high-risk a situation as is humanly possible. Then, you have the paradox of something so simple as a decision that people make many times during the day, the kind of mundane grocery store decision, and that's just overwhelming for him. I think that's an interesting aspect of war, or a look at the effects of war, rather. That's where I think the script was so well crafted, in how it just kind of sneaks up on you. This is where I think the characters were so carefully crafted by Mark, the writer.

Slant: You met a lot of these techs, these soldiers, in your research. By and large, did they seem to know who they were and what they were fighting for, or trying to achieve?
KB: You mean understand what they were fighting for, politically? I think it's hard to judge their level of self-awareness, but I did find them to be incredibly professional and, I suppose, they are grateful to be appreciated in a certain way. I think if you were to say to someone on the street "What is Explosive Ordnance Disposal?" you'd probably find that

it's a pretty fair assessment to say that the general public is not necessarily aware of it. They've certainly heard words like IED and they know what a roadside bomb is, but they probably aren't really aware of all the processes and the protocol and everything else that goes into identifying a live ordnance that's tucked into a rubble pile, you know? So, I guess this was an opportunity for me to kind of share that specificity, and I was just struck by each one. Each of them is an individual, and each one different from the other. I suppose I was just struck by their courage.

Slant: I think with my generalization, I was trying to move toward asking you about masculinity in general, which is something your previous work indicates much interest in, as does this film. I think you're our new Sam Peckinpah.

KB: [Laughs] Oh God, that's very flattering! I'm sure that you can look at *The Hurt Locker* as a portrait of masculinity, and that certainly did factor into it, but specifically my interest was just to humanize these particular individuals. It's more of a statement on that process of humanization. I make my choices about which films to do on a purely instinctual basis, and it's really not until I have the luxury of moments like this when I suppose I have to go back over the choices I've made and analyze either the processes or the thoughts that were behind them. So, I was really just drawn by the opportunity to humanize them.

Slant: Your choices never flow from a desire to operate in or improve certain film genres? I ask because you've certainly done much to elevate action cinema in your day.

KB: I never look at it from the standpoint of form. I always look at it from the standpoint of content. I've never approached [a project] as an opportunity to, let's say, expand a form. I'll approach it from the character and if the character takes me into a sort of presentation that necessitates tension, or suspense, or a kind of kinetic, experiential cinematic experience, then that's fine, but it's still informed and dictated by the character and the story itself. It's not from the outside in, it's always from the inside out. As long as it's a provocative story with some evocative characters, it doesn't matter whether those characters are sitting still and just talking in a room, or if there's bloodshed to be had, you know? It still goes back to the story and the characters, which is always what I find compelling, and that's what I found compelling with *The Hurt Locker*—not necessarily the form, but the authenticity of it, which was haunting and pervasive and provocative.

Big Bang Theory: Kathryn Bigelow Breaks out with *The Hurt Locker*

Peter Keough / 2009

From the *Boston Phoenix*, July 10, 2009. Interview conducted July 2. © 2009 by the *Boston Phoenix*. Reprinted with permission. All rights reserved.

Okay, so Kathryn Bigelow might be the only major filmmaker to have modeled for The Gap. And now, at fifty-seven, she could very well do so again. Though everyone makes a point of Bigelow's gender and height and good looks, what's germane is that even if she was short and had bushy eyebrows like Martin Scorsese, she still would be directing action pictures like no one since Sam Peckinpah and Sergio Leone. With her latest movie *The Hurt Locker* getting terrific buzz, maybe she'll start getting the recognition she deserves.

Here's another point that might cause some to pause: the new film is about the War in Iraq. Not only did that war undo a presidency and the country's image in the eyes of the world, but it also spelled box office death for all films on the subject. Until now, maybe. *The Hurt Locker* won't be doing *Transformers* numbers, but it will probably beat out *In the Valley of Elah* (also scripted, like *Locker*, by Mark Boal, based on his experiences as an embedded journalist).

Unlike those previous Iraq movies, and unlike almost every other film released this summer, *Locker* focuses on vivid characters in thrilling circumstances and renders what happens to them with lucidity, logic, and gut-wrenching suspense. It's the story of a bomb tech (Jeremy Renner) in Baghdad in 2004 whose job it is to defuse improvised explosive devices (IEDs). He does the job with uncanny skill and, more importantly, he enjoys the rush of danger, just like characters in almost all of Bigelow's movies, from *Near Dark* (1987) to *Point Break* (1991) to *Strange Days* (1995).

A thrill that might not be shared by Bigelow herself, who has just had a rough flight in from New York to attend a retrospective of her films at the Harvard Film Archive.

Q: How are you today?

KB: Fine. Other than the plane was hit twice in midair by lightning. Did you ever have that happen?

Q: Not that I've been aware of.

KB: Oh, you would be! It was like a bullwhip snapped the whole plane. Bam! It was very intense. So I'm very happy to see you.

Q: What an adrenaline rush. That's probably as close as you'll get to defusing a 155 (a howitzer shell used in IEDs).

KB: Let me knock on wood.

Q: After the screening of *The Hurt Locker* someone said that this makes Michael Bay look like a wimp. What is the key to making a powerful action movie?

KB: Emotional investment with the characters. Smart stories. If you're not emotionally engaged, cinematic prowess can't invent what is not there. And then there's keeping the audience oriented. Making sure the geography is very clear, especially in a movie like *The Hurt Locker* where that is the key to understanding what a bomb tech does on a daily basis in Baghdad in 2004.

Q: So, no Autobots.

KB: No tricks. If you're creating excitement strictly from an editing standpoint it has to be intrinsic to the story and the subject. It doesn't come from form, it comes from content. You are worried for the characters or even break down the fourth wall and become them.

Q: Do you find it ironic that this is coming out the same week the troops are withdrawing from major Iraq cities?

KB: I do. When the studio set the release date back in January I think the withdrawal date was set for August. I don't think they could have anticipated it.

Q: With the war ending do you think your film won't suffer the same fate as the other Iraq War films?

KB: This is the first that is, in fact, a war film. The others were not about combat. It's like if you were to go into Blockbuster and were looking for *Coming Home* it would be under "Drama." If you were looking for *Apocalypse Now* it would be under "War." This also would be in the war section. That's my scientific categorization.

Q: Is this the *Apocalypse Now* of Iraq?

KB: Our references are more *The Battle of Algiers* or *The Best Years of Our Lives*. But what I do think *Hurt Locker* does and *Apocalypse Now* did for that conflict is that it unpacks the abstract and makes it concrete and tactile. And if it makes it nonpartisan, then you have a more informed opinion. At the end of the day it's about a bomb tech walking down the street wondering if he's going to survive.

An Interview with Kathryn Bigelow

Peter Keough / 2009

From the *Boston Phoenix* website, July 4, 2009. Transcript of the full interview condensed in "Big Bang Theory" in two parts. © 2009 by the *Boston Phoenix*. Reprinted with permission. All rights reserved.

July 4, 2009

Happy Fourth of July, all. On this holiday celebrated with fireworks perhaps it is appropriate to talk about those heroes who put their lives on the line to prevent things from exploding. Kathryn Bigelow's *The Hurt Locker* tells the story of the demolition experts in Iraq whose dangerous duty involves defusing the lethal improvised explosive devices (IEDs) set by insurgents and which have been responsible for a frightening death toll, both military and civilian.

Plus, it's the best film so far this year. But don't let that dissuade you. True, *Transformers* opened with about $200 million last weekend and *The Hurt Locker*, which was released in only four theaters, made somewhat less (it will be expanding to more screens and cities on July 10, including Boston). But it did score about 91 on Metacritic. So I asked Bigelow how she might compare her film to the competition. A good question for Bigelow, no doubt, but when I spoke to her Friday, she seemed to have something else on her mind, as you will see.

PK: How are you today?
KB: Fine. Other than the plane was hit twice in midair by lightning. Did you ever have that happen?

PK: Not that I've been aware of.
KB: Oh, you would be! It was like a bullwhip snapped the whole plane. Bam! It was very intense. So I'm very happy to see you.

PK: What an adrenaline rush. That's probably as close as you'll get to defusing a 155 [an artillery shell used in IEDs].
KB: Let me knock on wood.

PK: The second time was probably already boring.
KB: Just old hat.

PK: After the screening of *The Hurt Locker* another critic said that this makes Michael Bay look like a wimp. What is the key to making a powerful action movie?
KB: Emotional investment with the characters. Smart stories. If you're not emotionally engaged cinematic prowess can't invent what is not there. And then there are so many other factors so I don't want to be reductive. Like keeping the audience oriented, making sure the geography is very clear. Especially in a movie like *The Hurt Locker* where the audience's relation to an improvised explosive device is the key to your understanding of what a bomb tech does on a daily basis in Baghdad in 2004. And so I'd say emotional engagement with carefully crafted characters and a great script.

PK: So, no Autobots.
KB: No tricks. You put the camera low and you dutch the angle and you hit the side of the magazine when you turn the camera over. But if the intrinsic investment is not there, you can't invent it out of whole cloth.

PK: And easy on the rapid fire editing so people can follow what's going on?
KB: And geography. So people can be oriented geographically. If you're creating excitement purely from an editorial standpoint it has to be intrinsic to the story and the subject; it doesn't come from form, it comes from content.

PK: Intensity and clarity.
KB: Exactly. And the intensity comes from, one hopes anyway, emotional investment in the characters. You are worried for them or you break down the fourth wall and become them.

PK: Was the point-of-view camera something you started using after *Strange Days*?
KB: I did some p.o.v. in *Near Dark* and I think . . . it's a really successful

tool if the story needs it and demands it. Total immersion and experiential cinema—I know I've talked about it in other interviews—where film and literature, not that literature can't be experiential, it is more reflective. But film is experiential. It can transport you to the desert basin of Baghdad in 2004 and put you up close and personal.

PK: Kind of like the SQUIDs [Superconducting Quantum Interference Devices, which record and replay personal experiences] in *Strange Days*?
KB: Kind of like that, but it's more literal. In the case of *The Hurt Locker* it's looking at a day in the life of a bomb tech in Baghdad in 2004. And you're walking toward what most people in the planet would run from. In the EOD [Explosive Ordnance Disposal, the units assigned to defuse IEDs] parlance they call it "the lonely walk." Because you're by yourself.

PK: With the big suit.
KB: Right.

PK: It's kind of like *High Noon*.
KB: I know. I saw that when we were shooting it. I kind of imagined it in the script stage but getting to the location, we were in the Middle East, and the nature of the light, the reflective surfaces of the sand, just creating this kind of classic palette and then this guy in the suit. The solo nature of the job.

PK: Is there a little bit of *The Wild Bunch* going on there too? The slow motion explosion for example.
KB: All of this came from Mark Boal.

PK: He's not here.
KB: No, he had to go to Florida with somebody.

PK: He had a bad feeling about the flight.
KB: He said if anyone is going to deal with lightning, it's going to be her. Anyway, he was on a journalistic embed in 2004 and ten, twelve, fifteen times a day they'd go to these coordinates that the ground troops had called in because of a suspicious rubble pile or a pair of wires or an empty garbage bag and . . . they're not all 155s, but they're fairly heavy ordnance. When they are detonated or, tragically, accidentally go off, there's something called overpressure. That's what those shots are meant to indicate. Before the particulate matter is expended it's the gas

that precedes the shrapnel. It travels at some ungodly speed. And that completely implodes any air pocket in your body.

PK: Ouch.

KB: That's what he means by, within twenty-five meters you're in the kill zone. The point of no return. Nobody can help you. These guys are like surgeons. Frighteningly intelligent. You have to have scored high on your IQ tests. [Only then are you] invited to the EOD. You need to have phenomenal motor skills and dexterity. You're able to make an extreme multitude of decisions under extreme pressure so it really self-selects. It takes a special kind of person to make that lonely walk.

PK: Are they addicted to adrenaline or do they have a death wish?

KB: It isn't meant to stand as a generalization and I wouldn't want to think of all of it as a death wish but I think they are incredibly courageous. If you've read Chris Hedges book *War Is Force That Gives Us Meaning* he . . .

PK: Did you read it before or after you decided to make the movie?

KB: Before. And Mark read it before his embed. James is not any particular individual, but a kind of composite and fictionalization. I think between James and Sanborn and Eldridge you get a nice myriad of personalities.

PK: You get that good angel/bad angel motif in a lot of your movies.

KB: That's true. I hadn't thought of that. That's why we need people like you. People to analyze. Not the gesticulators. Isn't that what the French critics say about American critics? "You gesticulate. We analyze."

PK: We blurb.

KB: Thankfully. So, anyway, Hedges talks about the allure of war. And, mind you, this is an all-volunteer military. It's a situation fairly unique to this conflict. So what Hedges tries to attack is that for some individuals combat provides an allure and attraction. It can provide that. Whether that attraction or allure, I don't know, intensifies your survival skills or not it certainly does with someone like James who has a kind of reckless swagger . . .

PK: He's intuitive.

KB: I think of him as an artist. Every IED, they are all prototypical. Not one is like another. And you have about forty-five seconds to . . .

PK: The red wire or the blue wire . . .

KB: Unfortunately, it doesn't work like that. It would be so much easier. But to make life or death decisions. If you're on the ground too long—first of all you're by yourself. You've got a two-hundred- to three-hundred-meter cordoned-off area. The guy in the balcony might be calling in your coordinates for a sniper or just hanging out his laundry. But you don't want to be exposed too long. And he's like a surgeon with this ability to analyze this prototypical wiring or pressure plate or secondary or single or double or triple initiating device. But if you make a mistake—it's not the patient who dies, you die.

PK: As the French critics would say, it's the ultimate deconstruction paradigm.

KB: Taking deconstruction to atomization. What would Lacan say about that?

PK: Deconstruct the artifice or it will deconstruct you.

KB: There's your lead.

NEXT: Beyond deconstructionism.

Part II: Outside the Frame, July 6, 2009

Now that I've shaken off all the fireworks, I can correct all the typos in the last posting and put up the second half of this interview.

PK: The immediacy of this film is similar to the immediacy of the real-time, embedded journalist reports at the beginning of the war. But they stopped doing that.

KB: They stopped doing that. For obvious reasons I suppose. But this conflict has been fairly abstract for the general public. I know when Mark [Boal, the screenwriter] was over there for his embed he came across maybe two or three other journalists. It was a multitude of reasons but mostly it was because it was just too dangerous. Certainly in 2004.

PK: The other films about Iraq also are political, unlike yours.

KB: If it's possible to make something nonpartisan, unpacking the abstraction, then you'd have a more informed opinion. We're filmmakers. It's not that the soldiers on the ground don't have diverse geopolitical perspectives. At the end of the day you're a bomb tech and walking down the street you're wondering if you're going to survive.

PK: And you're loving it. Or this guy is, anyway.
KB: That recklessness married to a profound skill set welded with a great authority may just be the combination that keeps him and his team alive.

PK: And then there's the pleasure of doing what you do best. As a filmmaker you identify with that.
KB: I suppose it is a bit like that, I mean production is a bit like the kind of a skill set that you wield with authority combined with a kind of, I suppose, maybe not a recklessness but a bit of bravado, in that there's no playbook. It's all prototypical.

PK: This reminds me of Hitchcock's bomb theory. I think it's another difference between your film and *Transformers* and films like that. He distinguishes between surprise and suspense. Surprise is when a bomb goes off suddenly but suspense is when you're watching people sitting at a table like this and underneath the table is a bomb and you know it's supposed to go off at a certain time.
KB: So you're ahead of the character. So surprise is when you and the character are in sync with one another, and suspense is like *Notorious* where you know that the key is down there and you know if they can— right, you're ahead of the character.

PK: So your movie is more about suspense. You know the bomb is there and you're wondering when or if it's going to explode . . .
KB: And the suspense is so pervasive.

PK: So you have a retrospective coming up at the Harvard Film Archive?
KB: Yeah, we're doing *Hurt Locker* tonight. I'm not sure what films they have been playing but I know they've been playing a few or they're upcoming or . . .

PK: They're showing all of your features, from *The Loveless* to *The Hurt Locker*. This isn't the first retrospective you've had, is it? I think you had one in '87 when you only had two movies.
KB: Yeah I had one in '87 and actually there was one in Los Angeles just recently for *Hurt Locker* that kind of culminated in our ad hoc premiere.

PK: So do you become reflective when you have—
KB: I don't think I'm old enough for a retrospective, though, I keep telling people.

PK: But you were in '87.
KB: I was old enough then, yes, exactly. I'm moving in reverse.

PK: But they could have included some of your artwork too; or did they?
KB: No, they didn't. They didn't. That's interesting.

PK: Didn't you have a short film where there was like two guys whaling on each other while somebody read critical theory texts?
KB: *Set-Up*—yeah.

PK: Is that your aesthetic in a nutshell?
KB: I don't know if you've seen Amy Taubin's piece on *The Hurt Locker* in *Film Comment*. I only bring it up because it's hard for me to kind of stand outside whatever these pieces are, these films are, and look at some kind of, the connective tissue from an analytical mind. I guess I try to but maybe, anyway, she does all [that] and, and speaks a lot about *Set-Up* and it's relation to . . .

PK: . . . *Hurt Locker.*
KB: Yeah, kind of pulling it all full circle. It's very interesting.

PK: Also, naming the character William James . . . ?
KB: The pragmatist philosopher.

PK: The author of *The Varieties of Religious Experience*; is that who he's based on? This is William James in Iraq?
KB: Well, you know, he's gotta be somewhere, right?

PK: One thing I noticed in the movie is that the character doesn't really start getting in trouble until he goes beyond that range—that three hundred meters—and wants to find out who the perpetrators are or the people that are watching him. So he's breaking through the fourth wall to find the person that's watching him and that engages him in more danger than just doing the bomb.
KB: What's exciting as a filmmaker is the kind of careful calibration of the effects of war on this individual. And you know, first you think this

is a man who is unmoved by anything. If you're standing over a daisy chain of six or seven 155s, how can you possibly be disturbed by anything, basically? And yet you realize in fact that the attritional effects of war are taking place.

PK: He goes home and demonstrates with the jack-in-the-box to his infant son how all thrills are illusory.

KB: Well, he's self-aware and, I think, he's kind of giving himself the permission to embrace what he, what truly gives his life meaning, and a kind of sense of purpose and at the same time you're able, I think, hopefully as a viewer, to understand courage and heroism, the price of heroism, you know, it all comes at a cost. And yet what he does every day is save thousands and thousands and thousands of little boys.

PK: Jeremy Renner, by the way, as William James. He was terrific. You saw him first in *Dahmer*?

KB: I think, you know, it's the new, new wave of talent.

PK: On the other hand, Harrison Ford with a Russian accent [in *K-19*] didn't really work for me.

KB: Well, you know . . . Jeremy Renner is, I think he's the real deal.

PK: Was working with Ford part of the reason why you didn't want to go and use a star again . . .

KB: Well, I wanted to keep the faces unfamiliar so you wouldn't have any anticipation or expectation on who's going to live or die based on their . . .

PK: Spoilers!

KB: Spoilers, exactly. I mean, you know, if it's Tom Cruise he can't die. Just there's that old adage.

PK: Or Janet Leigh.

KB: Well that.

PK: I'm giving that one away, too

A Discussion with Kathryn Bigelow at the Harvard Film Archive

David Pendleton / 2009

Discussion held July 2, 2009. Part of the retrospective "Kathryn Bigelow—Filmmaking at the Dark Edge of Exhilaration." Printed by permission of the Harvard Film Archive.

David Pendleton: Good evening ladies and gentlemen. My name's Dave Pendleton. I'm the programmer here at the Harvard Film Archive, and tonight—I love my job as few other nights—I'm very happy to welcome all of you to the local premiere of *The Hurt Locker*, and we're thrilled to have in person the director of the film, Kathryn Bigelow. [Applause].

I'm going to just gush for a little bit. I also want to say some thanks. Thanks to Summit Entertainment, the film's distributor, for making tonight's screening possible. The film does open locally a week from tomorrow. I also want to say thanks to Sara Rosenfield for her assistance in helping to make tonight's screening happen. We're very pleased here at the Harvard Film Archive to be hosting a full retrospective of Bigelow's feature films. Kathryn Bigelow—for those of you who don't know—has had a really remarkable career, truly unique, I think, in the history of American filmmaking. She's a California native. She began her career as a painter and then studied in the 1970s at the San Francisco Art Institute and at the Whitney. It was her involvement in the art world of New York in the 1970s working with such artists as Richard Serra, John Baldessari, Vito Acconci, and especially Lawrence Weiner that got her interested in working in the moving image. She went on to study film at Columbia and returned to California to become a filmmaker, supporting herself by teaching first at CalArts, until the release of her first feature film in 1982, *The Loveless*. This film, which we showed last night, instantly marked her as a filmmaker who worked in visually arresting images and who uses genre convention as a resource, a language that she can play with to communicate with an audience in ways that bear a fascinating relationship, actually, I think, to the world of conceptual art from the 1970s.

She followed *The Loveless* with a string of films throughout the eighties and nineties that brought her ever-increasing audiences and ever-greater critical prominence: *Near Dark, Blue Steel, Point Break, Strange Days.* Her two most recent films—*The Weight of Water* and *K-19*—extend the reach of the genres that she works with—the melodrama, the war film—as well as a renewed attention to character, and this fusion of character and genre, I think, bears fullest fruit in the film we're about to see, *The Hurt Locker.*

All along, Bigelow has carved out a unique place for herself in American filmmaking. Although her films are often distributed by the Hollywood studios, although they often feature stars like Harrison Ford, Keanu Reeves, Sean Penn, they're mostly independent productions, and they're remarkable examples of cinematic storytelling that keep an audience engaged intellectually, emotionally, and also physically, kinetically.

With her new film, *The Hurt Locker*, Bigelow reinvents the combat film for Iraq, a terrain where it's not always certain who is the enemy, where the enemy may not even be present. It's an act of reinventing the war film for an all-volunteer force also, as Bigelow herself has pointed out. In place of the patriotic soldiers of the WWII film, the bitter draftees of the Vietnam War film, the protagonist here enjoys what he does. He's a thrill seeker in a way that would be familiar to those of you who are fans of Bigelow's other films—the bikers in *The Loveless*, the vampires in *Near Dark*, the surfers in *Point Break*.

For the intelligence of her visual style and choices, for her inventiveness at working with the conventions of cinematic storytelling, for the cohesion of her body of work, there's no doubt that Kathryn Bigelow is an auteur, an important filmmaker, and we're very grateful to be welcoming her here. Please welcome Kathryn Bigelow. [Applause]

KB: Thank you for being here. That was an extraordinary introduction. I think I may have to cry now. [Laughs] This is a real, real honor, and I have to thank David and Haden [Guest] for making this possible. I can't imagine a more prestigious environment in which to show this film, or any film, and I feel like I'm a very, very, very fortunate recipient of this attention, not necessarily worthy of it, but I'll take it.

The Hurt Locker is kind of a true labor of love. It's a very independent movie. It originated with screenwriter and journalist Mark Boal, who was on a journalistic embed in Baghdad with a bomb squad in 2004 and 2005, just over the winter month there. There he encountered many different personalities, of which on the screen you will see kind of composites of those personalities and a fictionalization. It's definitely a movie. It's not a documentary. But nonetheless, our combined attempt and effort was to keep the piece, since it began as reporting, as reportorial as possible, to make it as realistic and authentic as we could and not diverge into unclassified or classified material.

So, with that in mind, I'm trying to think, it's really an opportunity to look at this particular conflict through the eyes of individuals who arguably have the most dangerous job in the world—that of a bomb tech—and they're there to render safe IEDs, Improvised Explosive Devices. I kind of think they're a bit like artists because it's all off the playbook. Everything is prototypical. They don't come to something that is like the one before. Every time it's absolutely brand new, and they have seconds on the ground, or else their coordinates are called in by sniper fire. So, it's a very unique set of skills that they possess, and I thought, and Mark thought, it was worthy of a film, so I hope you agree. I hope you enjoy it, but I'll be here for lots of questions afterward, and thank you very much. [Applause]

[Post-screening Q&A]

DP: So the way this will work is I'll ask a couple of questions just to start, once I turn my mic on, maybe a couple of questions about this film but also relating this film to the rest of your films and your career as a whole, and then we'll open it up to the audience to ask whatever you like. I wondered if maybe, just to start, you would say a little more about what drew you to the material. Did you know that you wanted to make a film about Iraq? Did you know that you wanted to make a war film? The reason I ask is because seeing this film after seeing *The Loveless* I'm struck by a certain similarity between the two, in fact something that shows up in your films time and time again, which is this focus on an isolated group of individuals who are sort of alienated from their surroundings and have to sort of depend on each other to survive but at the same time have these conflicts within them. I mean, there's a lot of dramatic material in that obviously, but I'm wondering if you're consciously attracted to that kind of a theme and what that enables you to do, or is it really about making a film about Iraq or both.

KB: Good question. I think I'm somewhat unconscious of the lineage, even though as you put it together so eloquently, it makes perfect sense, but I tend to look for material that has characters that are really provocative and evocative and allows me to work in the medium and keep the medium experiential, and that's been from the beginning. If it's artistically challenging and I can make it experiential, then I'm usually drawn to it. These guys or these individuals, this particular profession, is so inherently dramatic that I just needed to be very presentational, and in doing so, it would be an experiential look into a day in the life of a bomb tech, which, I think they can be appreciated to a certain extent.

DP: When you say experiential, are you also thinking of the film as a kinetic experience or sort of a physical experience for the audience?
KB: It's really an effort to humanize what it might be like to be a bomb tech in Baghdad in 2004, and in doing so I try to keep the shots sometimes very, very tight, you'll notice, but also very, very wide, because geography—it's a real geographic-centric piece because the audience as well as the bomb tech needs to know where you are in relation to the IED at all times, and that's what kind of dials up or down your level of attention and suspense. So, geography is very, very critical, so I intended to kind of work like that from a formalistic standpoint. But that does create a kind of experiential understanding of what it might be like to render safe these devices.

DP: There's a couple of moments, too, where it seems like you actually disorient the audience precisely in order to mirror the disorientation of the people on screen, like the use of jump cuts. Or, the shootout in the desert, I also wanted to talk about. It's almost sort of out of a spaghetti western, because you have these vast distances and you have the shot and the reverse shot that you would expect from a classic western. So, I thought that was a really remarkable use of the landscape, as was of the palette of the film, which was very different from the look of your other films.
KB: But again that distance, that's made possible, sadly, or however you want to look at it. But there's this weapon that's a fifty-caliber weapon that enables you to shoot and is utilized to shoot over a mile away—a surgical, a two-man process. One has to be the spotter, and the other is the shooter, and the person who's shooting has to literally almost still their heart to a point where they could—just even their breath could take the crosshairs off the subject. But anyway, again, that sense of geography and really hoping that the audience understands the logistical reality of the piece, and then therefore perhaps look at this situation through the

eyes of the soldier, and that was sort of Mark's mandate going in as he did his embed. He never knew from one day to the next if they were going to survive. And as the soldier doesn't know, I wanted the viewer to feel that same way, too. There's never a moment, hopefully, that you can relax. Until your tour of duty is up, there isn't really that opportunity. So I wanted to infuse the film with that feeling.

DP: So this idea of giving the audience an "experiential" experience—is it something you've come to over your years as a filmmaker? Or was that something you were interested in before you became a filmmaker? It seems like so many of your films are about placing the audience in the position of these people that they would never otherwise experience—the vampires, or the surfing gang. Is this something you've developed over your years as a filmmaker, or if it's something new with this particular film?

KB: Well I think, perhaps again, that we all work to a certain extent instinctually or unconsciously, but I did this short film that perhaps you'll get—I'm so sorry to mention it because he hasn't . . .

DP: I've been dying to see her student film from Columbia called *Set-Up*, which Amy Taubin called the Rosetta Stone to her work. Turns out it's at MoMA, so we're trying to add it to one of the screenings next weekend, so come back.

KB: It's very crude. It's very rudimentary. Anyway, I apologize profusely. But in it, I was trying—again, crude, in a rudimentary way—to understand what creates that contract between the screen and the viewer, in other words, why are you capable of having almost a physiological reaction. There was somebody who was writing about this film [*The Hurt Locker*], and I'm not saying it to praise the film at all, but he felt that in the scene when Eldridge has to clean the blood off the bullets that he was literally making saliva in his mouth. Obviously that's an impossibility, but anyway, I just thought that was such a wild . . . But in this short it's a moment of . . . It's twenty minutes. It's a bit of violence, and then it's deconstructed.

I was also at Columbia in the philosophy department reading Jacques Lacan, and so everything was about deconstruction. Now I've gone from deconstruction to atomization, I realized in an interview, we were talking about that. Anyway, so I'm still working on the same thing, but no. So, I had a couple of my teachers who were philosophers, really pretty amazing individuals, Sylvère Lotringer and Marshall Blonsky—this

sounds so erudite and intellectual and I don't mean it to be—but anyway, they were trying to deconstruct what makes it exciting and what's
transporting about this scopophilia, which is the joy of watching, what
makes that interesting, what creates that contract. So anyway, I feel like,
unconsciously, whatever, I keep trying to do work that has some elastic-
ity there, in areas in which film can still be really transporting. I think
literature—and this is a broad, horrible generalization—but literature is
much better at being more reflective than film, but film can be really
transporting. You can hopefully walk out of a film that takes place in a
desert and feel like you've got to brush sand off yourself. It really can take
you on a journey that you may or may not want to have in reality, like
being a bomb tech in Iraq. I know I don't want to be.

DP: That's really illuminating because one might expect that somebody
who came out of your background, working with these major names of
the art world in the 1970s in conceptual art, one might expect you to
make more experimental films, and yet you've been sort of consistently
drawn to narrative film, particularly genre films. I'm wondering to what
extent do you see your career now as a filmmaker a continuation of your
training as an artist or in the visual arts, and to what extent do you see it
as a change.

KB: The jump to narrative was a big, big jump for me. I had been working non-narrative for what seemed like forever, and the short was non-
narrative. But in embracing the narrative and realizing that—when I
was working in the art world it felt kind of like you're mining a narrow
bandwidth, and the opportunity to make something accessible and yet
have substance, that was sort of the Holy Grail. It's kind of wonderful
to have something that's really substantial but not necessarily if you're
interested in communicating, which I think any work of art tries to do.
But if it falls on deaf ears, it could be great still. Of course there's a whole
body of work that could justify that, but I guess what was interesting to
me was to—looking at artists like Warhol and how incredibly populist it
is and yet it's so sophisticated it's kind of off-the-charts.

DP: Well that's a great tradition you're working in, because a lot of the
early filmmakers were doing the same thing. Let's open it up to questions from the audience. Do we have anybody who's dying to . . . the first
hand is always the hardest to get up so—this gentleman right here.

Q: I want to thank you Ms. Bigelow for coming this evening. It's really
a fantastic treat for me to watch the film, of course, and watch yourself

speak about the film. I saw you years ago when I was a student at film
school in New York City when you showcased *Near Dark*, and so it's quite
a treat to see you again, but I think at that screening as well we did see
your student film in which the two young men are fighting in an alley
very graphically, and at the end, they make out. So there's always this homoerotic side to that. Of course, reviewers have spoken about that quality, potentially in this film with the fight sequence in Sergeant James's
room. But my question for you is the relationship Sergeant James has to
the boy, which jumps out at me immediately, especially in the sequence
where he assumes that the young boy laying there deceased is the same
boy, and his body then becomes the site of a bomb, and he actually utilizes his hands upon the boy, which one could push to be a homoerotic
situation. So I'm wondering how the boy fits in the larger story of *The
Hurt Locker* outside of this threesome relationship that you've developed
with just the soldiers.

KB: Well, Sergeant James is a pretty complicated character and one can
describe him many ways. He's capable in the heat of battle when one
of his teammates is self-destructing to provide an illicit tenderness, but
nonetheless it's a character that—what I think is interesting about the
piece is that the characters don't change. They're actually fully formed
when you meet them, but it's our relation to someone like James that
changes. First, you're kind of nervous. You're nervous for the group. You
don't know what's more dangerous—the bomb or the team leader. And
then you come to realize that kind of paradox of the skill set with a sort
of bravado is in fact what this man needs to keep himself and us, the
team, alive. So it's an interesting paradox. On the other hand, you add
to that the attritional effects of war and how you become maybe invis-
ibly and then slowly visibly unmoored in a way. You become . . . He really loses his bearings somewhat. It's invisible to him. It's apparent to
us, and you see him with the ravages—not ravages but the effects—of
war to a certain extent. So you see that he's actually not impervious. It's
very complicated. He's many people. He's many facets. But it's our relation to him that has changed at the end. We've given him permission to
actually leave a beautiful house and a family because in a way he's very
self-aware and he's doing what he has to do to give his life meaning and
purpose that he feels a need for. I don't know if that really answers it but
he's clearly a very complicated individual that is affected by combat.

DP: As you say, our relationship to him becomes very complicated as
well because typically in the war movie, the idea is when they go home,

if they want to go back, it's a problem, whereas there is a way it makes perfect sense that he goes back [to Iraq] at the end, and there's even a way that maybe even the spectator enjoys the fact that he goes back because the film has been so exiting and such a thrill.

KB: Right.

DP: So that's the way in which the thrills that he experiences loop into the thrills that one experiences as a spectator and we're drawn into that experience.

KB: Right, right. And you also see when he's overwhelmed—like in the cereal aisle. You know, with something so simple—yet he can pull up a daisy chain of seven or eight 155s, and—something like choosing a box of cereal is . . . is virtually impossible. And so, it's just interesting how, again—that's who he has been from the beginning, but it's our understanding of him that has broadened and deepened and hopefully been enriched, and has given us the permission in a way to forgive him.

DP: And in some way the payoff to the Beckham [the Iraqi boy he befriended whom he thought was killed] stuff comes at the very end when he sees that Beckham still is alive, but he [James] doesn't want to go through that experience of being hurt again, or he won't get close to it.

KB: Yeah, exactly.

DP: Alright, well we've got lots of hands up. Let's take this gentleman right here, in the front and then we'll go right there in the middle.

Q: Hi, you mention the word empathy, and I think what struck me so powerfully was love—the love that he had when his colleague punched him. Really hard. He didn't react, he shrugged it off. It was such a loving response in a way. You would expect a man like that to be enraged, but all of a sudden his character became terribly deep and terribly complicated and there were several instances which the only word that will really do it is love. That he felt—for his compatriots.

KB: That's interesting, we had an EOD tech see the movie recently, and that was something that he singled out. It is very gratifying, I think, for the writer of the script because he singled that aspect out, the tenderness in the film. He said usually, you know, the war film character stereotype, it's—it's usually admonishing of somebody who is in a place where normal mores are breaking down—and he said, in fact, what is rarely seen [in war movies], but often the case [in real life], in his opinion, is exactly what you're saying, that basically there is tenderness in that he puts this guy back together and doesn't make him feel ashamed and rub his face in his inadequacy in that moment or his limitation and fear. I thought that was a paternal thing. And that is when you start to adjust your affection for James.

DP: Okay, we have this gentleman right here.

Q: The gripping nature of the film, I think, was a lot due to the editing. And as a director, how did you—I mean you must have shot a lot to get what you did, and as a director how did you bring the editing together—you understand?

KB: Yeah, absolutely. We shot this movie in the Middle East in and around the city of Amman, Jordan, in the summer, very punishing temperatures but we shot for forty-four days. I had four cameras working nonstop fourteen hours a day and we came back with a million feet of film. And this movie is made for a microscopic budget, and so—I mean in kind of Hollywood terms—and so we didn't have to cut, but I had two editors, two really, really strong editors. And they, and I, worked through the material. I mean every day, twelve-hour day after a twelve-hour day—the hours are not great for this job. But then it ends and you come here and it's wonderful. But yeah—sifting through that material is like climbing a Mount Everest of material and I didn't think we were ever going to get through. Just watching dailies was an arduous experience, but you're absolutely right. The strength of the editing was, it really maximizes the strength of the photography of it. Anyway, thank you.

DP: This young man right here, wait for the mic.

Q: My question is: considering much of your audience will have not experienced war, what are your challenges in convincing your audience that your film is realistic when their sense of realism is likely largely influence by the previous canon of war films.

KB: Well, you know, I'm not sure empirically, unless of course they've been there. So, you know, I suppose—how does one judge a sense of realism? I mean—it's also meant to be a movie, it is not a documentary so I think that is clear going in it. It's a work of fiction, these are composite characters. However, I believe there is a degree of specificity—that certainly was in the script and that we tried to put up on the screen—an incredibly rigorous specificity, like the way he is lying on his stomach—they don't just bend over and work, they lie on their stomach and do it exactly the way he did. It's not just this sort of fictitious, I don't know, imagined universe, there's some kind of painful logic to the piece that could only be dictated by, let's say, the random chaos of war in this particular conflict, and that's not to say that in 2004 to 2006 all the technology is the same as today—today it's all different—but for that moment in time . . . And Mark's observations, I think, have been rendered certainly as accurately as we possibly could, given that we couldn't go into classified material . . . but really good question.

DP: Let's take this gentleman over here and then we're going to cut right through . . .
Q: How did you find and then push your actors to this, if you've shot that much, that's a lot of grueling hot and sweaty work. And your lead actor is so extraordinarily committed to that part, that it's amazing. So what do you do with them?
KB: For Jeremy it was the most difficult shoot, certainly, that I could imagine, that I think even he could imagine. That suit is not built by our wardrobe or art department, that is a one-hundred-pound suit made of Kevlar and ceramic plates. It was about 110, 115 degrees and I was very, very, very sensitive to his exhaustion level and ability to withstand heat. So we would constantly stop and break and make sure he was all right, and then shoot other things while he had a moment to take a breather. But on the other hand, he wanted to do it, and I think he did do it, in order to own the part, and he was kind of indefatigable. And we were very fortunate. He's an incredible actor with an ability to elicit truth and honesty, and there is also a subtleness in the script, which was written in a way that it was very naturalistic and there's a spareness to it. People do not, as one sees in most movies and it's something I'm not particularly fond of, relate all these, like, lengthy back stories that they have, and yet, you know, you're in the middle of a situation where you may live or die, you're making strategic decisions about doing something a particular way, you're not talking about your girlfriend back home. These are really grave circumstances that these guys are performing their job under . . .
DP: The juice scene comes to mind.
KB: The juice scene, yeah . . .

DP: Have people in the military seen this? And then the other question that I have is are there women in the military who do this job?
KB: Uh, yes and yes. So, we have shown it to people in the military. We've shown it just recently to an organization called EOD, Explosive Ordnances Disposal Memorial Foundation. They raise funds and scholarships for families of EOD fallen soldiers, and they've really embraced

it. They sort of feel like, every other sector of the military has had their movie like the Navy Seals, the Air Force pilots, the Army, the Marines, but they wonder, why not the EOD? They happen to be at the epicenter of this particular conflict, but nobody's really spent time with them, so they have embraced it. And I have gone to various screenings, and many veterans have come up to me, especially Iraq veterans, and said, that's exactly what it was like, even thought they might not have been in EOD, but they felt that it certainly replicated their experience. We've had a very positive reaction.

DP: And are there other women who work doing this too?

KB: And there are women who do the work; in fact, I was at Fort Irwin spending time with the EOD techs there looking at—for the first time— one of those robots, which is an amazing piece of technology, and it's even changed now. It's bigger and now even more dexterous, and in fact, they even have these tanks called Buffalos that have robot attachments. But anyway, there was a person in a bomb suit, and this person turned around, and took off the helmet, and revealed this shock of red curly hair and I realized that the EOD does not discriminate between any gender lines. You just have to be extremely, extremely intelligent. You have to have very finely calibrated motor skills, and be able to make a multitude of decisions virtually instantaneously under extreme pressure, and that's how it self-selects, so I thought that was kind of incredible.

DP: Okay, we just have time for a couple more questions, we'll take the two of you and then . . .

Q: This is just a very quick comment: the editing seems to also in part be complemented by the sound. And one of the most brilliant cuts was when Eldridge gets lifted up and he cries out in pain and we cut to the row of sinks, and you move, and it just seems like completely the next thing, but of course a lot gets left out between those two shots, but the cry of pain pulls us right from one moment to the next. And this happens then of course, when I saw that I realized, this technique is happening all the way through. You're using it. And somebody's making this decision . . .

KB: I wonder who?

Q: I wonder who! And it's wonderfully written, but there is a lot of direction going on here. And I also thought that the development of the relationship between Sanborn and James is really quite extraordinary. I mean, even on just very simple terms, I mean leading through even to the juice moment you know where it's something shared, where some moment of kindness is expressed, which is in a world where kindness is probably thought otherwise just a weakness. And, I don't know—the two on either side of me have a lot to say and they're women and I think a lot of men have said something.

DP: I think you had your hand up . . .

Q: I was curious about the title before I saw the film and I am still curious about the title of the film. Could you say something about why you chose that title and what it represents?

KB: Well, the "hurt locker" is a term that is used, that Mark heard when he was on his embed, which is used certainly in the time he was there—that was used in the military, but apparently it is also a sports term, and it means a dangerous place, a difficult place, like if you use it in a sentence, for example, as he heard once, "that if this bomb goes off we'll be in the hurt locker." So that's kind of it specifically, but what I liked is its sort of interpretive ability, and you know that's why it's never really spelt out exactly in the film and it has this provocative feeling of something that you feel, it certainly isn't a place, you know, of softness and kindness, but nonetheless is somewhat indefinable.

DP: Let us just do another.

Q: I think that I'm just stealing a turn. May I steal a turn?—It's hard not to notice that this is a war film about men, and you are a woman. I read about you in the *Times*, and I was actually sort of upset with the person who wrote the article noting first that you are a woman director, then claiming, but that doesn't matter. And then sort of going through the rest of the article talking about the fact you are a woman director. And so I hate asking this question, but I can't help but think about it, I wouldn't have expected to like this movie because it's a war movie—I am not attracted to war movies—but I liked this one, and I wonder if you are sensitive as to why this one might be more attractive to women than most war movies, because if you're aware of having put something into it that you feel is related to your female perspective, or if I'm imagining it, or if you're unaware of it?

KB: Well, complicated. I think that obviously who we are informs our perspective, and that as a filmmaker there is a certain transparency that's on the screen—I don't know, I feel like I can kind of get a certain sense of the person's personality by looking at their work, just as you can with a painting, you can get a sense of kind of who they are. On the other hand,

I don't know if I could pinpoint how exactly one's gender may influence what you do, but it does influence who you are and your sensibilities. I certainly know a lot of women like this movie, so I am very happy about it. But thank you, I wish there was a more concrete way to answer that, but I'm not sure how. Maybe you'll tell me how I can answer it someday.

DP: I promised this guy in the middle some time ago . . .

Q: First of all, I want to say that I thought that was a very haunting, beautiful movie, it was just breathtaking. I can't even believe what I just saw, but I want to make this quick because I know other people probably want to ask questions. I notice sometimes you choose the first-person point of view. Are there certain points of view that you favor or that you find more gritty or more realistic? I don't know if that even makes sense.

KB: Yeah, no, and thank you. I think when you go to point of view, it's used well as punctuation. I think it can be overused, but I think if it's used as punctuation, like in the case of him in the suit and in the helmet, you see the world through the helmet and you hear his breathing and that really does parachute the audience into what it might be like to be carrying that weight, and the creakiness, and with the Kevlar, and the kind of pressure on your chest as it labors your breathing. So I think if it's used as punctuation it remains a really nice, vital tool for your understanding and again back to that kind of experiential look at this conflict through these soldiers' eyes.

DP: Do you want to take one more question?

KB: Yeah let's take one more.

Q: I am a student director myself, so this very much applies to me and I am very glad to be here. My question kind of relates to everyone's with the "why does this feel so real." And for me, the first thing I thought was—the character. And I know that stems from the writing, and I know you are friends with the journalist, Mark, is that correct? It was experienced by him not necessarily firsthand, but watching everyone around him, so how much of this was reality? I mean, it does feel very much like a documentary in a lot of ways. But going from experience to writing to the screen, everything is going to change, so can you talk a little bit about that?

KB: Yeah, it's a good question. I think that virtually everything in here is either reported by him, or observed, or maybe a combination of some characters, and then a finalization, but it all came from fact. Nothing is really completely—yet, on the other hand the entire piece is invented because it is a work of fiction—but it is all so carefully observed, all the events, all the characters. Even when the guy takes the bomb suit off because there are so many bombs in the back of the car and he wanted to die comfortably, that was reported to him by, actually an Israeli tech who actually did that. He opened the back of the trunk, he kicked it first, then opened it up, and there were all these bombs, and he took his bomb suit off. You know it was kind of a legendary moment that circulates a lot in the world of EOD. So it's also really skillfully crafted, the calibrations of these characters and how they work together. The antipathy between the two of them [James and Sanborn] and then the structure that forms it really starts with really good writing. And I'd have to say as a filmmaker, both the actors and Mark and the crew, they sort of, in this case, made me look good. You can't do it alone. It comes from having firsthand observations and a degree of specificity that is . . . you know, we had tech advisers on the set. There wasn't a scene that we'd shoot and someone wouldn't say, yeah, that's how it's done on the field. So we just, we were kind of extremely rigorous, we weren't going to invent something out of whole cloth, on the fly, that's for sure.

Q: Well thank you, because I mean, I'm watching it and thinking of you and the crew and the writing, but—and I do that for every movie—but for this one, particularly, I kept going back to, "but I still *feel* for him!" And I can't get away from that. Despite the fact that I can see behind the scenes in my head. So I think you guys did a very good job researching the character.
KB: Oh, thank you, thank you, thank you very much.

DP: Well, with that I think we'll have to pull it (applause). That went really, really well.

[Post-Q&A conversations]
KB: Yeah, I think they liked it, they were all so sweet. I can't stand it, I loved them, every single one of them. It's interesting because that question of reality is very subjective and very interpretive. What's real to you, what's real to me, it's incredibly interpretive.

DP: Well, the interesting thing is that there is a sense of realism in this film that is very different than your other films. That—no doubt it was

a very realistic film in a lot of ways—they're really sort of like glued together, what is imagined and what is real, I think, is like, remarkable.
KB: Oh well thank you. Well that felt real to me then, but now it all feels just kind of fantastic, until this.

DP: But your use of detail . . .
KB: You know it just makes me want to go more into sort of topical and relevant material.

DP: Oh really, that's interesting
KB: . . . get into it further and further and get right in there next to documentary.

Q: [mostly inaudible question, ironically, about the sound design]
KB: The sound—I wanted to talk about that. I had this incredible sound designer. And I wanted to not have a score, because a score takes away the suspense because a score is repetitive. You know, you have a phrase, and you know it's going to repeat. Then go onto another phrase. There is no suspense there. Because you know it is going to repeat. But when you just have sound design, and you have no score, you can't telegraph what is going to happen. So, I think that helps out a lot in this sense of reality, it's not just in the character, but it's in the sound.

DP: I mean, the sound is amazing . . . It's even more forceful than the image. It's very kinetic, or rather very physical, your film is very physical.
KB: But then I tried to do those slow motion shots to give you a sense of overpressure, because there is the gas that is expanded before the particular matter that kills you first because it . . . it completely crushes in the air pockets of your body. So even before the shrapnel hits you, the gases . . .

DP: The forces . . .
KB: The force of the shock wave basically has—so that, so yeah. I was trying to give that sense. Because all the guys who were talking to Mark over there were saying that nobody understands overpressure. You know, they see the shirt fabric move and they just know that like two miles away something is going to concuss in a second—you're basically sort of liquefied or something which is how it is described to me. Which is what happens to Thompson in the beginning.
Q: Yeah, you kind of wonder why he died. [Inaudible]

KB: Yeah. It doesn't take a lot, he's actually a bit away from the detonation site and he's still wearing the suit. There's a point—it's so complicated. They have this way about talking about the relation to the IED, where at one hundred meters out you're thinking okay maybe there's a sniper out there, this and that, and then at fifty meters you're starting to think about your family, at twenty-five meters you're at a point of no return. Nobody can help you. At that point, nothing, no suit—there's no margin for error. You're either going to succeed or fail. And that's it. And then you go do it again, ten, twelve times a day.

DP: Well I think that's another way that the sound kind of helps to drive us into the isolation of the characters. They are sort of at the still center. At the eye of the storm, in some way.

KB: Exactly, and they call that the lonely walk. "I'm going to go take a lonely walk." And it is. It's the eye of the storm. I mean the ground troops, that's their job. They cordon off the city for you. That's the war. You are the war. That's it. That's what's being fought.

DP: I read something in an interview how you said this is a new kind of combat film, in some ways this is a new kind of war film—it is certainly new to film. It's new to cinema, as you said.

KB: But I will say that, something at least I am reminded of is—when I stand and talk to EOD techs—is that we know about the explosions because that's what we read about—but for every explosion, I don't have the fuzzy math on me, but there are dozens and dozens and dozens of these that are rendered safe. Countless lives have been saved, and sadly there are sacrifices.

A Maverick Female Director
Explores Men Who Dare Death

Carrie Rickey / 2009

From the *Philadelphia Inquirer*, July 9, 2009. Reprinted courtesy of the *Philadelphia Inquirer* and Carrie Rickey.

Slim as lightning, Kathryn Bigelow makes movies charged with adrenaline and electricity, action thrillers like *Blue Steel* and *Point Break*. The six-footer with the radiant presence of a Redgrave and the steel nerves of a high-wire artist is drawn to stories about daredevils addicted to the rush.

Her latest, *The Hurt Locker*, about a U.S. bomb-disposal technician in Baghdad in 2004, plugs viewers directly into the central nervous system of such a risk junkie, and it's earning Bigelow the best reviews of her career. "An instant classic that demonstrates . . . how the drug of war hooks its victims and why they can't kick the habit," the *Wall Street Journal* salutes.

The Hurt Locker is a topical exploration into mindful violence and one warrior's mindset: The acute focus that makes Staff Sgt. William James (Jeremy Renner) such a cunning creature of war is the very quality that makes him unsuited to just about everything else.

"He is walking toward what you and I and everyone else on the planet would be running away from," says Bigelow, fifty-seven, who made it her mission "to transport the audience into the mind of a bomb technician."

Is he a hero, this sergeant who unties improvised explosive devices (IEDs) as though they were shoelaces? Or is he a daredevil testing his mettle in the world's most dangerous job?

For Bigelow, who in her untucked black shirt and skinny trousers resembles a human exclamation point, Sgt. James is the kind of man attracted to no-man's land. And she is the kind of woman who's just as magnetically drawn there.

Over the course of eight films since 1983, Bigelow has mapped this uncharted territory variously populated by vampires (*Near Dark*), bank robbers (*Point Break*), and military men (*K-19: The Widowmaker* and *Hurt Locker*), and punctuated by random acts of violence. Some call her a "manthropologist," but she is loath to analyze her work.

"I try not to," she says, in a Philadelphia hotel room last week. "I work instinctually. Each film begins with characters. This time the opportunity arose to work with material that was relevant and topical.

"I read about the war in Iraq, about expressions like 'roadside bomb' and 'IED,' without fully understanding them," she says. When she read journalist Mark Boal's dispatches as an embed in Baghdad that are the basis of *Hurt Locker*'s screenplay, she grasped the risk and danger.

"Here was an opportunity to give meaning to the abstractions," she says.

As Bigelow pictures them, IEDs are assemblages, infernal and ingenious, potentially lethal sculptures that Sgt. James disarms while playing beat-the-clock.

"This is not your typical job," she says. "He has a special skill set, like a surgeon. Difference being," she adds drily, "if a surgeon makes a mistake, the patient dies. If a bomb technician makes a mistake, he gets atomized." Success means getting hooked on the adrenaline.

Born in the Bay Area community of San Carlos, Bigelow studied at the San Francisco Art Institute (where one of her teachers was experimental filmmaker Gunvor Nelson) before establishing herself as a sculptor. Awarded a fellowship to the Whitney Museum, she arrived in New York in 1972 when Lower Manhattan was a desert of abandoned warehouses.

Putting together an installation of scavenged six-foot steel tubes, she liked the reverberating music they made when they rolled against each other. She audiotaped the sound, which accompanied the installation.

By day she supported herself renovating lofts. "I did the drywall; (composer) Philip Glass did the plumbing." Still, money was tight and she knew how to stretch a dollar.

One summer she crashed at the loft of performance artist Vito Acconci, where other aspiring artists, including painter and future filmmaker Julian Schnabel, took advantage of a rent-free squat. Though her visceral, keenly observed films couldn't be more texturally different from Schnabel's surreal visions, there are few American filmmakers more alert to physical and psychological atmospherics than these refugees from the art world.

Excited by the sex-and-violence-charged imagery of Rainer Werner Fassbinder and Pier Paolo Pasolini, Bigelow moved from sculpture to film. Her debut was *Set-Up* (1978): Two fighters box while, in voiceover, two theorists hypothesize about the meaning of the punches traded. All but one of Bigelow's subsequent features resonate with such images of masculinity and aggression.

From the first, her heart-pounding films pulsed with adrenaline. In *The Loveless*, Willem Dafoe slices through space astride a motorcycle. *Point Break* is a triathlon of running, surfing, and skydiving.

The sinewy filmmaker is herself an athlete—"I hike, I bike, I ride horses"—who translates that physicality to the screen. Though some call her the only female action director, back in the day Ida Lupino mounted her camera on speeding cars and horses and between opposing tennis players. As with Lupino, for Bigelow action reveals psychology.

She lives near Hollywood, but except for a brief marriage to director James Cameron (1989–91) Bigelow is not of it. Her films are independently financed. She is the opposite of prolific, averaging a film every three years.

When *The Hurt Locker* debuted at the Venice Film Festival in September, some criticized it for not being more explicitly critical of the war.

"It seems pretty clear to me that it's a dangerous job and in a volunteer army, the psychology defines the people who fight there," she says of Sgt. James, the cowboy craving the increasingly intense highs that are soul-corroding.

"War's dirty secret," Bigelow has said, "is that some men love it."

Asked whether her enigmatic title alludes to the Kevlar suit worn by bomb technicians that make them resemble astronauts in their space suits, Bigelow shakes her head. "It's a slang term that Mark heard on his embed. Hurt locker is a place you don't want to be, like up s—- creek. It could also mean a coffin.

"I like the ambiguity."

The Hurt Locker Interview: Kathryn Bigelow and Mark Boal

Kingsley Marshall / 2009

From *Little White Lies*, September 1, 2009, reposted March 10, 2010. Reprinted by permission of Kingsley Marshall.

The Hurt Locker, Kathryn Bigelow's war film centered around a three-man U.S. Explosive Ordnance Disposal team, swept the Academy Awards in 2010. The movie collected six Oscars from nine nominations, including Best Director for Bigelow, Best Original Screenplay for its writer, Mark Boal, awards for Sound Editing and Sound Mixing, as well as Best Picture at the ceremony.

Bigelow's first feature since *K-19* in 2002 was a close collaboration with Boal, whose screenplay was seeded in his profile of elite bomb technician Jeffrey Sarver, entitled "The Man in the Bomb Suit," first published in *Playboy* magazine.

The resultant film was some distance from the adrenaline of Bigelow's breakthrough features *Blue Steel* or *Point Break*, with a tone closer to the war portrayed in David Simon's television series *Generation Kill* for HBO, in that it focused not on the wider context of conflicts, but those who fight them. Like Simon's account of the conflict in the Gulf, both projects were seeded in the observation of embedded journalism. The origins of *Generation Kill* were seeded in the book by *Rolling Stone*'s Evan Wright, who rode with a U.S. Marine recon unit at the start of the second Iraq invasion in 2001, while Mark Boal's script for *The Hurt Locker* came about through his experiences as a reporter embedded with a bomb disposal team in Baghdad.

"I had a desire to be more topical," explains Bigelow. "*K-19* came from *Pravda*, courtesy of Glasnost and, for me, *The Hurt Locker* was the opportunity to extend realism as a text within the medium and push film to be relevant, as opposed to fantastical. A colleague, Sally Cox, a senior agent at Creative Artists Agency, introduced me to Mark's journalism. I'd spoken to Sally at length about nonfiction material and had a deliberate interest in journalism and its potential application for film. I'd pursued a number of magazine articles through her, before she introduced me to Mark's work, and I became extremely interested when he told me that he was going off on a journalistic embed to Baghdad with the bomb squad."

The director had worked with the writer on the development of an article called *Jailbait*, which the pair developed into *The Inside*, a short-lived crime television series for Fox, though both felt that it was to be Mark's placement with the bomb squad which truly had movie potential. Boal had worked with Paul Haggis with a script that became *In the Valley of Elah*, but distinguishes this earlier Academy Award–nominated work from his work with Bigelow.

"We made a distinction from that film's focus on the reintegration of soldiers from the Gulf back into the home front," he explains, and details how his intention had been to make a concerted effort to distance *The Hurt Locker* from the glut of films situated in the Middle East. "We were very specifically thinking about this war. People talk about *The Kingdom*, even though it takes place in Saudi Arabia, *Three Kings*, which is primarily a satire, and *Jarhead*, which though it is a true story memoir, the source material isn't so much about the Gulf War, but the psychological state of being a marine sniper.

"Though the route from journalist to screenwriter is traditionally borne with a lot of pain and frustration, I've been incredibly lucky," he adds, laughing. "There's not a lot of social realism in film these days, which is a shame, as I've never really understood why those kinds of movies aren't made anymore. I think about that in the same way in that General Motors considered the taste of the American public with respect to automobiles, in that they were very scientifically certain that the Hummer, Escalade, and giant trucks would be the way to go based on extensive psychographic research into the mind of the American consumer. Five years later they're out of business, and trying to make small electric cars. Obviously I believed there was an opening there, or I wouldn't have spent the last four years working this, and I was naïve enough at the time to be excited about the value of importing some of the ideals of journalism into film. It was definitely worth an experiment, and has turned into something of an adventure."

Shot on location in Jordan the multiple cameras of *The Hurt Locker* lend an immersive, almost documentary, feel, where the action is entirely secondary to the visceral experiences of soldiers employed in the most dangerous of occupations.

"Mark's script carefully crafted the reader's orientation in any given bomb disarmament sequence," Bigelow explains. "Not only does the film try to humanize that event, but also be slavishly clear as to how important geography is in the process and protocol of bomb disarmament. Within Mark's script he so carefully crafted the reader's orientation in any given bomb disarmament sequence, so you are very clear where the bomb tech was in relation to the bomb itself. To achieve that, we needed a very dexterous camera, and it was important to be able to shoot both tight and wide; tight in order to capture the emotionality, and wide to make sure that the audience had a fundamental understanding of what was going on in any given environment. We chose Super 16 as our format and I've always worked with multiple cameras so that wasn't in and of itself that challenging for us to choreograph and stage, certainly once you've boarded it out and have a rough schematic in your head. Working with the cinematographer Barry Ackroyd it became a very exciting process of execution. Not only is the film trying to humanize that event, the day in the life of the bomb tech, but also to be almost slavishly clear to how geography works and the process and protocol of bomb disarmament. I guess what I'm saying is that the degree of specificity in the script was both exciting and inspiring, and also so important that we wanted to make sure we could capture all of it."

"Kathryn strove for authenticity throughout, and said that there was no off switch for the cameras," adds the film's editor, Chris Innis, who had the enviable job of trawling through over two hundred hours of footage. "Sometimes the scene would be staged the same way but in different locations, while the crew would also improvise their camera work and grab juicy documentary footage, like stray cats roaming in the streets and locals hanging out of windows. The producers saw that it was a tight, well-told film and left us virtually alone, which would be almost unheard of in a studio setting."

"On the page, scenes such as the sniper fight read not only in real time, but offered a highly nuanced examination of that kind of combat," explains Bigelow. "The high degree of specificity in Mark's script was both exciting and inspiring and I really wanted to protect that aspect, and make sure we could capture it all. In my storyboarding of the scene, I really wanted to protect that aspect, not just of the engagement, but the almost unendurable wait for yet another moment of engagement. That aspect was really palpable on the page and something that the film's cinematographer, Barry Ackroyd, Mark, and I spoke about in the desert—making sure that both the engagement and the wait for it were equally weighted."

"The independent financing was absolutely critical to many of these decisions," the director admits, "and I don't think we could have made the film under any other circumstances. To be honest, all of my productions have been technically independent, though this one gave me more autonomy than I've experienced before, Certainly we couldn't have shot it in Jordan, as I can't imagine a studio sanctioning that production, but it's absolutely a win-win scenario for a filmmaker. Even though the price you pay for that is working with an incredibly modest budget, the upside is worth any of the financial limitations in terms of content, substance, and cast; we had complete creative control, final cut, and the opportunity to cast break-out talent. For example, neither of us had anticipated that there would be close to a million Iraqi refugees living in Amman at the time of filming, some of whom were actors, but we were able to immediately fold them into the shoot. The result was that all of the speaking parts were played by Iraqis, as were most of the background extras, and the man who plays the suicide bomber at the end is a fairly well-known stage actor in Baghdad."

"That created a stage for people to be riskier I think," suggests Boal. "Jeremy Renner talked about how, at a certain point, it didn't feel as though he was acting at all, but reacting. After all, he may have been playing a white guy in the Middle East but, whether he was an actor or not, when he stopped acting he was still a white guy in the Middle East, standing amongst a crowd of people who didn't speak his language and with a cultural gap that's hard to bridge. The movie is a two-hour-long argument that encapsulates all of our ideas about the conflict, the war and the people that are involved in it. It's very difficult to take that argument which is so nuanced and complicated, that Kathryn has rendered in an incredibly artistic way and boil it down and reduce it to a good quote without feeling that you are doing violence to the work. It's a little reductive. It's hard to quantify, but it certainly felt like an adventure in filmmaking—a little like going up river in *Fitzcarraldo*."

"Or *Apocalypse Now*," adds Bigelow.

Shoot Shoot, Bang Bang

Paul Hond / 2009

From the *Columbia Magazine*, Winter 2009–10. Reprinted by permission of the *Columbia Magazine*.

"She's acting out desires. She represents what people want to see, and it's upsetting, because they don't exactly know what to do with it."
—cultural theorist Sylvère Lotringer

Baghdad, 2004. An explosive ordnance robot rolls along a dusty city street toward a pile of white burlap sacks. Soldiers, American, leap from armored vehicles, cradling their M16s. They must evacuate the women, children, and old men, who could be killed or maimed if they don't move faster. Cars race past, horns blaring. Soldiers yell and push. Closer to the kill zone, three members of the Explosive Ordnance Disposal (EOD) unit—Thompson, Eldridge, and Sanborn—huddle around a monitor, watching the feed from the robot's camera. Sanborn controls the robot by moving small joysticks on a board. The robot's pincer grasps a snatch of burlap and slowly parts the material, revealing the head of a dark gray bomb. "Hello, mama," Sanborn says.

The team calls the robot back and hitches a small wagon to it with a payload of charges to detonate the device. The robot goes off again on its miniature-tank-like tread. As it bumps over a pile of rocks, the rickety little wagon falls apart. *Shit.* Now Thompson has to go down there and lay the charges himself. Thompson, who has the heroic jawline of an aging quarterback, is the leader, the guy who wears the hundred-pound steel-plated bomb suit and the helmet and gets up close to the deadly thing and touches it. His buddies zip him up, set his helmet firm, and wish him well.

Thompson walks toward the pile, breathing heavily in the desert heat. There are sand-colored buildings, burnt-out cars.

Above, a shuddering helicopter crosses the sun. Eldridge and Sanborn cover Thompson from a distance, scanning the windows and storefronts through the scopes of their rifles. Thompson reaches the bags, kneels before them. Slowly, delicately, he lays the charges. Then he straightens up, turns, and begins walking back toward Sanborn and Eldridge and the Humvee.

Suddenly, Eldridge sees something. He looks through his scope: there, across the road, in front of a butcher's shop, amid the skinned animals strung up in the heat, is a man in a white smock, and he is holding something. A switch flips inside Eldridge: "Sanborn!" he yells, and runs toward the shop. "Butcher shop, two o'clock, dude has a phone!" The man in the smock waves, smiles, the picture of innocence, but Eldridge is locked in. "Drop the phone!" he shouts, sprinting now. Sanborn, in pursuit, calls, "Burn him, Eldridge! *Burn him!*" But there's no clear shot, and the man pushes the buttons, and we then see Thompson running in his bulky suit, still within the zone, and the ground behind him erupts in a gush of pewter gray, and you cover your eyes as Thompson, our quarterback, is blown forward in slow motion, and the earth spews skyward like a volcano.

You must be dreaming, because when you open your eyes, you find yourself seated at a table in the brick patio lounge of the Beverly Hills Hotel. Birds chirp. Across from you is a woman, tall and slender, wearing a black leather jacket, blue jeans, and a small crucifix around her neck. She has long chestnut hair and expressive hands. "The light is so beautiful these days because we just had this giant windstorm," she says, a poet of extreme conditions. "The clarity—it's just so magnificent."

Yes. Magnificent. Sunlight seeps through a canopy of blade-shaped leaves. There are pink stucco walls, and clay pots of luminous pink and purple bougainvillea.

The woman is Kathryn Bigelow, the director of *The Hurt Locker*, a psychological thriller involving a unit of U.S. Army bomb technicians in Iraq and one of the most acclaimed movies of 2009. Having just consumed all eight of Bigelow's feature films in seventy-two hours, your brain is revved up for blasts, killer waves, hunks of metal, erotic obsession, blood, guns, burning rubber. Bigelow has long been one of our most daring and original filmmakers, and *The Hurt Locker* is the most potent cocktail yet of her vast visual powers and her lasting formal and thematic concerns. The movie examines, in a war setting, the attraction to physical risk, which, for the freewheeling, industrial-metal-listening bomb dismantler Staff Sergeant William James (played by Jeremy Renner), has a chilling intimacy: "Hello, baby," James murmurs, brushing dirt from a plump, leaden bomb that he's uncovered in an empty square. Later, after snipping more wires, and coming within a whisker of his life, he retires to his Humvee and lights a cigarette: the Marlboro Man of Mesopotamia. "That was good," he says.

It's a classic shot from the Bigelow canon, where desire and death often converge, and heroes are seduced by things that might kill them. *The Hurt Locker* ups the ante by employing an immersive visual scheme—multiple Super 16 millimeter cameras, hair-trigger point-of-view shots, a 360-degree field of vision—that implicates the viewer in the action.

"It's an experiential form of filmmaking," Bigelow says between sips of fruit juice.

As she speaks, you recall standing outside a UN compound, within range of a carload of bombs that the unit has come to defuse. You are surrounded by apartment buildings, from whose balconies and windows Iraqi men gaze impassively, unreadable as the wind. Your vision whips from one potential trouble spot to the next, until it locks onto a man on a rooftop: he is aiming a small video camera directly at you. It's as terrifying as it is absurd. Should you kill him? Who is he? And who are you?

"The movie is looking at the humanity of the conflict, and the dehumanizing, soul-numbing rigors of war," Bigelow says. "There are soldiers who are either just numb, or who are so switched-on that they're capable of anything."

Switched-on. It suggests a high-tech adrenaline rush: a click, a spark, wattage to the blood. You then recall that *The Hurt Locker* begins with a quote from the *New York Times* war correspondent Chris Hedges: *The rush of battle is a potent and often lethal addiction, for war is a drug.*

"What switches *you* on?" you say. "As a filmmaker, what's the drug?"

Bigelow gives a sporting laugh. "That's tough," she says, but she thinks about it for a moment. Then, with care: "I suppose it would be the opportunity to provide a text that is provocative."

That opportunity arose in 2004, when the journalist Mark Boal was embedded for two weeks with an EOD unit in Iraq. Upon his return, Boal, who had worked previously with Bigelow, related his Iraq experiences to her, and "we both thought it would make a great entry point for a film," Bigelow says. Boal wrote the script, and when Bigelow read it, "I knew it was tremendous. No one had realized that the epicenter of the war was squarely on the shoulders of the EOD and that they *were* the war, basically. It was very timely, and I wanted it to be as expedient as possible." The movie became a financial reality, she says, when Nicolas Chartier of Voltage Pictures offered to raise the money. "I think this was a brave and creative choice on his part given that I didn't want to cast any major movie stars in the leads in order to preserve the naturalistic tone of the material, and to heighten the suspense." Bigelow also wanted to shoot in the Middle East, "as close to the war zone as possible."

To that end, she scouted Morocco. "Morocco could not provide that breadth of set, architecturally speaking—it looked like North Africa, not the Middle East. Baghdad, where the story was set, was a war zone and off limits as a film location, so we scouted Jordan, where the architecture was virtually a perfect match. The Jordanians were very receptive."

Bigelow now had a theater of operations—the capital city of Amman—that could pass convincingly for the war-rocked nation next door. As a bonus, the Jordanian military hardware—the Humvees, tanks, and armored personnel carriers—was American-made, and Jordan was also home to a community of Iraqi actors who had been displaced by the war. These resources, and the raw depiction of urban warfare, inject *The Hurt Locker* with the authenticity and immediacy of *The Battle of Algiers*.

It's a sharp turn for Bigelow, most of whose work, like the brilliant vampire love story *Near Dark* (1987), and the visionary cyberpunk thriller *Strange Days* (1995), has been fiercely fictional.

"I'm almost more excited by reality in some ways," Bigelow says. "Dealing with a conflict that's real and ongoing provides the opportunity for the material to be topical and relevant. If you can cause people to think about that conflict as they walk out of the theater, then I think you're really maximizing the potential of the medium."

Bigelow's mastery of that medium might be finally getting front-page attention (expect heavy Oscar action for *The Hurt Locker* this winter), but cinema hounds have been on the trail since her first feature, the art-house biker flick *The Loveless*, came out in 1982, starring leather-clad Willem Dafoe as the leader of a motorcycle gang that sojourns in a roadside town in the 1950s South. With its rebellious young bloods, simmering sexuality, and sherbet palette—the pinks and peaches of the women's dresses, the lemon yellows and pistachio greens of the cars—it evokes Douglas Sirk, and inaugurates a succession of bold, genre-bending movies. These include *Blue Steel* (1989), about a female rookie cop who falls for a psychopath with a deadly fetish for her gun ("Death," says the killer, "is the greatest kick of all"), and *Point Break* (1991), in which an

FBI agent infiltrates a gang of bank-robbing surfers whose leader, a high priest of thrills, counsels, "If you want the ultimate, you gotta be willing to pay the ultimate price."

Drawing inspiration from directors like Hitchcock, Peckinpah, and Fassbinder, Bigelow makes smart, violent, suspenseful, exquisitely photographed movies, shot through with grim wit and some of the most electrifying action sequences in the business: car and foot chases, shootouts, 100-foot walls of fire.

There's a maverick streak in her that enables her to handle these violent genres, but also to give them a very personal touch and deal with them in a very sensitive way," says film critic and Columbia professor Andrew Sarris ('51 CC). "I think *The Hurt Locker* is one of the best films of the year, and the best I've seen about the morass in Iraq." Sarris also singles out *Blue Steel* as a favorite. "Her style is—I'll use the word that *Time Out* used—seductive."

Bigelow was born in 1951 in the northern California town of San Carlos, where she grew up riding horses and painting. She has a kind of buoyant, outdoorsy vitality, a big-sky embrace of the visual world, and an intense cerebral energy cut with New York punk and what she has called her "semiotic Lacanian deconstructivist saturation."

A waiter comes by, and Bigelow indicates a nearby heat lamp. "If I could have one of these turned on to, like, nuclear," she says cheerfully. The waiter obliges.

You think: semiotic Lacanian deconstructivist saturation.

The heat lamp turns bright orange. It starts to get very warm.

That's when you remove your jacket and ask Ms. Bigelow about her time at Columbia.

"Her attitude: to formalize, to frame, to keep a distance, to control. I think control is essential."—Lotringer

New York City, 1972. Two strangers, a young abstract painter from California and a renowned cultural theorist from France, arrive in Manhattan. One heads uptown, the other, downtown.

The theorist is Sylvère Lotringer. He has just joined the French department at Columbia, where he will introduce, from Europe, the field of semiotics—the science of signs in society. He will also be the first professor in the United States to teach the works of contemporary French thinkers like the philosopher Gilles Deleuze and the psychoanalyst Jacques

Lacan, who claimed—intriguingly, for artists—that the signs and codes found in advertisements create, in the unconscious, desires that cannot be satisfied. For Lacan, desire is predicated on lack.

The abstract painter is Kathryn Bigelow. A student at the San Francisco Art Institute, she's been awarded a fellowship for the Whitney Museum's Independent Study Program. It's winter and freezing cold. The city is blighted, near bankrupt, dangerous.

"I've got a little Levi's jacket, sneakers, T-shirt. That's it," Bigelow recalls. "I decided that wherever my studio was, that was where I was going to live. It was in Tribeca before it was Tribeca—a *really* rough outpost. I've got my sleeping bag and a little dog-eared piece of paper that has my address: 'Basement of an off-track betting building, three flights down.' Someone takes me there. There's no light, footsteps resound off the walls, and the person says, 'Here's your studio.' It's a bank vault. I think, 'It's going to be a little chilly.' There's snow outside, and I can't feel my legs. So I gamely pull out my sleeping bag, praying that somehow the door to the bank vault doesn't close, because it's a 24-inch slab of metal. Mind you, there are gunshots echoing every night. And one of my creative advisers is Susan Sontag, which of course meant that I was never happier in my life."

"There's a maverick streak in her that enables her to handle these violent genres, but also to give them a very personal touch and deal with them in a very sensitive way."

After completing the Whitney program, Bigelow stayed in New York and began to work with conceptual artists like Lawrence Weiner and the British collaborative Art & Language, which was based on "an attempt to decommodify art, yet still have it be defined as art and justify its existence as art," Bigelow says. "We were in the Venice Biennale, where we put up a giant banner over the Grand Canal with an inversion of the famous Latin phrase, 'Art is long, life is short.' The group is always trying to subvert. Very political in its own way, and insidiously provocative. It made you think."

With Art & Language, Bigelow started making non-narrative short films. The group returned to England in 1976, and Bigelow, still in New York, applied for an NEA grant to make a short movie. She got the grant and shot the film, using her conceptual artist friends as crew. But the money ran out before she could edit the piece. "So I think, 'Aha. Graduate school. Free mix at Trans/Audio!'" She submitted the uncut footage to Milos Forman, who was head of the film department at Columbia. Bigelow was accepted and given a scholarship for an MFA in film criticism.

Sylvère Lotringer, meanwhile, was attempting to bridge the divide between downtown artists and uptown theorists. He taught Lacan and Foucault by day, and, by night, explored the downtown art scene and the prepunk happenings at CBGB and Max's Kansas City. In 1974 he launched a journal called *Semiotext(e)*, a watershed publication that brought art and theory together. The next year, he organized a conference at Columbia on madness and prisons called "Schizo-Culture." He invited French poststructuralists like Foucault, Deleuze, Jean-François Lyotard, and Félix Guattari, and artists like Richard Foreman, William Burroughs, and John Cage. The event drew two thousand people.

Afterward, Lotringer was approached by students from the Columbia film department. "Semiotics was in the air," he says. "Filmmakers were the first to pick up on it. Artists get excited by new ideas earlier than academics. They wanted to know more, so they came to my classes, and that's how I met them."

One of those students was Bigelow.

"She came to my class to understand what was going on with semiotics, and Lacan especially," says Lotringer. "It's a very controlling thing, to make films. And semiotics is a system of control."

Bigelow took classes with Lotringer, Marshall Blonsky, Edward Said, and Andrew Sarris, whose two-year film survey was another revelation. "I remember Sarris talking about Orson Welles and *The Magnificent Ambersons*," Bigelow says. "To this day I can see him against the screen; he had this almost cherubic smile, infecting everyone in that room with his pure love of film. You walked out of that class unrecognizable, even to yourself. All he did was give his love of film to you and defy you not to pick up on it."

In 1978, Bigelow completed her thesis, a twenty-minute short called *Set-Up*. In it, two men have a sloppy fistfight in a dark alley, trading insults of "fascist" and "commie." As the men tussle, two scholars—Blonsky and Lotringer—deconstruct the action in voice-over.

The following year, Bigelow began working with other students on an issue of *Semiotext(e)* called "Polysexuality," which, says Lotringer, "was meant to invent new categories for sexuality, like soft sex or corporate sex, so that nothing could be considered abnormal or deviant. The cover showed a gay biker in San Francisco with a leather jacket and bare ass. On the back was a picture of a man who impaled himself on a giant phallus. Seductive image in front, disquieting image on back. Sex and Death. You give people what they want, but you prevent them from enjoying it in full."

Fair enough. But what about that Lacanian saturation?

"In Lacan and Deleuze, you have the whole idea of neuroticism and perversion," Lotringer explains. "For French theorists, perversion is taken more positively than in America. The word has no moral connotation. It means experimenting with your desires, instead of repressing them, as most people do. Neurotics repress things. In perversion, you acknowledge your desires and try them out."

Cut to Staff Sergeant William James, encased in body armor, in punishing heat, plodding toward a roadside bomb.

Could his courage be a form of Lacanian desire?

"What becomes the discovery in the movie," Bigelow says, "is that James is actually quite self-aware. He knows what switches him on, and he accepts it. He's not living in a state of denial."

The temperature generated by the heat lamp approaches Jordanian highs, and Bigelow graciously asks the waiter to turn it down. She hadn't actually expected nuclear. "We could warm up half of Southern California," she jokes.

Just then, a woman comes over. She's an agent who has been lunching at a nearby table.

"Congratulations," the agent says to Bigelow. "What an amazing year for you, I mean, all of this attention! Welcome to the Oscars, dear, you're going to have a lot of opportunities. I think this is your year." She returns to her table, and comes back a moment later with a well-known actress, whom she introduces to Bigelow. There is no doubt as to which direction the compass needles are pointed.

When the women go, Bigelow returns to Columbia and *Set-Up*, to illustrate a central idea about her process.

"I began with *Set-Up* to provide a physiological and psychological connection between the audience and the screen," she says. "While you're watching it, you're deconstructing the connection. In a perfect world, theoretically, you're *experiencing* that connection." She then refers to a scene in *The Hurt Locker*, in which Eldridge, caught in a cross-desert shootout, is ordered by James to grab the ammo from off the body of a fallen comrade. But the bullets, blood-smeared, jam the rifle. With enemy fire whizzing past, Eldridge frantically wipes the bullets, spitting on them to clean them off.

"There was this one article," Bigelow says, "in which the writer talks about watching the scene and trying to get saliva in his mouth, so that he could help Eldridge clean the bullets."

It's what Lacanians call "scopophilia": the derivation of physical sensation through the act of viewing. Mostly, it is associated with pornography. But it can just as easily be something that makes you wince or cover your eyes.

The explosion rips through the ground, lifting earth in a rolling torrent. Dirt and rust loosen and fly from the shell of a junked car. As Sergeant Thompson is hurled toward us on the road, we see the inside of his helmet turn dark red. He falls, lies motionless. Smoke rises from his body.

The Hurt Locker has just begun. We are about to meet Staff Sergeant James, Thompson's replacement. With his record of disabling over eight hundred bombs—873, to be exact—James, the "wild man," as a giddy colonel calls him, has come here to do the one thing that makes him feel most alive.

As James is helped into his suit to perform his first death-defying mission with the unit, you seem to hear, in your mind, two disembodied voices, commenting on the text:

"Outwardly," says Lotringer, "the movie is against violence, but of course, violence is very seductive. And she played with the seduction. To have seduction and Iraq at the same time was a gamble."

And Bigelow: "The gravity of the subject is encapsulated within this physical beauty that creates a nice tension between the two elements. There's something interestingly, graphically provocative about a man dressed in a bomb suit lifting up six bombs strapped to a wire."

Kathryn Bigelow's 2010 Oscar Acceptance Speech

Kathryn Bigelow / 2010

March 7, 2010. Reprinted by permission of the Academy of Motion Picture Arts and Sciences and Kathryn Bigelow.

"This really is . . . There's no other way to describe it, it's the moment of a lifetime. First of all, this is so extraordinary to be in the company of such powerful, my fellow nominees, such powerful filmmakers who have inspired me and I have admired for, some of whom, for decades. And thank you to every member of the Academy. This is, again, the moment of a lifetime.

"I would not be standing here if it wasn't for Mark Boal, who risked his life for the words on the page and wrote such a courageous screenplay that I was fortunate enough to have an extraordinary cast bring that screenplay to life. And Jeremy Renner, Anthony Mackie, and Brian Geraghty. And, I think the secret to directing is collaborating and I had truly an extraordinary group of collaborators in my crew. Barry Ackroyd and Kalle Júlíusson and Bob Murawski, Chris Innis, Ray Beckett, Richard Stutsman, and if I could just also thank my producing partners, Greg Shapiro, Nick Chartier, and my wonderful agent, Brian Siberell, and the people of Jordan, who were, such a . . . so hospitable to us when we were shooting. And I'd just like to dedicate this to the women and men in the military who risk their lives on a daily basis in Iraq and Afghanistan and around the world. And may they come home safe. Thank you."

Introduction and Q&A for Museum of Modern Art Retrospective

Brett Michel / 2011

Introduction and Q&A at a screening of *Set-Up* and *The Loveless* for her Museum of Modern Art retrospective "Crafting Genre: Kathryn Bigelow," June 1, 2011. Printed by permission of the Museum of Modern Art and Brett Michel.

Kathryn Bigelow: I'm honored to be here in this extraordinary museum, and I'm not sure it's deserved, but I'm enjoying it! Again, it's such an honor; my head is spinning. So tonight, you're going to see *Set-Up* and *The Loveless*.

Set-Up was . . . actually, I began with an NEA grant before I went to Columbia University for my graduate degree, but I ran out of money to finish it, so I went to Columbia to use their editing equipment, and was able to go to school at the same time. So, I finished it as my thesis film, and it's a twenty-minute short. The audio mix—they did a great job with what I had—but it's a little rough. And so, the kind of idea behind it—I'll just be real brief—is that you're watching a cinematic episode—however you want to describe it—and then I have these incredible philosophers who were actually also my teachers at the time. When the film begins to split, they try to tell you, or deconstruct what you're attracted to while you're watching something that is somewhat violent onscreen.

What is the attraction while you're watching it? I only mention that because the sound is very rough, and you're going to be struggling to hear what these people are saying, perhaps. But hopefully not.

And then *The Loveless* was my first feature. But I did do that in collaboration with Monty Montgomery. We both wrote it together and directed it together. Collaborative directing is tricky. It's a bit challenging, but

213

very rewarding. This was my first feature, and Willem Dafoe's first feature, and I often say, it's kind of like the blind leading the blind. Hopefully, it's a little better than that.

And the last thing is just—because I come out of the art world—and the art world is sort of a non-narrative, or for me at the time, coming into New York in the early seventies, when conceptual art—clip art—was very, sort of, what's happening at the time, and I was completely immersed in that, and it was very non-narrative, very sort of ideologically based. So, transitioning into feature filmmaking, which is storytelling, making that transition from non-narrative to narrative, you'll see kind of the gears trying to turn, and yet trying to stretch that narrative as far as we possibly can, so it's almost nonexistent. So you'll see it—hopefully, you'll see it as a transitional phase, and be a little bit forgiving. Anyway, on that note, thank you, and I'll talk to you afterward.

Post-screening Q&A:
Brett Michel: Is it true that you just turned in a new script on the killing of Bin Laden?
A: I can't talk about future projects.

Q: Can you talk about how you achieved the level of detail from a different era in *The Loveless*?
A: It was, again, an early, early, early work, and all those motorcycles are actually vintage motorcycles. We were really trying to be as fastidious with the production design as possible, and Willem, when I first met him, he was performing in one of the Wooster Group performances at the Garage, in downtown Manhattan, and I spoke to him and said, "Do you want to be in a movie?" And he said yes. And I said, "Can you ride a motorcycle?" He said yes. And you know, I learned my lesson. So we were in Georgia. It was like three days before we were going to shoot, and he's in these leathers, which were of the period, and it's summer, it's August, in a little town just outside of Savannah. It's about 115 degrees, and he's in this heavy leather outfit. We put him on this Electra Glide—I don't really like motorcycles, and it's huge. He promptly goes off the road. And this was just to line up the camera shot. We never imagined that, oh, maybe we should have gotten him comfortable with the bike. Anyway, he goes off the road, he goes up the front lawn of the house, the bike goes through the hedge, hits the front door, and this woman comes out. . . . So anyway, the long answer: yes, we were trying for as few anachronisms as possible.

Q: Can you talk a bit about the inception of the script, and what drew you to the subject of biker gangs?

A: I think I'd been looking at a lot of Kenneth Anger. *Scorpio Rising*, specifically, and also, having just come off of *Set-Up* and thinking about iconographies of power, spending time with those two philosophers, and it all kind of coalesced in this idea of doing something in the fifties that was very sort of nihilistic, and stretching the narrative. So I think that Kenneth Anger and *Scorpio Rising* was probably the biggest single influence on that piece.

Q: Would you say that violence is a common theme that runs through your films?

A: Well, it certainly is—I suppose if I was to generalize and try and contextualize it, it might be. But it's not perhaps quite as deliberate as maybe it might feel. The material itself is really about trying to understand what is it about a very kinetic piece of footage that attracts you? I had taken a class, and the professor was applying Freud's interpretation of dreams to film. And he was talking about the subconscious, and why you identify with the character onscreen. Why, at the beginning of *Strange Days*, when the guys are running up the stairs, and I'll look at the audience, and there will be people, and their legs will be moving. In other words, there's this kind of subconscious identification that happens, and so I was trying to understand that, and I think in trying to understand that, I became fascinated with that process. But again, it always starts with the character, it doesn't start with the form, so it's not as deliberate as it seems.

Q: Are you consciously trying to work your way through different genres?

A: Interesting. I think of genre as kind of something that is very handy— and I don't mean this in a pejorative way, necessarily—but handy for critics or historians to catalogue and categorize filmmaking processes, techniques or subject matter. I don't look at it from that standpoint. Again, it's like from the character and—*The Hurt Locker* was a study of these EOD techs, and what is the psychology of somebody who walks toward what you or I, and I'm sure most people in this room would run from—so that's where it starts, and then you realize after the fact—or simultaneously—yes, it's a genre, it's a war genre, it's the military, it's drama, but it really starts with character, and trying to understand that psychology.

Q: What does filmmaking mean to you, how did filmmaking become that to you, and is there a common theme in your films that you try to express?

A: Well, how much time do we have? I'm kidding. Um . . . humpf! Good question. I think that because I came from making art, and I thought that's what I'd do my whole life, I think of making films as a very similar process to making art. I know it's not the same. It's extremely complicated, but it's a little like breathing. You just do it because you have to. And if I was to stop and question it or, worse, perhaps censor ideas, then I wouldn't be able to do anything. So, I tend to try and be as fluid and as expansive and as exploratory as possible, and so I see it as a process of maintaining an exploratory frame of mind. It's kind of more of a state of mind than a vocation, I suppose. And early on, as I mentioned in the introduction, involved in conceptual art, and political art, and I think that's where I sort of became fascinated with topicality and how art can speak to our time. And it's a great delivery system, so to speak, to comment about the world in which we live. Taking genre, and kind of exposing it, if you will, or looking at the world through a different lens. It's a great opportunity to do that, and that's what I think the beauty and the value of the artwork can give you.

Q: If you look back, what would you say was your most transitional time from being a visual artist, to being a moving picture artist?

A: Huh. Interesting. It all seems difficult, but I'd say, I suppose, when I made this. I didn't actually know it was called directing, I just knew there was somebody who would set up the shots, and I would work with the cameraman and working out the storyboards. So, I think it was moving away from the static image and the non-narrative image, to the moving image and embracing—or trying to embrace—the narrative. It was kind of a rough beginning, but trying to embrace that. And I was excited by that, because I felt that film has this great opportunity across all cross-cultural lines. And sometimes art, sadly, can be a little bit more rarified, and maybe miss certain parts of the population. And so what I like about film is that it doesn't require that sort of . . . and yet, on the other hand, if the film is somewhat smart, there are many, many layers to it, and there can be multiple interpretations, and that's when it's very exciting.

Q: [inaudible]

A: Well, I think that gender is curious because, again, not to kind of keep kind of going back to the same source, but coming from the art world, I'd never felt any kind of disparity. Like, you would think in terms of schools of art, but not the gender of the artist. Like, I wouldn't think "that's an amazing woman sculptor." You just wouldn't talk like that. So, moving into film, I remember, in fact, screening this in Italy. Actually, in the Locarno Film Festival, and the interviewer said, "but you're a woman, and you make this movie!" And I couldn't understand why that was a question. It is what it is, you know? So, I don't know. It still to this day is kind of a curiosity to me. And I tend to be drawn toward stories that have a lot of dramatic conflict and, yes, in that case, certainly the military, as both of my last two films dealt with the military—one the Russian, one American. Again, it's the character where I start, and not the gender.

Q: The difference between being a visual artist and being a filmmaker strikes me as working solo as opposed to working tremendously collaboratively, even down to your co-directing a film. Do you see it this way?
A: Yeah, I kind of felt that there was something a little too solipsistic about sitting in my studio and painting. You don't know; it's painful. It can be a very painful process, but early on, I began working with a group of conceptual artists, political artists, whatever you want to call them, and so I kind of started with sort of a group psychology, a group collaborative effort, in working with them. And that just crossed over to film really easily. And politically. I really love the collaborative process. I think that, in a way, the fact that, yes, there's a structure and, yes, there's a director, but I really feel that all films are made by teams, and teams of potentially extremely talented people who contribute an enormous amount. I think that's one of the great, great gifts of filmmaking.

Q: What was the best lesson you learned as the writer or director of *The Loveless* that you were able to bring to your films after that?
A: Oh, I don't know that there was a single lesson, but I really felt that a hunger for narrative and plot was kind of like a character tone poem. And so that's what I felt I wanted to focus on. Which is what I really did try to focus on in *Near Dark*. And so *Near Dark* is really the attempt to try and immerse myself and embrace narrative, as opposed to *The Loveless*, which was sort of one foot in one world, and one foot in another. Yes, it's going to be an intellectual exercise, and oh yes, you're going to have to enjoy it. Oh! That's a problem. So, it's about trying to find the boundaries, and then trying to go into narrative.

Q: No one has ever considered me a prude, but why is it that filmmakers make films with the f-word running through them? I happen to love old,

old movies, your *Gone with the Wind*'s. Why is it that so many modern filmmakers keep doing this?

A: Oh, I don't know. I can't speak for anybody else, but I suppose in the case of *Set-Up* it was a very deliberate desire to create a very provocative text against which these two philosophers would deconstruct it. So the more provocative, the better. That would be more grist, more material for them to work with.

Q: Would you share with us whether and how you experience filmmaking, or yourself, since winning the Oscar?

A: I don't know. If there are differences, I'd have to ask my friends. They could probably better answer that. It was such a surreal moment. I was absolutely not expecting that outcome. I think I wasn't prepared for it, and I still probably feel that way.

Q: How closely are you working with your editors, or have you created enough of a film language in your actual shooting of the film, that you don't really need to interact with them very much for them to become almost like little teeny sculptors on your massive finished piece?

A: Well, I love the editing process, and I'm in the cutting room every single day. So it's maybe kind of surprising, but I love it. And again, it's that sort of collaborative process. But I also think that editing is when you get to kind of rewrite the movie for its final time. From soup to nuts. You can scrub it of what you had imagined, and start from scratch. Like Walter Murch used to say—I was working with him, obviously one of the great, great editors, on *K-19*—and he said, "you can't muscle it into being something until it wants to reveal itself." So, I think the editing process is fascinating. I just love it.

Press Conference for *Zero Dark Thirty*

Peter Keough and Brett Michel / 2012

December 4, 2012; New York City. Participants were Kathryn Bigelow, Mark Boal, Jessica Chastain, Jason Clarke, and Kyle Chandler. Reported by Peter Keough; transcribed and edited by Brett Michel. Printed by permission of Peter Keough and Brett Michel.

Sony Publicist: Hey everybody! Thank you. We are at the *Zero Dark Thirty* press conference with Kyle Chandler, Jason Clarke, Jessica Chastain, Kathryn Bigelow, and Mark Boal. And our first question.

Question: Good morning. Thank you all so much for this wonderful and so important film. I have a question for the cast. I wondered what beyond the script you looked at in terms of your research and considering some of the very dark and murky content of this piece, how you were able to extricate yourself at the end of the day once Ms. Bigelow had called "cut."

Jessica Chastain: It wasn't really any—at "cut"—being able to just kind of go back home and be normal because we were shooting in Jordan and India and we were really immersed in the story we were telling. I had the props person print out all the pictures of the terrorists that Maya looks at, and I actually hung them in my hotel room, so even when you go home from set, it was always around me. In terms of research, you know, there was a great deal of information in the script, every scene gave me clues and little things she would say as to who the woman was, and of course our screenwriter's an investigative reporter, so that was very helpful! [Laughs.] I nicknamed Mark "the professor," and I had three months of going to school before we even started shooting. I read books like *The Looming Towers* and the first book on Osama Bin Laden. It was a full-immersion school.

Jason Clarke: Yeah, I agree with Jess. On a secondary note, we went to

219

the Taj Mahal, you know, to Jerash in Jordan, just do a couple of things to get out and see a pretty amazing part of the world we were in. First and foremost, Mark's script—stick to the facts, get your ducks in a row, then *The Looming Tower, The Black Banners*—there's some great material out there. And on a personal note, you know, psychotherapy books helping me along, just to work with in terms of creating relationships, to understand what it is to be a man that is out there playing a number of different roles, and has to have a great relationship with people that he meets, and understand them.

Kyle Chandler: The reference material that was brought forward, ideas in different books. And of course, it's not too far away from all this, so it's just a click away on your computer if you get yourself involved. One of the greatest things for me was this travel, going to Indian land. And all of a sudden, that's your other partner in the show, to wear just like your costume. You're sort of there. My guy makes decisions. Hard, difficult, and life-and-death decisions. I'm a father of two daughters—no problem, done. [Everyone laughs.]

Q: Congratulations on your New York Film Critics Award yesterday . . .
Kathryn Bigelow: Thank you.

Q: . . . and for Kathryn and Mark, could you talk a little bit about your research and getting involved with this project from the start . . . ?
KB: Well, originally we were working on another project still about the hunt for Osama bin Laden, but it was about the failed hunt in 2001, and this all took place in the Tora Bora mountain range in Afghanistan between December 6 and December 20 of 2001. And while Mark was working on the screenplay, actually quite far along in the screenplay, May 1, 2011 happened, and we realized after some soul-searching that it was going to be a little bit difficult to make a movie about the failed hunt for Osama bin Laden when the whole world knew that he had been killed. So, after much debate, we pivoted, and Mark being an investigative journalist, set on his way to report the current story as of 2011, as history revealed itself and created a change for us.

Q: This question is for Kathryn. Unlike the military revelry when Bin Laden is killed, Jessica's character is depicted as unhappy, even crying. Talk about the thinking that went into the making of that decision about her political or emotional reaction.
KB: Well, that was beautifully articulated in the screenplay, and we never

deviated from that. So that's a creation of Mark's. And I think what's so interesting and so poignant for both Jessica and myself—for all of us—is this idea that this woman has spent the last ten years exclusively in the pursuit of one man. And yes, at the end of the day, she triumphed. But it's not a victory because finally, at the end of the day, it's . . . you're left with much larger questions like, where does she go from here? Where do we go from here? Now what? So I think that was . . . the human element of it and the sense of that kind of question and what the weight of that question on your shoulders is.

Q: During the making of the movie, there was a lot of news about a congressional—a possible investigation into your help from the CIA. Could you discuss that, and also, how much assistance did you get from the CIA and the Defense Department, and whether that had any influence in the final film?

Mark Boal: As you're aware, there was a bit of election-year controversy about that. I'm probably not going to get into great detail, except to say that the movie was made independently; it was independently financed. We're very lucky to have Sony's support in distributing it, but I emphasize the independence of the film because there was no arrangement or deal of any kind with either of those two agencies. And as far as the research, we approached it as any reporter probably since the dawn of time has approached reporting a story, which is to say you work through every channel you can, including public affairs, and departments at those agencies. It was a distraction in terms of the filming of the movie, but ultimately, I think the movie speaks for itself.

Q: This question is for Mark. Transitioning from the other project to this one, can you speak a little bit more about how you structured the character of Maya, created the character and developed the film around her journey?

MB: Can you be a little more specific?

Q: Just in terms of, I guess, the previous project was a different subject matter, and it had different characters, and then in your research, did this character present itself in the reporting you were doing? And then you decided to build around her?

MB: A couple of months into the reporting, I don't remember exactly when, I had heard about—well, first of all, there was the discovery that I made relatively early on that women had played a prominent role in this hunt, and that was surprising to me, and so that became a focal point of the reporting. And then we ended up deciding to tell the story through the eyes of this character, and I want to emphasize that it's a character in a film, but based on a real person. And of course, there were many other women in the CIA who we didn't represent. But it just seemed like the right way to tell the story. We always knew we wanted to tell the story through the eyes of the workforce, through the eyes of the people on the ground, as opposed to the command-and-control political story that people thought that the film was sometimes mischaracterized as being about. So we just kind of went with it.

Q: I have a producer or director question, and by the way, congratulations to all of you. Terrific film. I'm just so curious how you shot this thing, and the crowd sequences. Kathryn, I know you're not afraid of crowds; I looked at *Strange Days* again recently—the New Year's Eve thing. [Laughter.] How did you go about, you know, the big crowd scenes in India, was it guerrilla filmmaking, and what were these supposed fake shoots you did to distract people? Could you, or somebody, talk about that?

KB: Well, yeah, we needed that sense of a teeming environment in which you're looking for a sharp needle in a very large haystack. And so, getting the sense of being lost in this sort of human deluge—and these marketplaces in India were just exquisite, beautiful to shoot in—but what happens when you pull a camera out—and I like to work with a lot of cameras, which is good in this case—but what happens when you pull a camera out is you get about two thousand faces looking at the camera. And so that would have broken the illusion that this is a movie and a story is unfolding in front of you. It sort of pierces that illusion. So what we had to do is we began to set up these diversionary film sets where we would have an actor who wasn't in the key scene that I was shooting and a camera, and we would set up. They would be doing something like walking through the marketplace two hundred feet away, while the shoot I needed to do, let's say with Edgar in the van, was happening two hundred feet away in the other direction. But eventually, you're found out, and you have to swap it. I mean, you don't get all day; you get maybe another half hour or something, so you're constantly leapfrogging sets, from one set to another. But it's worth it. The sort of life and vitality and immediacy of those environments; you can't re-create it. If we could have gone to Pakistan, we probably would have, but we were about two hours from the border, so between pre-partition and post-partition Pakistan,

I think visually, all the architecture's identical and probably a lot of the wardrobe and all of that.

Q: Good job.
KB: Thank you.

Q: Good morning. Kathryn, job well done. Has the president seen the movie, and if so, any comments? Or do you plan on him seeing the movie?
KB: Good question. I don't believe he has, and I'm sure at some point he will.
Clarke: We hope he will.
KB: We hope he will, yeah!
MB: That brings up a larger question, which is we've shown the movie basically to some small movie audiences in Los Angeles. We just finished it two weeks ago, and so you guys are really among the first group to see it, and we will be bringing it to Washington for the national premiere in January. But you guys are among the first.

Q: I have a question regarding the character that Jessica played, Maya. Since she was based on a real person, could you talk a little bit about . . . you talked earlier about where does she go from here, any debriefing that she or any of the other agents had that you know about accomplishing this mission and where they went from here after this incredibly history-making event. And also, anyone on the panel can answer this, but what do you think about the tug-of-war between journalism and government when it came to reporting this event? Because there was some controversy over things that were classified that a lot of journals felt should've been made public, and maybe that affected your research, some things that maybe you couldn't find out because it was classified. So if you could talk about the real-life person or people, how they were debriefed, and also the journalism question.
MB: I'm going to step on that for you, Jess.
Chastain: [Laughs.]
MB: One of the things just as a general sort of principle that we're not going to do is talk about the real-life people that the film is based on because many of them are still working, and we take protecting their identities very seriously. So, unfortunately, while that's a really interesting question, I probably won't answer that here, today. The issue of

government transparency is obviously going to become more and more important as the war on terror continues and sort of expands. We got, I think, sucked into that debate a little bit, but we're trying to make a movie here. [Laughs.] With all due respect to that debate, we just hope that people view this as a film.

Q: For Jessica, I'm just wondering if you had the chance to meet the person on which Maya was based, and I know you can't talk about the actual person. But, did meeting that person or meeting any other agents—how did that inform your performance?

Chastain: I never met Maya, because she's an undercover CIA agent, and it would've not been a good thing to do. However, I got a lot of research from Mark. It really, really helps when your screenwriter's an investigative journalist, and I had to approach it like any other character I was playing, so any questions I could answer through the research, I did, but questions that I couldn't answer through the research, I then had to use my imagination and Kathryn's imagination, and Mark's, to create a character that went along the lines that respected the real woman. You know, I'm playing a character who's trained to be unemotional and analytically precise, and as an actor, you spend your whole life [laughs] trying to be emotional and keeping yourself emotionally open. So to find the humanity within that, and that arc, was a great feat that would've been impossible without Kathryn and Mark's leadership.

Q: In a film like this, do you have a favorite scene, or a favorite part, and was there anything about this story that surprised you a whole lot?

Chastain: My favorite moment is the last scene of the film. There were a lot of scenes that are fun to do as an actor. It's so fun to do the big scenes, like when you're yelling and you're . . . because it feels really good to emote as an actor. It's very hard to play something that is subtle and specific and really tiny in the arc. It's really fun to play the scene where I'm chewing out Kyle in the hallway. That's great!

But, for me, in the film, my favorite moment is the very end of the film, because it says more than just what this woman did. It's not a propaganda movie—"go America"—it's through the eyes of this woman who has sacrificed, become a servant to her work, and she lost herself along the way, and she realizes that. It's bigger than that because then it's like what Kathryn said: where does she go, but then also where do we go as a country? Where do we go as a society? What do we do now? And

I find that to end the film on that question is far more interesting than providing an answer.

Q: For Kathryn and Mark, can you tell me a little bit about handling the facts and the sensitivity of the material, but also keeping the film's entertainment value in mind?

KB: Do you want to start with him? Go ahead . . .

MB: I'm the least entertaining person here so . . .

Chastain: Not true!

MB: . . . so you don't want me to answer that. Look, the material's inherently dramatic, is what I would say, and if you grew up like I did, reading James Bond novels and that sort of thing, to get a chance to work in a kind of behind-the-scenes of the real thing is pretty exciting, and you've got a story with people running around Pakistan chasing dangerous terrorists, so that's pretty fertile ground. Not that it wrote itself—there was a little bit of work involved—but I think it's kind of one of the great stories.

KB: And I think, you know, in terms of, like Mark was saying, it's inherently dramatic, but at the same time, I think as a filmmaker it was very interesting to stay within the sort of longitudinal, latitudinal guidelines of history, and reality. So there was never a moment you could just say, "Oh god, wouldn't it be great if we could . . ." You can't do that; you can't even think like that. So the beauty of this piece for me—and I love working like that—is within a sense of naturalism and realism and specificity. I mean, there was nothing that was done that didn't come from the research, so that, as a filmmaker, is thrilling.

Q: This is for Kathryn. You've been making films for thirty years or more, and it seems like you started with very formal, avant-garde kinds of interests, and then you moved on to genre filmmaking, and now you're into journalistic filmmaking. This film is actually, in many ways, similar to *K-19*, I thought, which was maybe the first film where you had a historical incident. Could you describe this progression, if indeed it is a progression, and do you intend to continue along the journalistic line?

KB: Both Mark and I talk about this as a kind of reported film, in a way. In other words, the story and the film are sort of contemporaneous. In fact, when we were shooting the raid, we were actually shooting it in May—in late April, and into May—and on May 1, 2012, I'm looking at my crew and my cast and realizing that the event had only happened just a year prior. It hadn't even been a year old. So there was a kind of urgency in the timeliness of it. And yes, I'm excited by that space. I think it's very interesting. You know, having gone through different permutations, I've been fascinated by different schools of filmmaking, let's say, and then prior to that the art world, I think there's something very freeing about constantly, well, moving forward? But at the same time, I'm very excited by this kind of reportorial filmmaking. I think it sort of fills a space, like a kind of imagistic living history, is how I think of it.

Q: This is a question for Kathryn, Mark, and anyone else who'd like to chime in. How would you define a good soldier, and what do you think are the basic elements that turn a war film into a classic?

KB: [Laughs.] That's an easy question.

MB: I don't know why you people are looking at me . . . It's a very easy answer. If you want to make a classic war film, as a producer, you hire Kathryn Bigelow.

Everyone: [Laughs.]

KB: No, I don't know. I don't know how to answer that. I don't actually know how to answer either of those. But, the soldier question is an interesting one. In a way, the characters in the film are soldiers of a different type, right? And they're not in uniform, and they're not on the front lines, but they're warriors, I guess, is the word I'd use, and it's a fascinating archetype, but I don't know that I could pin it down on my second cup of coffee.

Q: This is for the cast. I want to know when the story was unfolding in the press, how attuned you were to the story, and if at any point, did you think you'd be part of the storytelling?

Clarke: I followed it all. I mean, I was in Pakistan when it all started, I was up in the mountains, and then went back into China and read it on the Internet. You know, it kind of filled and consumed everyone, so when word went around, they came knocking on my door, I was over the moon, you know? These things come along once in a lifetime. I mean, touch wood. I mean, touch wood, yes or no that it does happen! [Laughs.] Yeah, so I think everybody has ownership of this story in some kind of way. I think it's very rare—particularly here in New York City—that someone doesn't have one, two—let alone six—degrees of separation, and to know that you're going to be part of something just so interconnected in the galaxy is, it's like picking up Hamlet for the first time, and all of a sudden, you're going to be in the original production. I'm very grateful.

Chastain: I never, ever imagined I'd be involved in telling this story during those events. I was in New York during 9/11, and when I found out that Osama was killed, and when I was reading the script, every page that I turned was a shock to me, especially . . . especially Maya, and the role she took in it, and then I got upset that it was such a shock to me, but why would I assume that a woman wouldn't be involved in this kind of research. The wonderful thing about working on this film is, historically in movies, lead characters are played by women who are defined by men, whether it's a love interest, or they're the victim of a man, and Maya's not like that. I don't think . . . I don't know that Kathryn Bigelow would make a movie like that, because she's not . . . she stands on her own . . . she's capable and intelligent, and I think she represents this generation of woman, and that was really exciting for me to discover on the page in the script, and to discover about our history.

KC: I think I had lost touch—until I saw the movie—I had lost touch with what had happened in the last ten years, and that's what I really . . . it really surprised me while watching the movie, because it's two hours and forty minutes—it goes by so fast—in the first ninety seconds, and the last ninety seconds, if you will, everything in between there—and it was evident as I sat there watching it, and I was able to watch it with Katherine—not this Kathryn, my Katherine—the two of us in the theater by ourselves, so we really . . . I was just right there with the film, and what was so wonderful, was everything in-between was so . . . earned, as the chapters went through that decade or more, there were little parts in the script, little, little tiny lines, little pictures that showed me, "oh, yeah, I remember," that that's a political change right there, or there's that moral dilemma that was brought up. And it's still going on, and everything was marked so subtly, and so everything throughout the movie was just morally and emotionally earned. There was a truthfulness that kept it what it was, and the facts, I'm sure, helped keep that, and it was really seamless. I'm just so proud to be part of this, and I have a lot of military friends, and so when I found out I was doing this, I was like, "guys, guess what I'm going to do?"

Chastain: [Laughs.]

KC: And they laughed, like you did. But, it's just . . . I'm really proud to be part of this, and to Kathryn—such a filmmaker—and Mark. It's just been a great ride, and I think that this is one of those movies that ten years from now, you'll be able to look at it again and go, "yup, that was my time, that was our time," and again, you saying over ninety countries are represented in that initial strike. This is almost like a global . . . everyone owns it—galactic, if you will. And it's just an incredible piece to be part of, so it's pretty amazing.

Q: I'm really fascinated to hear the story of the editing process, because it says in the production notes that this could've easily been a movie over three hours. To the filmmakers, can you talk about some scenes that may end up on the DVD, Blu-ray, will there be a director's cut? And also, to the actors, were there any scenes that were cut that maybe you'd like the public to see, but didn't make the final cut?

KB: Well, we shot almost two million feet of film, so it was a lot of film. We only wrapped photography on June 1, and so, gratefully, I had two of the most talented editors working in the business today—Dylan Tichenor and William Goldenberg—and through their tremendous talent, we were able to winnow it down to 2:35, 2:40. It was interesting, I went back and looked at a couple of the scenes that we had taken out—for time, and also for narrative, kind of urgency—and, you know, kind of spending some time away from them, and then looking at them again, and we realized, we had made the right decisions, and that there was a kind of narrative coherency that we were very, very happy with. Whether there will be perhaps a little more raid footage, if down the road we decide to put some back in for a DVD bonus piece, I don't know, but right now, the film stands as it is, and I'm very proud of it.

Q: Kathryn, given your background in painting, do you—in your preparation—do you do storyboarding or paintings based on concepts that are turning up in the screenplay as it's being developed, in trying to figure out how you want to stylize the film?

KB: I always storyboard, not sometimes personally, but I always have a storyboard artist, because I think what's great is to, as quickly as you can, once you have the script, is to begin to see it, to open up, and to visualize it, and begin set construction, and of course, the designs for that. But, yeah, I love storyboarding. I think it's really a necessary tool.

Q: This question is for both Mark and Kathryn. How would you say this film has been shaped or influenced both by your feelings about 9/11 and your feelings about bin Laden and the importance, or not, of the pursuit of bin Laden?

MB: Well, 9/11 was, as I've said before, a personal day for me. I was born and raised in this town, and so bin Laden basically attacked my hometown. I grew up on 11th Street, and . . . with this piece, in particular, I didn't approach it with any agenda, beyond . . . I didn't know what the story was going to be when I sat down. The characters that these guys portray, as I've said, are based on real people. That's what emerged from the reporting. It could have been something else. Whatever it would've been, is what I would've tried to piece together, but I think there's, for all of us . . . as Kyle was saying, it's been a decade that in a lot of ways was shaped by 9/11, so it's hard to draw the really precise lines of influence. And as Jessica was saying, hopefully the piece captures some of the ending of a particular chapter. At least I'm hopeful that this is the ending of a particular chapter.

KB: Yeah, obviously, I suppose from a certain standpoint, it's been a very long and dark decade, and my hope is that some of those more difficult images can be replaced and/or that narrative can be amplified by another narrative, one of courage and dedication and a kind of nod to those men and women who work in the intelligence community to try to make our lives safer.

Q: The torture sequences are some of the most harrowing, and hardest to watch I've ever seen a narrative film, and considering this is such near history, I wondered, Ms. Bigelow, as a filmmaker, how you judged how hard you were to go on that, where to stop before it became too gruesome, and also it gave you a very, very interesting insight into the mindset of some of these folks who do this for a living, and for the cast—particularly Jessica and Jason—what in your research, in performing those scenes, changed your perspective, or perhaps altered your perspective on what those people have to do for a living?

KB: Hmm, very good question. I mean, there's no question that that methodology is controversial, and . . . but there was no debate on whether or not to include it in the movie, because it's part of the history, so that was an element that we were working with. And then it was a question of working with the material and finding the right tone and balance, and I had also explored other methodologies, like electronic surveillance, and over the course of the decade, many, many different tactics were utilized. I think that's what's interesting and magnificent about the screenplay, and what Kyle was saying as well, is that over that decade, you see all that . . . you see all the different permutations, and all the different applications of surveillance that were utilized in order to track this courier, and then track the courier to the compound, and now of course, the rest is history, so it was really a question of finding the right balance.

Chastain: Those scenes . . . I think . . . they were tough—to be honest—to

film, and we filmed that section in a Jordanian prison, so we really were—
well, we weren't on a soundstage in Los Angeles—and I think, about the
film, you can see how important the location of being—of shooting in
India and Jordan was to the film—because it creates an atmosphere that
is absolutely in those scenes. That was a tough week, but, you know, it's
like Kathryn said, it's a part of the history of the characters, and instead
of looking at it and making my own judgments on what I personally believe is right and wrong, I try to look at it in terms of the character. I
mean, this is the introduction to this woman who was recruited right
out of school. She shows up in her suit to go to what she believes is going
to be a normal interrogation. It becomes much more intense than she
imagined, and an introduction to a woman like that, and to see where
she starts to where she ends in the end of the film, I found that very useful in playing the character.

Clarke: I think it would have been remiss of Kathryn and Mark to not
tell the story. Mark said: he followed the facts. He did the work, followed
the story, found the story, and Kathryn sculpted it, with a surgeon's scal-
pel, and really followed that river where it went. There's big choices in
watching two-and-a-half hours, but the honesty and integrity of that
sequence—you're not going to feel the weight at the end, and I know for
myself, and for Reda [Kateb], who shot the scene, we were . . . we were
grateful. You know, Reda's a French/Moroccan actor, and he was grateful
to get in there and explore that part, and ensure the story, as we know the
facts demonstrated it. It's out there in the public arena already, without
marketing to make it up, or whatever, and then I think that's the integrity of their work, you know, it's there, and you get the whole story. You
get the whole 360 degrees as much as you can in two-and-a-half hours,
and it all accumulates and adds up to this piece of work which speaks for
itself, I think.

Q: This is for Kathryn and Jessica. The last scene in the movie reminded
me a bit of the last scene of *The Hurt Locker*, and I was wondering if you had
thought of the characters as similar, and also, for Kathryn, whether you
identified with Maya as a woman in a very male-dominated profession?

KB: I think what I found very surprising about Mark's research is that
women were central to this operation and so that's what excited me
about it, not the fact . . . I mean, yes, it's extraordinary that women were
pivotal, but . . . it's also just that, those were the facts. That was the story,
that was a hand we were dealt, and so that's the lens through which we

chose to tell the story, and I think keeping, as Jason was saying, keeping the kind of honesty of the piece, the most important element of it, I thought, was . . . that's what drove me, that's what motivated me, more than anything else.

Chastain: I didn't think of Maya in terms of . . . I didn't connect her to the character in *The Hurt Locker*. When I was doing my research and I was thinking about her, I was thinking about her as like a computer, almost—a woman who's really good with facts and details, and putting a puzzle together, and what happens when that woman is put in a situation that is much bigger than she ever imagined she'd be involved in. And the stress of the interrogations, or being in that part of the world and not only dealing with the interrogations of the terrorists, but also coming up against superiors who don't believe in your lead; how she starts to unravel within that, just because she's trained to be unemotional and analytically precise doesn't mean she's unemotional. And what I loved so much about the script is we do see moments where she falters in this . . . in the hallway with Bradley—with Kyle—she's basically blackmailing him. [Laughs.] You know, "if you don't give me what I want, I'm going to put you in front of a congressional committee." I mean, that's a very emotional reaction. So, I found it to be a very compelling piece with a lot of complexities of a lot of depth and I really saw her as her own woman, and I never really connected her to another performance.

KB: And it's also such a testament to the talent of Jessica to find the beautifully calibrated, finely calibrated nuances of the emotions within a character that had to be so precise, and that's something that I don't know if I've ever seen, and I think that it's certainly a testament to her, but also to Jason and to Kyle—that these are really . . . these are characters that have to operate with a tremendous amount of precision, and as beautifully written as they are in the screenplay. And I think that the emotion that they're able to generate within the calibration of that precision is pretty extraordinary.

Clarke: That scene is also confirmed in the Seal's book, as you said, in *No Easy Day*. Mark got it right! The first firsthand account to come out, is . . . it's right there in his book, he saw it . . .

Chastain: Yeah, she was crying there on the airplane.

Clarke: Which is . . . it's not invented.

Q: For Jessica, you clearly have a firm sense of the journey the character takes through the movie, but like you mentioned before, she is recruited straight out of high school, which made me wonder what kind of girl was she before all this began? Did you do any backstory work for that part of it?

Chastain: Anything that I couldn't answer in research I had to answer in my imagination. But do it in a way—because she's so opposite of me, of the life that I've had, and the life that I still have, so yeah, I had . . . I knew why she was recruited out of high school . . . in my mind, I knew what her favorite American candy was when she was homesick, I knew her favorite music. Whenever I approach a role—even Celia Foote—what I couldn't find from the novel [*The Help*], I had to answer questions in my imagination, but stay along the line of honesty that the writer has put out. It's like they create the spine of a character, and then as an actor you have to fill out the rest of it.

Q: Jessica, after this dark film, what did it take for you to go on stage every night in *The Heiress*?

Chastain: I don't know what . . . I'm a crazy person. I think my first films came out a year-and-a-half ago. I'm really lucky to do what I do, but I'll tell you right now, it's a very strange thing to be talking about this film, and to be talking about Maya, and then think "okay, at 6:30, I'm going to start putting my nose on, and my thin curls, and go on stage as Catherine Sloper in *The Heiress*, but it's a great gift. Even though the character of Maya is very different from me, because I am a very emotional girl and very sensitive, and I like to have a good time, I'm very smiley—even though she's very different, there is something that is very similar and it's this being in love with your work. And I can understand that passion and . . . servitude, some might say—not quite to the extreme that she does and I'm nowhere near the amazing woman that Maya is, but I do understand that, and that's what gets me on stage every night. Thank you.

Q: This is a question for Mark and Kathryn. How challenging was it to find moments of levity, and what do you think is so appealing about dark themes?

MB: Well, I don't actually think that this movie is dark, but that's probably more a comment on me than it is the film. I actually find it encouraging to tell a story, that even in the fairly ruthless world of counterterrorism, to discover that there are real human beings there and not just killing machines; maybe that is dark, now that I say it. [Laughs.] Levity. . . . You know, a lot of that comes down to performance. I mean, there's a few little political jokes and so forth in the film, but it's not . . . it's obviously not at the level of slapstick, so it really just comes down to, I mean, the line about "we don't know what we don't know," and Kyle's response of "well, what the fuck does that mean?" and there's some people get that as a joke, but a lot of people don't. But it just comes down to the performances really, and being able to find a little bit of humor in what's otherwise a fairly buttoned-up professional environment. And Kathryn should talk about casting people who are funny, like Chris Pratt. That doesn't hurt.

KB: Well, I think it's not just somebody that's funny, it's somebody who has a tremendous facility to convey humanity, and that humanity takes on a lot of different permutations, and the beauty of this cast—of the whole cast—is that everybody was, I don't know, just very giving, and very human and very spontaneous. They trusted the material, enormously, and the environment, and felt where they could give all different colors to their character.

Additional Resources

Books

Hedges, Chris. *War Is A Force That Gives Us Meaning*. New York: Anchor Books, 2002.

Jermyn, Deborah, and Sean Redmond, eds. *The Cinema of Kathryn Bigelow, Hollywood Transgressor*. London: Wallflower Press, 2003.

Lane, Christina. *Feminist Hollywood: From Born in Flames to Point Break*. Detroit, MI: Wayne State University Press, 2000.

Prince, Stephen, ed. *American Cinema of the 1980s: Themes and Variations*. New Brunswick, NJ: Rutgers University Press, 2007.

Shreve, Anita. *The Weight of Water*. Boston: Little, Brown, and Company, 1997.

DVDs

Bigelow, Kathryn. *The Hurt Locker* (2009). Summit Entertainment. Includes audio commentary by Bigelow and behind-the-scenes featurette.

Bigelow, Kathryn. *K-19: The Widowmaker*. Paramount. Includes commentary by and interview with Bigelow.

Bigelow, Kathryn. *Near Dark* (1987). Lionsgate Home Entertainment. Includes Bigelow's audio commentary and a making-of documentary with a Bigelow interview.

Bigelow, Kathryn. *Point Break* (1991): The Adrenaline Edition. Fox Home Entertainment. Includes interview with Bigelow.

Bigelow, Kathryn. *Strange Days* (1995), Blu-ray Edition. Kinowelt Home Entertainment. Includes interview with Bigelow and her commentary in featurette extras.

Sirk, Douglas. *Magnificent Obsession*. The Criterion Collection. Includes an interview with Bigelow.

Articles and Interviews

Benson-Allot, Caetlin. "Undoing Violence: Politics, Genre, and Duration in Kathryn Bigelow's Cinema." *Film Quarterly*, Winter 2010.

Boal, Mark. "The Man in the Bomb Suit." *Playboy*, September 2005.

Carr, Jay. "Bigelow Makes a Wake-Up Call." *Boston Globe*, October 8, 1995.

Cieply, Michael. "Film About the Hunt for Bin Laden Leads to a Pentagon Investigation." *New York Times*, January 6, 2012.

Dargis, Manohla. "Action!" *New York Times*, June 18, 2009.

Dargis, Manohla. "How Oscar Found Ms. Right." *New York Times*, March 10, 2011.

Frank, Michael. "Canyon Zen." *Architectural Digest*, May 1998.

Diamond, Jamie. "Kathryn Bigelow Pushes the Potentiality Envelope." *New York Times*, October 22, 1995.

Innis, Chris. "Between Iraq and a Hard Place." *From the Guild* website, March 15 and March 23, 2010. [On location diary by *The Hurt Locker*'s editor.]

Hoberman, J. "It's Alive . . . Again" [includes a review of *Set-Up*]. *Village Voice*, November 28, 1978.

McGavin, Patrick Z. "One Director's Reality Check: Kathryn Bigelow Confronts Life's Horrors." *Chicago Tribune*, October 15, 1995.

Nine, Jennifer. "Gory Daze." *Melody Maker*, March 2, 1996.

Paskin, Willa. "What Kathryn Bigelow Learned from Rembrandt." *Slate*, March 2, 2010.

Sharkey, Betsy. "Kathryn Bigelow Practices the Art of the Kill." *New York Times*, March 11, 1990.

Susman, Gary. "Kathryn Bigelow Says Her Bin Laden Film Is Not a Security Risk or an Obama Campaign Ad." *Moviephone*, August 11, 2011.

Tasker, Yvonne. "Bigger than Life." *Sight & Sound*, May 1999.

Taubin, Amy. "Hard Wired: What Makes Kathryn Bigelow's Iraq War Procedural Tick." *Film Comment*, May/June 2009.

Travers, Peter. "Women on the Verge: Four Women Attempt to Infiltrate a Male Stronghold: The Director's Chair." *Rolling Stone* (New York), September 21, 1989.

Index

118, 148, 168, 197; on clichés and
stereotypes, 31, 69, 101, 133, 187;
on collaborative process, 119,
133, 144, 166, 199, 212, 213–14,
217–18; Columbia University
graduate film school, xi, 22, 26,
34–35, 41, 45, 48, 67, 88–89, 95,
107, 113–14, 132, 140, 180, 184,
207, 209–10, 213; commodification of culture, 19, 92, 96; conceptual art, influence of, 35, 48,
88, 96, 180, 185, 216; on editing
process, 28, 33, 44, 64, 80, 96,
111, 127, 145, 170, 188, 190, 201,
218, 228; elite groups, interest
in, 76, 182, 187–88, 197, 199; elit-
ism of art, 49, 62, 67, 70, 90, 114,
140, 185, 216; entertainment
with a conscience, xiii, 47, 58,
65, 106, 114, 116; escapism and,
74, 76, 98; females in traditionally male roles, 12, 13, 47, 61, 66,
68, 71, 101, 115, 230; feminism
and, 47; filmmaking style, ix,
xiii, 54–55, 95; Milos Forman as
teacher, xi, 22, 35, 48, 67, 206;
found objects and, 87; gender
and women filmmakers, 34, 40,
47, 60, 61, 64, 65, 66, 67, 69, 72–
73, 94, 105, 107–8, 110–11, 117,
135, 139, 191–92, 216–17; genre
and, 31–32, 46, 168, 180–81, 206,
216; on geography and action
sequences, 54, 78, 79, 144, 148,
150, 151, 170, 173, 183, 201; independent filmmaking, merits of,
149; on individual vs. collective,
58–59, 99; *Inside*, shooting of,
xv, 161; instinctive method, 132,
145; on interest in film, 35, 70,

92, 96; lens choices, 84; lighting
strategies, 86; masculine qualities, attraction to, 13, 47, 68, 101,
139; movies as political scape-
goats, 94; on myth and film, 57;
narrative and, 54–55, 70, 90,
185, 214; New York University,
graduate student at, 113; on
noir, xiv, 19, 38, 73, 74, 76, 87,
95, 96, 99, 102; as outsider, 107;
painting, visual arts background
and, x, 21, 35, 40, 48, 50, 70,
86, 92, 95, 96, 105, 107, 112, 116,
145, 180; parents and family, 14,
86, 113, 118; peak experience,
attraction of, xiv, 65, 74, 76,
114, 159, 168, 169, 181, 186–87,
196, 197; physical appearance
of, x, 17, 20, 26, 27, 47–48, 105,
109, 110, 117, 169, 196, 204; POV
sequences, 54, 77, 79–81, 93, 192;
on propaganda, 58, 224; realism
and, ix, xv, xvi, 86, 123, 144, 145,
147, 148, 152, 158, 165–66, 169,
174, 182, 183–84, 188; Edward
Said as teacher, 96; San Carlos,
Calif., upbringing in, x, 30, 35,
44, 48, 86, 107, 113, 115, 131, 197,
207; San Francisco Art Institute,
attendance at, x, 17, 21, 30, 41,
44, 48, 67, 87, 96, 107, 113, 126,
132, 140, 180, 208; on scene
composition, 53; on science fiction, 22; scopophilia, voyeurism
and, xiv, 76, 85, 92, 98, 105–6,
185, 211; *Semiotext(e)* and, 45, 92,
96, 209; on shelved projects, 34;
steadicam and, 80; storyboards
and, 13, 78, 81, 89, 116, 125, 126,
144, 201, 216, 228; structuralism

CPSIA information can be obtained at www.ICGtesting.com
Printed in the USA
BVOW02*0652040913

330219BV00003B/49/P